Fisherguman

—

Living the Dream

Ian Hall

Ian Hall

Orchard House Books

Published by Orchard House Books 2014

Orchard House Books
Raven Lane
Applethwaite
Keswick
CA12 4PN

A CIP catalogue record is available from the British Library

ISBN 978-0-9928156-1-5

www.orchardhousebooks.co.uk

For Jen, Anne-Marie, Geoff, Catherine, Sally, Elizabeth, Claire and Philip, my fellow travellers.

Plan of the buildings at Fisherground

1970

1996

Chapter 1

Pen-pals plus: 1962 – 1972

Anne-Marie was born in Perpignan, in the South of France, a very long way from Eskdale, in the English Lake District. Her father, a bank manager for the Banque de France, was transferred to Brittany and by the time she was 13 she had been a proud Breton for many years. On her 14th birthday, she met Jen, and a little twig of history branched off in an unexpected direction.

July 1962: a steam train draws slowly into Keswick station, with a joyful blast on its whistle. People lean out of the windows above the doors and turn the brass handles. The doors swing open and from one a fully wimpled nun steps out onto the platform, looking round for the small reception party she knows will be there to greet her and her group of French youngsters. Among them is Jen's father, Norman Wake, an English teacher at a Keswick Secondary School, where the French teacher has set up the exchange visit. There are kisses all round, two on the left cheek, one on the right, as they are introduced to the various parents who have agreed to play host to these French teenagers for the week they will be in Keswick. The nun is Soeur Lazare, and she distributes her youngsters in what proves, for one at least, to be a life-changing lottery. Anne-Marie is allotted to Norman, and, back at his home, meets his daughter Jen, her sister Barbara, and Marjorie their mother.

A butterfly clapped its wings in the Amazonian jungle.

That week Jen played the genial host to her new French friend, showing off her favourite places, down by the River Greta, making dams on the old mill race, picnicking on the island, trespassing through the long railway tunnel on

1

Sunday, when she knew there were no trains - but Anne-Marie didn't. Barbara, now a sophisticated 18 year old, was too grown up for such trifles. A-levels just completed she preferred the company of her peers... with just a brief nostalgic glance back at her own childhood, so recently gone. Then, as abruptly as it had started, the week was over, and Soeur Lazare gathered her girls on the station platform, thanked Norman and all the other hosts, and began the weary journey back to Brittany.

Anne-Marie and Jen, Summer 1966

Fast forward to the Summer of 1966: World Cup fever grips both nations, and in France Anne-Marie's father, whom Jen must always call, rather formally, Monsieur Angin, sits her ceremoniously on the hideously uncomfortable Louis XIV chair beside him in front of the television and insists they watch the England vs. France match. England win 2-0, ending

France's bid for a place in the quarter finals. Monsieur Angin is devastated; Jen would rather have been on the beach with Anne-Marie and the others. But she has all Summer, for by now she and Anne-Marie are the best of friends and Jen is in France until school starts again in early September. This time it's Anne-Marie's turn to play host and show her friend around, and as an 18-year-old 'around' is a lot further than just down to the river. En masse, French fashion, the group toured the villages and towns of Western Brittany, a laughing, lounging, Gauloise-smoking clique that made Keswick and Jen's friends back home seem parochial indeed. Ten days after her enforced sojourn by the television England beat West Germany in the final. Neither girl cared one jot: the sun shone, they were carefree, together in a world full of possibilities. Four glorious weeks on, it was time to go home, to an England still delirious from that historic victory. I was to meet Jen off the plane at Newcastle airport for the start of her A-level year. The airport tannoy in Nantes announced that due to bad weather –'une tempête' – the plane couldn't fly. The next plane would be in a week.

The butterfly's great grand-daughter clapped her wings in delight.

Anne-Marie was studying English as her main subject at university in Rennes, and was required to spend the third of her four years' course in England, teaching in an English school. There was no question as to where that would be. Jen was in her final year at Leeds, studying Sociology. Anne-Marie joined her and her friends in a squalid student house, where they shared a room, their secrets, and a growing delight in Christianity. I was an occasional presence, hitching up from Oxford for a weekend and somehow we were the exception to the rule that 'Three's a crowd'. Her English became fluent, but never quite polished, always retaining a delightful Gallic lilt.

There are two obvious career choices for a French woman with a degree in English. She can teach English in a French school, or vice versa. Again, there was no question which Anne-Marie would choose. Her time in England had convinced her that she preferred our way of life: long evenings to spend with friends rather than the family; comfortable furniture; friendly pubs; cosy firesides. France seemed so formal in comparison, with Catholic families interconnected, forever spending interminable meals together. She had manned the barricades in '68, she was a revolutionary at heart and, Mon Dieu, she was born on 14th July, Bastille Day. Every year the nation put out the flags just for her. But for all that her future lay in England.

Easter 1971: Jen and I needed jobs, teaching jobs, and had spent a year in Leeds on the newly compulsory teacher training course for graduates. Anne-Marie was staying with Jen in Keswick, and I was with my parents on their rented farm in Borrowdale. Jen had an interview with the Head of a primary school in Whitehaven, West Cumberland. It was a walk-over, the Head couldn't believe his luck. A graduate, and she could teach French! He was a great believer in Primary School kids learning a language. That year, anyway. So hard to come by, French teachers in Whitehaven: why, his friend, the Head of the secondary school in town had been looking for weeks for a French teacher for next year. Oh really, well, guess what...? I, on the other hand, got a job in Windermere, 40 miles away, but at least all three of us were in Cumbria, and in work. In September, we were all teachers and the world had become a more serious place.

Instead of hitching up the M1 to see them, I now had a motorbike, and regularly rode over to the flat the girls had taken on the Solway coast, in the ancient village of St. Bees. Though I didn't realise it I regularly passed Fisherground, as I took the short cut over two of the steepest passes in the country, Hard Knott and Wrynose, and on through Eskdale en route. I had my own flat near Windermere, and Jen and Anne-Marie were my guests some weekends. One such weekend there was one other guest, Geoff, Jen's cousin, also a Wake.

Geoff was five years older than us, mature, his own man. He was a rock climber, which is why he was often in the Lake District, and he occasionally visited his Uncle Norman when in Keswick, which is where he came across this intriguing French girl. Unlike us he hadn't spent years in universities; he left school at fifteen to take an apprenticeship as a fitter and engineer. He had had time to make a living, to spend hours under an ancient AC sports car that he loved and to learn to climb. He'd also spent a few years in the Merchant Navy, making sure the cruise ship got from port to port, and the single ladies successfully back to their cabins from the bar. He knew the world, and was recently back from the Great Expedition.

After his time in the Merchant Navy, free as a bird and with money in his pocket, Geoff, his girlfriend Avril and his great friend Johnnie set off to drive round the world in an already world-weary Land-Rover that needed an engineer on board. Without Geoff's mechanical skills they would scarcely have made Dover. As it was, they made their way slowly across Europe, down through Turkey, and picked up one of the Silk Routes through Iraq, Iran and on into all the various Soviet 'stans'. Geoff insisted they weren't hippies -"Far too working class to be hippies!" Actually, he abhorred the genuine hippies they did come across, sponging on the local impoverished population in Pakistan and then in India. No, Geoff, Johnnie and Avril paid their way, and took occasional jobs on their journey to help make ends meet.

Wherever they went at least one member of the party had to be with the Land Rover at all times. Left alone it would have been stripped clean in less time than it takes a plague of locusts to clear a field of grain, so they slept in or around it, and two visited the sites along the way, while one was always on guard. The Land Rover became their fortress and their tank, as they made their way tortoise-like, instinctively withdrawing into its shell at any sign of danger. Ironically, then, it was the Land Rover that was their undoing. India's roads, or rather India's drivers, are legendary in their capacity to maim and kill. Only sacred cows are safe on an Indian road, and one such brought about their downfall. An oncoming lorry driver swerved to miss one and crashed into the Land Rover which somersaulted into a ditch. Geoff and Johnnie crawled out but Avril could only moan in pain. She was suffering from a badly twisted back and several broken bones. It was only after two weeks in hospital that she was deemed well enough to get on a plane home, leaving Geoff and Johnnie to nurse their beloved, battered and bent tortoise shell back to Britain.

Geoff and the Land Rover in Afghanistan: 1969

So this was the Geoff who was the other guest for a weekend in my new home near Windermere. We all went to a nearby pub for an evening out, and as I drove home with Jen beside me, Geoff and Anne-Marie were in the back and I inadvertently saw their first kiss in the driver's mirror. Jen saw I was ready to leap in with some bright remark, and

6

silenced me with a warning look. Our trio had become a foursome.

Jen and I were married that Christmas, 1971; Geoff and Anne-Marie 18 months later. We grew together almost organically, both couples buying neighbouring properties in a hamlet - though in our case it was a dilapidated barn in need of total renovation. Geoff helped me with the big stuff, and when it was complete I helped him extend and modernise their bungalow. At the same time Jen and Anne-Marie alternated babies. Catherine, our first, was born just before Geoff and Anne-Marie were married, and they had Elizabeth 16 months later. Sally, our second, followed just six months on, and Anne-Marie was pregnant all through the time we were negotiating to buy Fisherground.

We? 'We' was the four of us, partly because there was no way Jen and I could have raised the money alone, but mainly because we really wanted to continue the closeness that we'd experienced as friends and neighbours. We relished the challenge – even if we had little idea just how challenging it would be.

Chapter 2

'A hogg, a hogg, my kingdom for a Herdwick hogg' 1976

"If we don't get those hoggs, you don't get a sale. What good is a farm without its next generation of sheep?" I was angry, and I'm always aggressive when angry, especially on the telephone.

"Sorry, Mr. Hall, take it slowly, please." The estate agent hadn't a clue what I was getting so upset about. "I didn't think any pigs were included in this sale. What is a hog, exactly?"

"Oh for goodness sake! Hoggs are last year's lambs, and I need them because they'll be next year's ewes, part of the whole flock."

"Oh, right. Tell me again, Mr. Hall, where exactly are they?"

Well, it was rather complicated, to be fair. Mrs. Gingell was selling Fisherground, but she also had an old farmhouse and some poor land on the opposite side of the valley, just across the river, which she was keeping. And she seemed to think she could keep the hoggs too.

"They're on her land across the river. Mrs. Gingell, your client, seems to think they aren't part of the sale. Either they are, or there's no sale. "

"Ah: could they get across the river to your side?"

"Well, there is a bridge, though it might spook them, seeing as it's a swinging suspension bridge. Why?"

"I understand the farm manager has gone back to, ah..."

"Scotland. You can hardly blame him. Told he's got a job for life and then finds she's selling the farm. Why?"

"Well, look, I'm in London, the farm is in the Lake District, and there's nobody there who could get the sheep, the, ah, the hoggs back if they did cross the river, I don't suppose…"

What was he suggesting, this estate agent?

"No, I can hardly see Mrs. G. gathering hoggs."

These were Herdwick hoggs, the native and most robust breed on the Lakeland fells, and to my mind were essential to Fisherground and its future as a farm.

Mrs. G was a civil servant who had spent most of her life in London. She was probably a very good civil servant but she had only had Fisherground four years and now it was bankrupt. Mind you, this was no surprise. Lakeland farms could barely support a family, all working hard, never mind a farm manager, paid a proper salary. And she'd spent a fortune building a big daft cattle shed. Presumably she was going to try again on her side of the river, with the hoggs as the start of a new flock. I felt a bit sorry for her. It must have been a great disappointment to see her dream of making what she called 'the best farm in Eskdale' fall apart so soon.

Not sorry enough to give in over the hoggs, though. I didn't want 'the best farm…' but I did, desperately, want a farm, a farm with a proper fell flock, including its hoggs. In some ways, my credentials were little better than Mrs. Gingell's. I was a teacher, a Maths teacher, and had been for the last five years. But I had been brought up on a very similar farm in Borrowdale, and I'd spent the last year moodily staring out of the classroom window at the groundsman on his tractor, wishing I could change places.

It was Jen who first heard Fisherground was for sale. It was early in 1976, and we had two young daughters, Catherine and Sally, and the district nurse still popped in 'for a cuppa and a pee'. And a gossip; Joyce could talk for England, and she was a font of local knowledge. Jen told me that night, after we'd got the girls to bed.

"For sale? How the hell can we afford to buy a farm?" I asked in my usual roundabout manner. My parents had rented their farm in Borrowdale, and retired from it last year, pretty well penniless, so they wouldn't be able to help.

"Well, we could sell this place. We'd make a fortune, seeing as we did all the conversion ourselves." Sell? I was amazed; her dream home, picture windows, fitted kitchen, open plan lounge, all lovingly created by the sweat of our brows from a derelict barn. But then, Jen had also always wanted a farm.

"It's in the Lake District, Jen, Eskdale. It'll cost far more than we'll get for this."

"There's no harm in having a look, though, surely. I've got a really good feeling about this - I mean, it was pure luck Joyce dropping in."

Since there was indeed no harm in having a look, that's what we did, that very weekend. Drove into the valley, through the little village, Eskdale Green, with its village shop and opposite it the 'new' church, built over the village hall.

"Oh look, a basket-maker, William Hartley" Jen read, from his sign. "Blimey, when did you last see a basket-maker's shop?" On, past what looked like a sort of castle, incongruously sporting a sign proclaiming it was the Eskdale Outward Bound Mountain School. On, over a very hump-backed bridge with, of all things, a brightly painted red miniature steam engine passing under it, with a pall of black smoke billowing from its funnel, pulling a few hardy holiday makers huddled in winter woollies in open-topped carriages.

A little further on I suddenly yelled "Stop!" Jen drew up beside some metal railings enclosing a field opposite a pub, proudly displaying that it was the King George IV. "What?"

"Those railings, that's where that photo of me as a two year old was taken, standing just there, look, between Mum and Dad, just … here." We got out and Jen stood back a bit: "You're right, that little black and white square photo. Just about the only one there is of you as a kid. It is, it's right here.

What a coincidence - I told you, I've a really good feeling about this." Coincidence? Well, yes and no. I was born just eight miles away from where we now stood, and no doubt my parents had taken me for a ride on the very train line we'd just crossed. The Ravenglass and Eskdale Railway is its official name, but it's always known locally as t'La'al Ratty, perhaps to confuse visitors who can't pronounce the name.

Mum, Dad and a two-year-old me at the railings near the farm: 1950

We got back in the car and drove on, and almost immediately the farm came into view on the left, as the road narrowed down to a single track between dry stone walls. Tantalising glimpses over the walls showed a perfect setting, the farmhouse almost glowing in the low rays of the winter sun. At the end of the lane leading to the farm a crooked 'Footpath' signpost gave us permission to walk up the lane, parking the car in a nearby gateway. Feeling like spies casing the joint we sidled up the rough, rutted lane, hoods up, pretending to be normal walkers out for a hike. A mighty ash tree, skeletal against the sky, stood at the entrance of what was clearly an ancient orchard, the apple trees all wearing their own coats of moss. A stream burbled through it and Jen gasped in delight, as she took in the full panorama. The Georgian farmhouse was splendidly symmetrical, looking for all the world like a house young Catherine might have drawn, in its own walled garden - even if that garden was hideously overgrown. To our right was a truly magnificent bank barn, the traditional Cumbrian barn with a ramp at the back to fill the upper storey with hay and various byres and a cart-shed at yard level. It was just like the barn at Thorneythwaite where I had spent my happy teenage years. Other stone buildings formed the left side of the yard, and the whole scene was open to the south and the sun. Jen fell in love with it there and then, love at first sight.

We dawdled through the cobbled yard, largely covered with a hair shirt of grass and nettles, and up the walled lane that led towards the fellside and t'La'al Ratty line, which separated the lower fields from the intakes - enclosed fellside, full of bracken, rock and trees. The backs of houses, viewed from a train, are rarely things of beauty, and from this angle the ugly new cattle shed and the vast new slurry pit did their best to dampen Jen's ardour – but to no avail. I could see that if there was a way, any way, we could find the money to buy this glorious place, then find it we must.

The sale took four months to complete, four months of negotiating, dealing, crying with frustration, and finally agreeing a price and a contract. And now, to cap it all, Mrs. Gingell wanted to keep the hoggs, claiming that because they had spent the winter on her land across the River Esk they were legitimately hers. It took huge anger and frustration on my part to make that call to the estate agents, knowing that if they called my bluff we would have to make the hardest decision we'd ever made. But I had to have those hoggs, it just wasn't a real farm if it didn't have ewes of every age to make a proper fell flock. I reported the phone conversation to Jen, and we made the decision. At least for the time being we would keep those hoggs on 'our' side of the river, till the issue was resolved. With a mixture of bravado and trepidation we crossed the Rubicon, by the bridge, and tried to gather together the hoggs from Mrs. G.'s fields and bring them to the bridgehead. With only Jen's pet dog, Tess, and old Beaut, pensioned off by my parents after they retired, we struggled to keep the wilful delinquents in a flock and move them along. My blood-pressure, and the inventiveness of my language, rose exponentially as one after another broke away and had to be chased back into line, but eventually we were at the bridgehead. Impasse: no sheep would venture on that undulating platform.

"Now what? How are we going to get them on?"

"How the hell do I know, I've never had to drive sheep over a suspension bridge before."

"Keep your hair on, Ian, it's not helping, you losing your rag."

"I know, sorry love, but I just feel so exposed and ridiculous. This is supposed to be an undercover operation, and the whole of Eskdale must know by now. Why won't the bastards just give it a try?"

"Look, you try to hold them all together – you've got Beaut and she knows what she's doing. I'll grab one and take it over – see if others follow." Jen leapt in among the scrum and caught a smallish hogg, and straddled it and sort of shuffled it across to the middle of the bridge, while I did a fair impression of a demented leprechaun shouting and yelling behind the rest of the flock. Eventually, tentatively, another followed to join the one Jen held in the middle, and as she retreated with it slowly, Indian-file, others followed, clearly very nervous of the swaying suspension bridge. I held my breath, and my language; Beaut lay down panting while Tess kept up a steady bark that was really getting on my nerves. Then the file broke: one nervous little bugger refused to follow and we were left with half across with Jen, half still with me. Wearily Jen came back over, grabbed another, and, infinitely slowly, the process started again. It took four forays, and well over half an hour, before they were all over, and of course by now all over the field as well.

Running now, to help tired old Beaut, we gathered them together, Jen and Tess barking together to make the stupid things move, and we got them across the road, through the cobbled yard, still overgrown, up the walled lane and so into the rickety sheep-pens that looked as if they had been in place at least since the first World War, if not before. Drawing on my experiences as a teenager on my parents' farm in Borrowdale, I mixed the recommended strength of dipping fluid in the tub, and an hour later 60 hoggs stood drying in the sun.

Now, quickly, we needed to get them out onto the fell. Mrs. G. could come for them if she wanted. Next problem: how to get them over the railway line with just two people and two pet dogs. Jen stood down the line while I chased them out of the pens. Being teenage delinquents the hoggs had no intention of making it easy, and instead of crossing and going through the intake gate they trooped off up the line, me in hot pursuit. Once they were through the gate, however, it was fairly easy going, up the main track to the fell gate and out onto their fell; the fell they were heafed to.

Heafing is the critical factor with Herdwicks, and the reason I felt so strongly that we needed these particular hoggs. They had spent the last summer on the same fell as lambs with their mothers, and left to themselves would stay on the fell where they were raised - essential on fells with no boundaries. I could have walked from the fell gate at Fisherground to Thorneythwaite – and many miles further –

without crossing any wall, fence or boundary. Theoretically, then, so could the hoggs and sheep, but for that vital heafing instinct.

I hoped Mrs. G. would come to see it that way.

Fisherground in 1972, as Mrs. Gingell bought it

Chapter 3

Bending the rules: January to July 1st 1976

Going into Fisherground as a partnership still fell a long way short of the finance we would need to buy the farm. We also had to strike a deal with the next door neighbour, Michael Postlethwaite, who had his eye on some of the land that would be sold with the farm. Once again my past poked its head over the parapet of time. Unusually for a man who rarely volunteered any information just in case it might be used against him, I had told my parents about our first visit, thinking they would be interested in the railings where the photo had been taken. I hadn't anticipated the reaction.

"Eskdale, oh, what a lovely valley. We spent our honeymoon there. You remember, Jim?"

"Would I dare forget? Yes, and many trips with friends when we were in Corney. Spent our honeymoon with Possie and his Missus -what was her name, Betty?"

"Mary, Mary and Jimmy. Spout House, right beside Fisherground if I remember right."

"Let me get this straight… you two know the people next door?" Parents! Full of surprises.

"Well, we did. It's a long time ago now, but I did see Jimmy a few years ago when we last went to Eskdale Show. Look, why don't we ring them up and sound them out about the place. They'll know what's what."

It was a strange feeling, at 27, to find your parents' honeymoon figuring in your own plans, but if there was a chance they could help make our dreams come true I was very ready to use any lever available. Two days later Jen and I stood dutifully in the shadows while Dad knocked on Jimmy's door. We were taken into what was obviously the front room, the fire banked up and cheerful, every surface polished to perfection, rosettes proudly announcing many firsts, seconds and a few thirds in sheep classes at various shows. Dad introduced us both and Jimmy introduced his own son, Michael. We all sat as directed and Mary bustled in with tea and cakes, delicately displayed on a three tier cakestand. She handed round plates and doilies, and we obediently made our choices. Jen surreptitiously held her little finger out at the soirée angle and I suppressed a giggle.

Cumbrian conversations can be convoluted, and protocol demands a lot of nibbling at the edges before you tackle the main course. So for an hour the older generation caught up with what each had done for the last 30 years or so and we realised that Michael was born on the same date as me, but a year later. We three youngsters sat obediently on the side-lines. Only when it was time to go did Dad casually mention Fisherground. The story went that the farm had become very run-down over the years as the previous farmer had grown old and tired of milking by hand. He had died in 1972, when it had been bought by Mrs. Gingell who intended to make it 'the finest farm in Eskdale'. She was Principal Private Secretary to Michael Heseltine, then shadow Environment Spokesman, later Secretary of State for the Environment, so while she may not have known much about fell farming in deepest Lakeland she clearly knew a great deal about affairs of state. She approached Fisherground with the open wallet typical of Civil Service contracts.

For three years she invested heavily in Fisherground, but to cut a long story short it hadn't worked out, and Knight, Frank and Rutley, perhaps the most prestigious estate managers and agents in the country, had been instructed to sell. The advert even appeared in 'Country Life'.

Michael was now very interested in buying the prime 32 acres, to augment the farm he was inheriting from his parents. This would leave just 35 acres of poor bottom land, 60 acres of scrubby intake, (enclosed land on the side of the fell,

17

full of rock and bracken), and the fell rights to go with the farm itself. We were still adamant we wanted to buy, even though Mum and Dad cautioned that it was unviable as a farm without those prize 32 acres. Days later we agreed to submit a joint offer with Michael under which he'd get his 32 acres, us the rest. It wasn't ideal, in fact it would hardly really be a farm, more a smallholding with fell rights, but buying Fisherground had become a possibility.

"Oh my God, they've accepted our offer. Now what?" Now it was time for solicitors, for selling both our houses, for looking for a mortgage. Time for second thoughts, for doubts, for wondering how all this would work. How do you fit two families into an old farmhouse? How do you split up incomes, outgoings, duties, responsibilities, rights? We should have been thinking all this through - our worried parents certainly were – but none of it seemed to trouble the four of us one whit. With the sublime folly of youth we simply assumed everything would be fine, and somehow it was. Both our houses found buyers, at prices that would make it all happen. All we needed now was a mortgage.

On the practical side Jen and I were busy. Charlie, Mrs. G.'s farm manager, could see no merit in going down with a sinking ship, and once he knew our offer had been accepted he rang to say he was leaving with his family, going off to a possible job back in Scotland, and would we come down so he could hand things over.

"Aye, I thought it would be you two. Ye see I saw you standing in the yard, luking around sae keen, back in January, and I thought to myself, 'Aye, they'll be the ones, jist you wait and see'." He gave us a big brass key for the front door, and said he'd leave the back door Yale in the house when he left. It was March, and lambing would start in April.

Here was a nice moral dilemma to start our farming career. Who was to look after the 200 odd Herdwick ewes? We didn't own them, but if everything went according to plan we soon would. Mrs. G. did own them still, but was busy in

Whitehall. Whose sheep would be on the 32 good acres that Michael hoped to buy? It was all a splendid muddle, and in the event Michael and I sorted it between us. He expanded his flock onto 'his' acres, but kept an eye on 'our' flock, while Jen and I made the fifteen mile journey at least once a day, after school, to deal with any problem mothers - several of whom ended up back in our garden for Jen to keep an eye on. Of course we set up camp in the farmhouse, proud owners in a 'nine parts of the law' sense, with a kettle, coffee and picnic facilities.

Enter Major Thompson, stage left, valuer for the National Farmers' Union. Were we fit to gain a mortgage from this august society? As we walked around the farm, marvelling at the fine buildings, making up our plans as we went along, he quizzed us about the unconventional partnership we envisaged. I assured him Geoff and I would carry on working, (fingers firmly crossed behind my back), and that we both made good money. The Major's bushy eyebrows lifted a little, quizzically, when we invited him in for a cup of tea.

"I say, you do seem rather well established!"

"Yes, well, you see, the previous manager has abandoned ship, so we're having to look after things. We are just camping in the kitchen…"

"Quite so… quite so, em, how came you by the key?" I told him about Charlie and the lambing we had done.

"Um, established on all fronts, then, quite so."

"Well, someone has to look after the lambing ewes, and we do enjoy it, to be honest."

"Quite so… tell me, would you be down-hearted should I turn down your application?"

Down-hearted? We would be devastated: but he didn't. The NFU offered a mortgage at a rate bordering on usury, of 14¼ %, fixed for the next 25 years. Naturally, we accepted, eagerly.

With our offer accepted, the NFU mortgage available, and our own house sales proceeding at the usual crawl, we started to think of Fisherground as ours, very much against the advice of the solicitor, who had seen many a purchase fail at the last hurdle. It was at this crucial stage that Mrs. G. claimed possession of the 60 hoggs, and I lost my temper. To have come so far, to have spent so long dreaming about escaping the classroom, to have put so much effort into helping our, yes, dammit, OUR ewes to lamb successfully, only to be told she was about to make yet another monumental agricultural mistake was more than I could bear. In the first place, it was a ridiculous argument she was making - that because the hoggs had spent the winter on her side of the river they would be heafed to her land. In the second place, she had no fell fit for sheep, just a boggy, wooded scrubland that would kill them all in their first year. But above all, a farm without all generations of ewes was a non-starter. That hurdle side-stepped, if not jumped cleanly, we really did start to think the farm was ours.

There were developments on other fronts. Anne-Marie grew bigger as she entered her second trimester, the baby quickening and beginning to make its presence felt. Ever since finishing teaching, with a sigh of relief, to have Elizabeth, she had marked papers for examination boards, and she spent that May and June busy with scripts, busy with Elizabeth, and resting at every possible opportunity. Somehow she could never find the time or the energy to make the journey to see what, fingers crossed, would be her new home. Besides, if it was good enough for Geoff, if it kept the families together, if her English dream remained intact... She had a hazy memory of a trip on the little train back in the '60s with Jen and had thought the valley beautiful then. 'Thy will be done, on earth as it is in Heaven'. Anne-Marie was content to let Jen, Geoff and me take care of the practicalities.

*****

"Ian… it's stupid to have the kitchen at the back of the house, and a parlour nobody uses at the front."

"Um, well, I see what you mean Jen, but the Rayburn is in the kitchen…" The Rayburn was a poor man's Aga, cast iron, weighing half a ton, and with a flue going up the chimney.

"Can't you move it? Somebody put it there, it must be possible for you to put it here."

I gave her that long, slow, appraising look that always made her wonder if she'd pushed her luck too far, but was really just giving me time to think. She held my look, smiled winningly, and I sighed, resigned to trespass on an industrial scale. It's one thing to camp out in a house you don't technically own yet, it's quite another to alter said house fundamentally.

I thought Geoff might be an ally, a male voice of reason, but he was all for making a start. After all, he and Anne-Marie would be living upstairs, and there was no kitchen at all there, yet, so the next job after moving the Rayburn would be to tackle upstairs as well. Together, he and I undid the flue, brought in rollers made from old scaffolding pipes, and between us managed to manoeuvre the beast onto them. It was a piece of cake then to trundle the range along the corridor, Stonehenge style, into the kitchen-to-be. Connecting the flue was more of a problem, and it simply disappeared into the chimney with no fancy flue liners. But this was the 1970's, and nobody ever died of Carbon Monoxide poisoning in those heady days.

Between us, me after school, Geoff after a shift at Sellafield, sometimes with small girls in tow, we made workman-like kitchens upstairs and down, and a new bathroom downstairs. Jen peeled off acres of woodchip, painted walls, and took several doors to a place that stripped all traces of paint and varnish - and most of the glue holding the joints - in a vat of caustic soda. All in all we thought it better not to tell the solicitor. He'd only have worried.

Fisherground in 1976, as we bought it

Chapter 4

The long, hot summer: 1976

1st July 1976: the middle of the longest, hottest, sunniest Summer anyone could remember. Carting our clutter in a hired van and my parents' trailer, over several journeys, we four adults, three young girls and a baby in waiting finally took legal possession of Fisherground. Anne-Marie gazed, rather awestruck, at what was to be her new home and new lifestyle. Geoff took her upstairs, to what would be their home. Strictly, it should be called a flat, but we'd never thought of the house that way: it was far too interconnected in so many ways to be reduced to mere flats. She could have been upset at the loss of her lovely, independent bungalow. She could have been oppressed by the pine-boarded kitchen, the dowdy wallpaper, the prospect of coming and going through the downstairs hall and communal stairwell. Perhaps, had it ever rained in that first two months she might have been. As it was she was entranced.

We had all lived closely enough before, cheek by jowl in a small hamlet. Now we were literally on top of each other, just a stairwell apart. Inevitably the two women spent most of the day together, while Geoff and I were out at work. The toddlers loved it too, rolling naked on what was becoming a lawn, after I attacked it with a scythe and Jen tidied up the stubble with one of the two mowers we'd brought. We also had a spare washing machine and tumble drier stored in a shed outside: sharing a house meant only enough space for one of everything inside. It all felt a bit like being students again, sharing a house... except for the toddlers, and Anne-Marie being pregnant.

We must all have had conflicting emotions at the reality of what we'd taken on, but somehow being so busy in those first few months, with wall to wall sunshine every day, made it all seem so natural, so right. We settled effortlessly into the new regime, and there was no looking back. Traditionally farms change hands on Lady Day, March 25th, which long ago was New Year's Day. It's the start of the growing season: grass begins to shoot, cows to have their calves, sheep their lambs. Fields were ready to plough, corn could be sown. It was the sensible, logical day for new tenants to start on a farm. Coming in on July 1st, even though we'd overseen the lambing from April onwards, conflated our year terribly, and not having any machinery made it vital to get on with things. Top of the list was a tractor. What is a farm without a tractor?

Leaving Anne-Marie at home in charge of all three girls, Geoff, Jen and I went to buy a tractor at the nearest machinery sale, fifty miles away in Carlisle. Me, as the would-be farmer, to bid; Geoff, as the knowledgeable mechanic, to sift out the hopeless wrecks, and Jen because she loved sales… any kind of sales! We were badly strapped for cash, and with our selection limited to older, smaller models, I picked out an International Harvester that Geoff thought ran well. Michael had already warned us not to buy a four cylinder Massey Ferguson 35. He had one and said they were notoriously difficult to start from cold. Sure enough there was one in the sale that in all other respects looked good. Being warmed up anyway it started easily and Geoff thought it ran smoothly, but we agreed to go for the International if it was in our price range.

This was my first experience of bidding in an auction, and as the auctioneer moved down the rows of machinery with his coterie of dealers and farmers in tow I got increasingly nervous, till at last we were in front of the International.

"Nice little International here, come from a good home. Who'll start me at £200. 200, gentlemen, 200 anywhere?"

I kept my hands in my pockets, not wanting to declare an interest yet.

"Well all right, then, 175, somebody will... thank you Frank, 175 I am bid."

Frank, eh, a dealer then I supposed. He wouldn't go beyond a fair price.

"Come on gentlemen, 175, 175, who'll give me 190. Ah, thank you, Sir, 190 I am bid, 190."

Oh God, that was me. £190, and we'd said £200 was our maximum.

"190, then, 190, 200 bid, thank you Frank, 200, 200 any other bids?"

It was this or the Ferguson, that might be hard to start, and how much would it be? Oh hell, we couldn't come all this way for nothing. I nodded my head, trying to appear casual.

"220, 220 I'm bid."

220? I thought we were going up in tens.

"220, 220, last chance gentlemen.... 220 it is. Thank you, Sir, give your details to my clerk here."

We weren't prepared to pay a haulier good money to bring it home, so I decided to drive it the 50 or so miles to Eskdale, which we reckoned would take about four hours. We agreed to meet up in a pub about five miles out of Carlisle to eat, after which Jen and Geoff would go on without me. 'The best laid plans of mice and men gan oft a'glee...' and this plan soon looked a bit shaky as I struggled to steer a straight line through the streets of Carlisle on a tractor whose front wheels preferred to go in two different directions. By the time I got to the pub I was very sure this wasn't a machine I wanted to spend long hours on in a field, and certainly not all the way to Eskdale. A hasty confab produced plan B which was to return to Carlisle and see if any of the traders would do us a swap.

Leaving the wayward International in the pub car park we dashed off back to find the auction over and only one professional trader, Frank, co-incidentally, still loading his purchases, which included the MF 35. I explained our dilemma and asked if he would swap the Massey for the IH, and take it to Fisherground.

"It'll cost you £75 plus the VAT for me to do the swap and bring the Massey down, but of course you can claim the VAT back."

"Em, no, no, we're not VAT registered, we've just started you see, and we haven't got round to registering yet."

"Oh hell, that's going to make it very complicated, and expensive. I've paid VAT on it, and I have to charge you VAT or I'll lose out. Listen, tell you what, we'll pretend I'm selling you, oh, I don't know, a load of hay. More or less the same price, but there's no VAT on hay. I'll give you an invoice for it to keep you straight, and you can keep the invoice for the International."

We were completely lost by this time, unused either to the vagaries of VAT or the machinations of dealers but we agreed what we thought was the deal and gave him the keys to the International. Despite our worst fears that Frank would just disappear into the blue with both money and tractor, he did indeed turn up the next day, and we were the proud owners of a Massey Ferguson 35. Jen painted it back in its original red, and it got us safely through that first year's fieldwork. And yes, it always was a bugger to start from cold.

A farm sale just down the valley provided most of the rest of the implements we needed: a knife-bar mowing machine, a 'Wuffler' hay tedder, and a Vicon-Lely Acrobat hay rower, and a small trailer to go behind the tractor. None of these was in the first flush of youth, and Geoff was hard put to keep them going, but hay-making was so easy in that glorious first summer we could almost have done it with scythes and rakes. The sun was so hot that by mid-July the grass was withering on the stalk and had to be cut or lost, so I cut fields before going to teach, starting more or less at sunrise, leaving Jen to turn them with the Wuffler - if she could get the Fergie to start.

We had no baler, that year, and called on the services of a neighbour, Tom Bowes, who was even younger than us, and who would turn up dressed entirely in cowboy gear, with boots, jeans and ten gallon hat. He drew the line at the spurs. Tom made short work of our few acres and the crop was so sparse it took little effort to get it in the barn, even with our tiny trailer. It was a far cry from my teenage years struggling to help my parents make hay in Borrowdale, just a mile from Seathwaite, the wettest place in England, where some years the job dragged on into September. My parents, Jim and Betty, had retired from Thorneythwaite only the year before and were keen to help at Fisherground, both with advice and with muscle. I had chafed, as a son does, under their yoke at Thorneythwaite, and was determined now to be king of my own midden.

My parents had spent their own first two haytimes working purely with horses and the primitive machines they could pull. Manpower was essential, and the more the better, to turn wet grass over to dry, to rake in from the edges of the field, and, if rain threatened, to construct what were known as 'pikes', carefully constructed huge piles of still drying grass around a tripod that kept a hollow centre. They had only grudgingly moved on to baling and mechanisation, forced by the lack of manpower, and in perennially wet Borrowdale had suffered many a fraught haytime. Now they turned up unannounced at Fisherground eager to help, forks and rakes in hand. At the same time Jen was equally eager to make something of the garden which was overgrown and overshadowed by several fruit trees that had been allowed to grow wild. She and I were chain-sawing when Mum and Dad arrived, horrified by such tom-foolery when the critical task of haymaking loomed large over the day. I was caught, skewered on the horns of a dilemma that went back years. I knew they were right, that farming should be single-minded, that the critical job of the day was to get the hay dried and baled. And I knew Jen was right, too. This day was so sunny,

27

and the crop so thin, that it would dry with or without our input. So why not attend to the garden's needs too?

Dad mowing with horses, 1948, the year of my birth

Instead of making the case gently and carefully I reacted badly, making it more than clear that I was the boss now, and that everything was under control, the weather set fair and the machines eminently capable of turning wet grass into hay. And that we really didn't need their help. Wordlessly they returned to their car and the 15 miles to their home. As soon as they were gone I abandoned the tree and the garden, got on the tractor and unnecessarily turned the grass over one more time. Nothing more was said, no apologies offered, and it was something I came to regret profoundly. I threw myself into the farm work for those six blessed school holiday weeks, while Jen and Anne-Marie explored our beautiful new valley. They discovered Turn Dub, a lovely pool in the River Esk, and were frequently there with the toddlers, picnicking on the bank and paddling in the beautifully clear waters. I discovered wall gaps to be mended, fences to be fixed, systems to be set up, and sheep to be clipped. Geoff had a new journey to Sellafield, and machinery to tinker with in the evenings.

'Boon day' clipping at Fisherground in the 19th Century

There were sheep to clip, over 200 ewes and the 60 odd hoggs 'retrieved' from Mrs. G, and we had no clipping machine. However, we had another neighbour in Eskdale, Maurice Steele, whom I'd known since we were kids, as he was born and brought up on the next door farm in Corney, just eight miles down the coast. I asked if I could maybe hire his machine just for this year, as we could ill afford to buy one yet. Maurice turned me down flat, saying he would never let anyone else use his precious machine. Then with a twinkle in his eye he added that he would be delighted to come and clip our flock for free. We were given a photo of the 19th century 'boon day' equivalent of this good neighbourliness, where all the valley farmers spent a day on each farm clipping all the sheep.

*****

On another front, Lake District National Park byelaws allowed anyone with land to use it for camping for up to 28 days a year, and with the temperature in the 70's every day this looked a good year to use the allowance. A hand-painted sign at the end of the lane designated the front left field for camping and we waited expectantly for customers. We didn't have long to wait, and soon the field was buzzing with tents, cars - and lots of people wanting a loo. We quickly set up a single 'Elsan' portaloo in the old dairy, the building nearest the campers, and allocated a standpipe outside for their use. Two or three times a day I hauled the Elsan up the yard , opened up the top of the septic tank, and poured it in, washed it out, reprimed it with the fluid, and replaced it for the next onslaught. This first venture into camping was manic, unsanitary, but very profitable. At 25p per adult, 10p for children and 10p a car we were taking some real money. And when the sun shines every day nobody minds a smelly loo too much.

Chapter 5

Outward Bound!: 1976-7

There were tensions, that first Summer, of course there were tensions. Living so close to each other the only way a couple could argue was to go into the middle of a field, and as we struggled to accommodate each other inevitably there were frictions. But the sun shone relentlessly on and by and large we were carried along by the great adventure. Jen and Anne-Marie started to make new friends in the valley, discovering a rich vein of ladies of similar age and interests. Next door (half a mile away) was the Eskdale Outward Bound Centre, run by fit, active instructors with kids at the same stage as the three Fisherground girls. Jen, taking our three-year-old Catherine to a playgroup in a nearby village, found herself accosted by a stressed mother thrusting her own three-year-old into the car with the scantiest of introductions. More properly introduced a little later this was Hilary Duncan, the key to unlocking the Outward Bound treasure chest of friends, children and parties.

In 1950 the Outward Bound Organisation took over Gatehouse, an imposing castellated example of the Victorian country houses that sprang up throughout the Lake District in the 19th Century. This was a late specimen, built in 1896 by Lord Rea of Eskdale, a Liverpool shipping magnate and millionaire. Gatehouse itself is magnificent, inside and out. The south façade looks out over the six acre shallow tarn Lord Rea had constructed, surrounded by rhododendron gardens kept more or less in check by the full time gardeners Outward Bound employs.

"Thomas Mawson, you know" said Hilary, airily. Jen looked at her blankly.

"Mawson, the Edwardian Capability Brown?" Jen nodded warily, Capability Brown she had heard of – must be talking about the gardens.

"Go on...."

"Well, Lord Rea managed to tempt him over here - hell of a coup - height of his career and all that. He designed lots of the stately home gardens in Cumbria. Brockhole and Holehird in Windermere – oh, and Blackwell."

"Oh, I know, the famous Arts and Craft house above Windermere."

"That's the one, did you know he even invented the title Arts and Craft?"

"Hilary, you amaze me!" Hilary grinned wickedly: "Not really, they do lectures on him to every new course in the Centre."

Eskdale Outward Bound Centre looks out over its tarn

At Gatehouse the main entrance opens to a hallway sporting an immense fireplace with the homely motto inscribed: 'East, West, Hame's Best'. This leads through to a dining room, a large library and then on to a snooker room where the full size table rises from the floor at the turn of a capstan. Parties here were of a completely new order; rowdy, boisterous, and sometimes all-night long.

During our first December in the valley Hilary invited us all to the 'Farmers' Party', an all-night do with a lot of style that the staff of Outward Bound (OB) put on each year as a sort of thank-you to anyone in the valley who had helped them in any way. Fisherground would have qualified anyway as OB used the crags and rocky outcrops on the intakes and fell for lots of training exercises; but by that stage Jen and Anne-Marie were firm friends with many of the wives and staff. My parents, summer slights forgotten, volunteered to sleep over in the farmhouse and baby-sit for what were now four girls, and we set off in our best bib and tucker for the party of the season.

Squashed into the fine main entrance, with a roaring fire under the motto, we mingled with new friends and neighbours, accepted the proffered glasses of wine, and listened in some awe as Roger Putnam, the eminently smooth and civilised warden, gave a run-down of the past year's successes and thanked all villagers present for their help. In those days OB offered month-long courses in August, with much of the time spent out on camp, and the crag behind the farm regularly rang to shouts of encouragement as another youngster had his first abseil or scaled her first pitch.

Supper was a sumptuous buffet with silver plates presenting, as I moved on down the table, a full salmon, opened out for best display, a succulent side of ham, a roast of beef showing that delicacy of pink that promises juicy perfection and a Lamb Henry that must have come from a truly mighty Texel. Geoff, a lifelong vegetarian, made a gargantuan meal of samosas, Yorkshire pudding, delicious crackling roast potatoes and glacéd carrots, all rounded off with not one, but two puddings. The bar did a roaring trade and the guests drifted off, some to the billiard room, where the table was raised in readiness. A quartet in the musicians' gallery overlooking it re-created the atmosphere of the house's Edwardian heyday as those not playing chatted in the ingle nook. Others took to the dance floor in the library where a folk dance band and caller led the revellers in various rumbustious country dances. The four of us joined in lustily, Geoff and me whirling our womenfolk off their feet in the notorious 'Cumbrian Basket'. We might not have got Anne-Marie off the ground a couple of months earlier, but now she was back to her trim size ten.

Just past midnight, ties loosened and tongues the more so, shoes kicked off along with inhibitions, I was suddenly called to the telephone. First thoughts, 'Oh God, the kids. What can have happened?' But no, an anxious Mum with the news that it was snowing hard, and she and Dad really felt I should come back now and go up the fell to open the gate in case the sheep needed to come in, and maybe carry on round the fell wall to make sure no ewes were getting covered over in drifts. They'd learnt from bitter experience, having started farming in March 1947, just at the end of the cruellest winter on record, when the fells and even the villages had been cut off for many weeks. The flock of sheep they took over, that should have numbered two hundred, was down to less than a hundred, and very few were still in lamb. These things stayed with them. I stayed at the party.

There was an historic connection between Gatehouse and Fisherground. Lord Rea, real name James Hall Rea, had bought a considerable chunk of Eskdale at the turn of the century, Fisherground included, and had upgraded the farm around 1910. All the roofs dated from then, and one of the 'new' buildings had a plaque with his initials JHR inset. I was intrigued by the coincidence as Dad was James Hall; all the more so when I discovered another plaque in St Catherine's church to a previous vicar, one James Wharrier Hall. The squire and the parson – it seemed appropriate somehow.

The only other plaque at the farm was much older and well-worn, but it was still possible to make out the names and date: John and Hannah Sharp, 1795. This was on the front of the house and entirely appropriate for an obviously Georgian farmhouse, but surely the farm was much older than that? The mystery was solved by a teacher friend who presented me with a photograph, produced as a sepia postcard in the style of the late 1800's, showing the proud owner with his horse and trap in front of not one house, but two. The present house stands proud, neatly covered with Virginia creeper, its roof and slate chimney guards clearly pre-Lord Rea, looking prosperous and well kempt.

Fisherground in the 19th Century, the older, white property to the left

To its left is a much simpler dwelling, fully a yard lower, with two tiny windows, each with a centrally pivoted 'tilt and turn' opening pane. Beside the oak-planked door stands a braffin, the neck collar that is a fundamental part of a working horse's harness. This house, though ancient, is also clearly well maintained, with good slates and a fresh coat of lime wash, and was doubtless home to farm workers. In those pre-mechanical days each farm supported and needed a work force of at least three or four men and as many women.

We four new-comers had great fun piecing it all together, looking for clues in each of the many buildings, old maps and other photographs that turned up here and there. That original house was contemporary with what was now the oldest building left. Running at right angles to the old house, separated by a narrow lane through, was the original farm building, probably from the 16th Century. The ground floor held the remains of a stable and two small byres, each with its own wide doorway and a small window. Upstairs, reached by an unprotected stone stairway, was what had originally been the storage barn for hay and oats, now cut in two by a lath and plaster wall. This building remained, but the original house was gone, though it is still shown on the 1899 Ordnance Survey map - presumably a casualty of Lord Rea's modernising. Though it was gone some physical evidence remained, for the west wall of the new house was the original east wall of the old, and a bulge halfway up told of a fireplace long gone. There were very few windows on this west wall, and what there were but recent, as it had been the solid party wall between the two houses, separating master from workers. When Geoff and I came to knocking through more windows later we found old bottles and clay pipes buried in the stonework.

Across the yard, running true north-south, was the magnificent 'new' barn, built by John and Hannah Sharp, but re-roofed by Lord Rea. This was a classic Cumbrian bank barn, built to store oat straw and hay on the huge top floor, and with byres and a cart shed below. The oats were originally winnowed (separated from the straw) by beating them with flails on the threshold floor in front of the great east doorway, with the small west door wide open to catch the prevailing wind and so blow the chaff away from the threshold. Lord Rea, however, had improved on this ancient method by installing a small threshing machine beside the great doorway. This was driven by a horse-powered gin wheel which still stood outside. When we came in 1976 all the machinery was rusted and inoperable, but many years later we donated and transported the threshing machine to Eskdale Corn Mill and museum, just up the valley in Boot village. It is still there. The Corn Mill, the threshing floor and the new-fangled threshing machine all testify to a very different valley, one where self-sufficiency was the order of the day. When travel to other centres was too time-consuming to be standard. When the village had its own butcher, baker, chair-maker, basket maker and cobbler. When everything they ate, or needed for the animals, had to be grown in the valley fields.

Our arrival in 1976 came at the very end of this era. William Hartley still ran his basket shop, though he had bought the willow baskets in for the last decade. John Porter, the last cobbler, had retired but loved to tell the tales of the Eskdale he had known since the first decade of the century. The amateur dramatic society was putting on its last show in the village hall, and the last of the Hunt Balls which had been such a feature of Lakeland life were puttering to an inglorious end. There were still the occasional whist drives in the village hall, but they too soon petered out.

At Fisherground there were two pieces of evidence of the previous 40 years, and how the farm had been run. Attached to the south end of the fine bank barn was the milking parlour, built in 1935 to modernise Fisherground's dairy enterprise, based as so many were then on Shorthorn cattle. Another photograph turned up, of a farm boy proudly holding the Shorthorn bull in the yard, just where the horse and trap had stood half a century before. The parlour held 16, a fair herd in those days, and was light and airy. But they all had to be milked by hand, for there was no trace of pipework for a machine, and Michael-next-door told how the hardship of it all had led to the previous tenant's having a nervous breakdown.

The only other stone building, in the garden, was the privy.

Boy with bull, about 1930
Note the decorative ball and its mount in the previous
picture has been displaced – the ball alone just sitting on the wall.

One relict of the previous century did remain, though, and went from strength to strength. At the back of the farm, between the fields and the intakes, ran the miniature railway track, the Ravenglass and Eskdale Railway, t'La'al Ratty. It's a 15 inch gauge seven-mile track originally used to haul iron ore and granite from Boot, the village in the middle of Eskdale, to the main line station at Ravenglass on the West Cumbrian coast. It was saved from extinction in 1960 by a consortium of far-sighted business entrepreneurs and a preservation society, and kept going by the trickle of visitors drifting over from the busy Central Lakes. A trickle that was by now building to a stream. The Ratty celebrated the new ownership of Fisherground in spectacular fashion - it had its only major crash the day after we moved in, just half a mile up the valley from us. On a very busy, very hot day as many extra trains as possible were running to cope with the unprecedented hordes of visitors. An 'extra' train coming down the valley met the scheduled train going up at the worst possible place, Gilbert's Cutting, a blind corner. Fortunately no-one was killed in the collision, but there were 13 injured, four of them quite seriously. The first Jen knew of the crash was when Norman, her father, rang from Newcastle to ask her to fill in the gaps in the news bulletin he had just heard.

Chapter 6

Showtime: September 1977

I missed Eskdale Show the first year we were at the farm. It seemed more important to sort through the sheep, weaning the lambs: 'spayning' as it is called locally. By late September the lambs are five months old and shouldn't need their mothers any longer, while the mothers need a couple of months' break to get in condition for tupping. Every Lakeland valley holds its own show over the summer, Eskdale's, on the last Saturday in September, being one of the latest. As I was back at school I only had weekends free for the big jobs, but Jen and Anne-Marie went, with the three girls, Anne-Marie by then feeling elephantine, just a month before her due date. They didn't stay very long, with fractious children and Anne-Marie's discomfort, but long enough to get a flavour of what was on offer.

The main purpose of the shows is to judge the livestock brought in by the local farmers. The more adventurous venues had categories for sheep, cattle, goats and horses, and even ran gymkhanas, and were a draw for large numbers of visitors. Eskdale thought of itself as purist, and only offered sheep judging - and only Herdwick sheep, at that. There was a certain historical appropriateness in this, as it was held in the fields of Brotherilkeld Farm, at the head of the valley, at the foot of Hard Knott pass. Brotherilkeld has a good claim on Herdwick history, as one of the summer farms that the monks of Furness Abbey sent their flocks to way back in the 13th century, right up to the Dissolution.

Fisherground's own flock of females arrived too late for the judging, but they wandered past the pens admiring the primped, rudded rams, ewes and gimmer hoggs, Catherine trying out her dialect calling them tips and yows as if born to it. She got excited in the produce marquee where the school-children had made animals from vegetables. First prize went to a cunningly constructed crocodile made largely from cucumber. Jen was more drawn to the photography section, one of her skills, and was fascinated to see my friend Maurice had won first prize with a moody shot of an oak tree set against a dark cloudy background and highlighted by a shaft of sunlight.

Anne-Marie was under a different kind of cloud and badly needed to sit down, and they made their way to the tea tent, realm of the Women's Institute, and full of neighbouring farmers' wives eager to have a look at the newcomers who, rumour had it, were part of a commune down at Fisherground. Jen and Anne-Marie spent a slightly fraught half-hour putting people right on that score, reeling in the girls as they explored this strange new world, and fending off invitations to join the WI . They then beat a hasty retreat back home for Anne-Marie to put her feet up, to change the girls' nappies, and to regale Geoff and me with their stories of neighbours and the show.

A year later I had retired from school-teaching for ever and Anne-Marie was back to normal size. We could all go together to the next show. More accurately, Jen, Anne-Marie and Geoff could come up to the showfield straight after an early dinner to join me. I had been arm-twisted into entering four of the Fisherground flock in the sheep judging and had passed an embarrassing morning - the auction experience in spades - realising our sheep had no place among these prize specimens of Herdwick grace. My attempts at rudding resembled rouge on a whore's face, and the judges passed over our pen rapidly with barely suppressed grins.

I fared no better in the sheepdog judging. Knowing Moss's limitations - or perhaps my own - I wouldn't have gone in for a 'one man and his dog' sheepdog trial, but this was altogether different and simply required man and dog to walk round the ring in the company of the other competitors. There was a category for 'rough haired sheepdog' (maybe I should have entered myself!) and another for 'smooth haired'; the problem was that Moss was sort of in between! I chose rough haired and Moss finished a highly creditable fourth - out of a field of four.

Moss and me in the ring for the rough-haired sheepdog class

Jen fared much better in the photography section, where her careful composition of a ewe and lamb came second. Anne-Marie had helped the kids with their 'vegetable animals', and their creative potato and carrot dog won third place. Geoff and I eased away the humiliations of my morning outside the beer tent, chatting to friends and neighbours, while mums and girls competed in the various toddlers' races. The sun shone and gradually I put it all behind me and cheered up, ruefully swearing never again to expose myself and my lack of knowledge on the finer points of sheep showing.

Anne-Marie and Geoff, with Elizabeth, at the sheep judging: 1977

The afternoon's events included a hound trail, and Edward, one of my A-level students the previous year, had misspent one of our lessons bringing the small class up to speed on this quintessentially Cumbrian sport, and its potential for betting. I'd justified the time wasted as a practical lesson in probability as Ed took us through the meaning of 11 to 3 on, spread betting, betting both ways and so on. Ed, it turned out, moonlighted as a bookie's clerk, had a couple of hounds himself, and knew the sport and its main characters very well.

Before a hound trail begins two fit runners (of the human variety) set off in opposite directions from the mid-point to 'lay the course', trailing behind them sacking that lays a trail of paraffin and aniseed, easy for the trail hounds to follow. These hounds are related to the fell packs which were used for fox hunting, but are smaller, better fed and bred for speed and stamina. Ed told tales of the hounds being fed on best steak while the families made do with fish and chips, such was the potential for large winnings if you owned a winner. He also spoke of dark skulduggery where leading hounds were sometimes nobbled in the out-of-the-way parts of the course - lured aside by juicy morsels, and held back just enough to fail to win. Alternatively a poor hound would be released at the start, and then pulled out and replaced by a much fresher, almost identical hound, at the halfway stage.

The course itself was ten miles long, leading way up into the hills. The start was sheer mayhem with a baying mass of hounds straining at their leashes, ready for the off. The tired runners came in, dragging the by now bedraggled aniseed bags, and as soon as the bags were safely retrieved the judge gave the signal for the off. With a mighty whoop 40 or so hounds lunged forward, cleared the field wall with a liquid leap, and made for the nearby intake, so recently vacated by the trail-layer.

There was none of the mystified snuffling about that you get with fox hounds who seem to lose the scent of the fox at regular intervals. Then again, the fox is actively trying to shake them off, diving into streams, swimming down-river, deliberately crossing tracks with another fox: employing any devious tactic to avoid being torn limb from limb. The trail layers had left an unmistakable scent of aniseed and all these hounds had to do was breathe it in and run like hell. They did, while Geoff and I sought out Ed to wager a pound apiece according to his advice.

Would he be generous to his old teacher, or would he protect his employer by giving rubbish advice? He explained recent form and advised us to bet on Crackenthorpe, and took our pounds at 3 to 1. We wandered off to the finish to await developments, which weren't long in coming. The loudspeaker announced "all betting to stop now" and a few minutes later the leading dog appeared on the skyline and led the charge down the hillside, over the last beck, and into the top of the showfield by the intake gate.

Bedlam broke out behind the finish line with owners whistling, shouting, hallooing their dogs home to a large plate of lights, and as they crossed the loudspeaker gave their names. Whistlers Spring was first and I gave Geoff a rueful grin: Ed had stuffed us. Crackenthorpe was a miserable fourth. We returned to the beer tent to drown our sorrows and commiserate on the ingratitude of youth. After all, under my guidance Ed had passed A-level Maths with a creditable grade B.

That's where Ed found us, half an hour later, wearing a big soppy grin and carrying eight pound notes. Mystified, Geoff asked him to explain. Apparently hound trailing sometimes has such powerful top dogs that you can place bets ignoring those dogs, if you want to. Ed had placed our bet 'without the first three', a new form of handicapping to me. On that basis, we had won. This called for another pint, obviously, and the afternoon was wearing on quite nicely. The kids had long since grown bored, and Jen and Anne-Marie had taken them home. Geoff and I ambled amiably round the showfield, chatting to the vicar, the bank manager, who inevitably doubled as the show's treasurer, and our growing number of Eskdale acquaintances. Geoff was particularly impressed by the display of shepherds' crooks, showing real artistry in the ornately carved horns that formed the crook above the hazel stick.

The announcer on the tannoy called for competitors in the open class fell race, and it seemed rude to leave without placing another bet. Ed warned that he had no idea on form here, so we were on our own. I resorted to the usual amateur's technique, betting my pound on a runner sharing the Hall surname, though unrelated. Geoff decided not to risk it as there were about 30 runners, all unknown quantities. They were dressed in a variety of garb (with an equal variety of footwear), ranging from lycra shorts, singlet and mean-looking trainers to the more usual jeans, shirt and light boots. Some were local lads testing their prowess against runners from other valleys.

They all lined up, and at the whistle sprinted off for the gate out onto the intake. It seemed important to get on the narrow track in pole position. The race led them up a good old quarry track for so far, then up hard going to the top of Harter Fell, and along the ridge to a poor track down. The first man appeared on the skyline to a few shouts of encouragement he was too far away to hear. A string of runners soon became visible. As they turned to descend the shouting started in earnest, cheering the front runner, and the first local to appear. They flew down the stony track at breakneck speed, the cliché looking all too likely to be fulfilled. There was to be no overtaking the front man, a well-known member of the famous Borrowdale fell runners, and he cruised through the gate and across the line to rapturous applause. He wasn't called Hall.

Back in the beer tent, this time to mourn my losses, Geoff and I settled down to what must have been our fourth pint. As we did the loudspeaker started giving out a rather jaunty melody and Michael from next door, who was always ready to join in a round, explained what was to come, as the evening wore on. These reedy notes were a tape recording of last year's singing, designed to get drinkers in the mood to make a new tape of this year's. Definitely not karaoke, definitely no backing tapes. These were the hunting songs of all the Cumbrian packs, and it wasn't long before old Teddy Foster started the evening's proceedings with a song neither of us had ever heard. But then, we thought *D'ye ken John Peel* was the only one in existence.

There turned out to be dozens of these hunting shanties, all designed to have solo verses and rumbustious choruses where everyone joined in, in whatever key suited them. Michael, our guru, explained there were six different Lakeland fox-hunting packs, none of them using any horses but all with a huntsman who tried to keep up with the hounds over the rough terrain, and a 'whipper-in' who chivvied along any straggling hounds that got left behind. There were usually lots of hunt followers, but instead of riding to hounds they drove along the country lanes in their Land-Rovers, catching up with where the hounds had got to using Citizen's Band short-wave radios, and watching the hunt through binoculars.

By about ten o'clock we reckoned we'd better make our way home before the ladies sent out a search party. As we left the merriment was still in full swing, and Geoff walked up to the telephone box at the foot of Hard Knott to ring Anne-Marie to ask her to come and get us as we were definitely the worse for wear.

Next morning the show secretary rang me about 8 am to ask whether I intended to take our sheep home, as the committee members were dismantling the pens.

Chapter 7

The Green Shed Rodeo: 1977

September brought an end to that idyllic summer. The government appointed a Minister for Drought - and the heavens opened with a thunderstorm that was greedily soaked up by earth that hadn't drunk in months. Too late for the fell on the other side of the valley which had burned for weeks, fuelled by peat laid down over thousands of years, till it was back to the bedrock. I had to return, unwillingly, to school and the insistence of the bells, and it fell to Jen and Anne-Marie to manage the day-to-day running of our small-holding. This was the era of the TV programme *The Good Life*, about a couple who eschewed paid work to subsist on a suburban garden in Surbiton, and I became quite annoyed by the frequent suggestions that Fisherground was its Northern incarnation.

Keen to establish proper farming credentials we started two enterprises designed to make best use of our many buildings, while not needing many acres to support them. For the first of them the four of us and the children made the trip to Broughton auction, eleven miles over the fell road over Birker Moor. I would have preferred to have gone alone, trying to merge into the background, but this was designated a family day out, To Be Enjoyed By All. Our brightly coloured assembly jostled together on the top row of seats around the ring, surrounded by a sea of brown and grey: brown sunburnt faces under drab caps, sporting every shade of old, ripped Barbour jacket and cord trousers. And all male. So much for merging into the background. At dinner-time we shuffled into the steamy little café that served those who didn't slake their thirsts in the three pubs this little market town supported, and again felt conspicuous as the girls squabbled.

By the end of the sale we were the proud possessors of 100 wether hoggs. These are the castrated male lambs born in Spring, and ready now to be fattened up for sale after the turn of the year. The plan was that they would spend four or five months in what we called the Green Shed, 120 feet long, 40 feet wide - big enough to take more cattle than Fisherground even at its zenith could ever have supported. Late that evening the hoggs arrived on a lorry and were released into this strange new environment of timber and corrugated iron sheet, the first animals actually to use it. For a couple of days they raced around in the straw and one by one slowly took to eating the hay and barley designed to fatten them up.

After a couple of weeks, however, it was clear all was not well, with several coughing and one dead. I called the vet in Broughton and was told that if another died I should take it to them straight away for a post mortem. Two days later when I was at school, Jen checked through them and found another dead. She wasn't strong enough to lift 30 kilos deadweight into the Renault, so she press-ganged her very unwilling new friend Hilary into helping. Dissecting it before their eyes the vet pronounced Pneumonia - very infectious and nearly always fatal - then loaded the slopping remains in a bag and back into the Renault, saying they had no means of disposal. Hilary, who had gone with Jen as moral support, turned a delicate shade of green on the return journey and refused point blank to help unload the stinking bundle back at Fisherground. That's when she introduced Jen to Gin.

The vet said the answer to our pneumonia problem was better ventilation, so that night when Geoff and I returned from work it was out with the hammers and jemmies. Two hours later the bright shiny new building was looking decidedly the worse for wear, with sheets ripped off the sides all round and even a row along the top. No more hoggs died of pneumonia, but Geoff swore that if he had to spend any more time in there with the wind whistling round him, he certainly would. We had probably paid too much for the hoggs in the first place, and together with odd losses from pneumonia and other ailments, and the poor price for finished lamb in spring, we made absolutely nothing on the enterprise, and had to put it all down to experience. We were on the lower slopes of a steep learning curve.

Lots more ventilation, as prescribed. Jen, 'helped' by her dog Meg.

The same was true of the next bright idea I thought might produce a decent profit. Again, looking for an enterprise that used buildings rather than land, I suggested we buy in week-old calves and rear them through to 'stores' – year-old, half-grown calves that are ready for someone else to take on and fatten. Back we went to Broughton auction, this time just Jen and me, dressed scruffily (in brown). This time lunch in one of the pubs, for this was <u>our</u> day out. But still Jen was the only woman round the ring, and still we stood out as the 'green welly brigade'. By now I'd crashed our old car, a Renault in a sickly shade of green. Michael was very sympathetic, reckoning everybody who came to live in the valley smashed at least one car in their first year, on the narrow, stone-walled, twisting roads. With farm life in mind we replaced it with an old Vauxhall van, and this time brought the purchases - half a dozen Friesian calves - back home ourselves.

Geoff and I had spent a happy day making suitable rearing pens in the milking parlour, and Jen and Anne-Marie, surrogate mothers to the new orphans, made a fuss of them, bedding them in with straw. That evening we gave them their first feed of formula milk in the warm glow of the heat lamps hung over the pens, with varying degrees of success. Up to now the calves had followed their instincts, with heads turned upwards to find a teat and suck. They didn't take kindly to the idea that they should lower their faces into a bucket and gobble milk instead. Jen was best at cajoling them, by putting her hands in the milk and then popping a milky finger in a calf's mouth for it to suck. In time she managed to get it to lower its head in and continue to suck on her fingers.

There are those who enjoy this sort of sucking. I wasn't one of them, finding the whole process vaguely disgusting, especially when an over-enthusiastic calf decided I was mummy and started sucking every part of me it could reach. However, neither Jen nor Anne-Marie could be persuaded to give the early morning feed, pleading the need to see to the children, so it was down to me. After all, I was the one who was desperate to be a farmer. This all meant a pretty early start, as I had to be at school, 20 miles away, by 8:45, clean and tidy and, ideally, not smelling of calf milk. Geoff also started very early, Sellafield running a work day from 7:00 am till 3:30 pm.

Our two families were sharing cars, so generally the Renault 4 was available for Jen or Anne-Marie to take the kids places, but occasionally there was an overlap and one of them had to use the old Vauxhall van. Jen was out in it, fortunately without any children, when she was pulled over into a layby by a policeman. As she got out of the driver's side, the passenger door opened spontaneously, and an officious looking man with a clipboard pounced.

"Now then, Madam, do you know why we've pulled you over?"

"Nooo, but I see other vans so I suppose…"

"Quite so, Madam, we're testing commercial vehicles, and your van is one such."

"Ah, right, well, what do you want to know?"

"Firstly, Madam, why is the passenger door hanging wide open?"

"Ah, the door catch isn't very good, and it sometimes does that."

"Really, Madam, do you think that's safe? What happens if it springs open when you're driving? Someone could fall out, or you could cause an accident, don't you think?"

"Oh no, it can't fly open when I'm driving, because there's a bit of string tied to it and I sit on it to hold it tight."

"Really, Madam…. I think I'm going to enjoy this one!" She had to ring Geoff to pick her up in the Renault, and we had to pay a scrap merchant to come and take the van away.

By this time the first batch of calves, and a few more, had grown beyond needing milk and needed larger premises. The wether hoggs had gone, sold as oven-ready lamb, so where better than the Green Shed. The dozen or so calves rattled about a bit in the huge space, but they were happy to kick up their heels and run around. One started to limp so, mindful of the problems we'd had with the sheep, I called the practice to ask a vet to come out and have a look. Again, when he came, I was at school, Geoff at work; so Jen took him out to the shed leaving Anne-Marie in charge of the four girls. He introduced himself in a distinct Northern Irish brogue.

"Call me Ricky, if you would now. What would we looking for here, then, Mrs. Hall?"

"Ian said one of them is limping, oh, look, that rather bigger one, with the small horns."

"Right-oh, I see him. I don't suppose you'd be having a cattle crush….?"

"Sorry, what's one of them? Anyway, I'm sure we haven't… we've hardly any tackle at all."

"Not to worry, we'll just use a gate to trap them in this corner. Look now, I'll tie this end here, so we can swing it across when they're in."

It all looked a bit make-shift, but by driving the small herd right down one side of the shed and then up the other they ended up in the cul-de-sac, and Ricky quickly pulled the gate across to contain them. It wouldn't actually close on them, but he yelled to Jen "You hold them in as best you can, now, while I dive in and pull him down." It was as well he was quick, because as he jumped in among them and grabbed the stirk by its handy horns the rest backed up hard against Jen. One stood on her wellingtonned foot and as she jumped and howled they pushed past and out to the relative freedom of the shed. Ricky had his quarry, though, and putting his left hand in its mouth, behind the top teeth, and twisting its head to one side he bore it down to the ground.

"So far so good, then, would you not say. Now, let me be showing you how to hold him down, while I have a look at that foot." Jen looked nervously at her charge… how was she going to control such a beast?

"Sure, 'tis no problem at all, just you hold him like this, with your hand in his mouth like this and keep his neck twisted right round. You'll come to no harm." Anxiously, Jen did as bid. She couldn't be having me come home to find she couldn't cope, now, could she? Damn, this Irish was catching. "Are you sure I can do this?"

"Undoubtedly, Mrs. Hall, you'll be fine, so you will."

Jen lay all her weight on the beast, tugging his head round, grateful for the horns to hang on to, as Ricky started to investigate the foot. For several minutes all was well, as he scraped away the dirt and straw from the foot, but as he started to cut into the rot the stirk gave a mighty bellow, threw off Jen's left hand from his mouth, and struggled to his feet. Jen still had his horn in her right hand, and found herself, instead of weighing him down, somehow now mounted astride him, feet well off the floor. Ricky threw himself at the gate to hold them captive, but too late. The stirk beat him to the exit and set off back down the shed, Jen hanging on grimly to the horn, bouncing up and down at every stride. Hang on or fall off? Some atavistic instinct insisted she held on to her quarry, and she grabbed the other horn with her left hand and settled into the ride. And what a ride it was, right down the full 120 feet of the shed, skidding round the corner at the end, then right back up the other side.

Beside himself with fear at the potential for disaster, Ricky yet had the presence of mind to close the gate against the corner, and as the stirk, Jen still astride - just, came up against it he quickly trapped it, sides heaving after its gallop, and helped Jen dismount, with as much dignity as she could muster.

"Sorry, Mrs. Hall, farmers' wives generally come in larger sizes!"

It was June before we could eventually let the calves out to graze. They went mad with joy, kicking their heels and racing round the field for all the world like delinquent teenagers let loose in a shopping centre. It was September when we loaded them in a lorry to take back to Broughton to sell as stores. I discovered that it's a lot more nerve-racking to sell than to buy, as I waited for my turn in the ring. Somehow what had seemed quite big stores at home seemed to have shrunk in the auction pens, and they looked scruffy compared to the sleek beasts in the neighbouring pens. My pen was the last in a long line, and I waited with rising nervousness as batch after batch disappeared up the alleyway and into the ring.

Jen helping a ewe to lamb

I could hear the bidding over the tinny tannoy, and the prices didn't sound impressive. My brain ticked over the break-even price I'd worked out at home the night before and I could see long before I got to the ring that there wasn't going to be much in it. I steeled myself for my turn. It wasn't long in coming and suddenly I found myself walking into the ring with contrived nonchalance behind our six prize cattle that had somehow shrunk to the size of slightly overgrown sheep. Someone handed me a stick and I mooched around the ring trying to keep the cattle prominent and myself invisible.

Bidding was desultory. I was an unknown upstart and the cattle I was trying to sell were only moderate, at best. You are permitted to refuse to sell, of course, and I had heard quite a few pens 'passed' (withdrawn) during the day, but I didn't want to start our selling career that way, and in any case Fisherground's few fields hadn't produced enough hay for more than the sheep for the coming winter. So the cattle were sold, and I sought out the buyer, a local dealer, to give him his 'luck money', that traditional gesture between seller and buyer. I wanted the dealers in particular to remember me favourably, so I slipped him a fiver. To my astonishment he said he was sharing the pen with the dealer sitting beside him – and tore the fiver in two!

Back at Fisherground I licked my wounds and went over the figures again. If I was generous and ignored a few incidental expenses, didn't charge anything for time and forgot about the auction's commission, then we'd broken even. The same had been true of the fattening wether hoggs. Don't give up the day job, then.

Chapter 8

Entertaining angels unawares: 1976-7

Eddie came that first Christmas. He just turned up on the doorstep, saying the vicar of a nearby parish had found him sleeping in the church boiler house and had told him Fisherground was a new commune and he'd find the peace he was searching for there. Jen opened the door to him surrounded by Catherine, Sally and Elizabeth, squabbling ferociously, and upstairs the new-born Claire bawled lustily for another feed. Eddie didn't turn a hair. He had a lot of hair he could have turned, tied in a ponytail and beginning to go grey, and five days growth of beard, but his brown shoes were pretty new and well-polished, though his corduroy trousers were worn thin where his thighs rubbed together, and his Parka had seen better days. Even one step down from Jen at the doorway he still towered over her, and he spent his first few days with us banging his head on the squat doorways. Farmers in 1795 must have been short, because there wasn't a doorway higher than six feet.

Not knowing what else to do Jen invited him in for a cup of tea, and hoped that I would soon be home from school, and Geoff from work. But it was only early afternoon and she and Anne-Marie made heavy weather of small talk with an ex-hippy who was either a bit slow by nature or had taken too much LSD in his flower power days. When he said he played the piano they led him to it and begged him to play - and then left him to it while they took the girls upstairs to try to think what they should do. He was still playing, if that was the right word, when Geoff and I got home. We met round Anne-Marie's kitchen table and Geoff voiced everyone's first reaction. "What the hell is that vicar playing at? What gives him the idea we're a commune?"

"Well, maybe it is that we are a bit unusual, cheri. All living together."

Jen joined in: "Even so, even if we were a commune, surely we'd have the right to pick and choose. I reckon this vicar was just trying to get rid of a problem – pass it on to us."

"Well, whatever, he's our problem now. It's nearly Christmas, and it's freezing out there. We can't just throw him out." Me, voicing what we all knew.

"Mais non, that would be terrible indeed."

Geoff, ever the practical one: "Where's he going to sleep if he stays tonight?"

"The salting room is nearly ready, we could put a bed in there…" I'd spent the last month ripping out the slate slabs where generations of farmers before us had salted hams and bacon. It still just had a tiny window though that was next on the list. It could make a bedroom, at a pinch.

"Well, if it comes to that I suppose Claire could sleep in our room, but we've only just got her used to being on her own." Geoff was mellowing.

"No, the salting room is fine. Let's not make him too comfortable, or he might stay forever." Jen looked at me sharply, contrasting emotions fighting for control. "How long is he staying? I know the Bible says we have to welcome strangers, but how long for?"

" I don't think it sets a limit, love."

So Eddie stayed, a bedroom hastily furnished for him, and Christmas crept closer. There was a sort of agreement that he would do odd jobs in return for his keep, but he seemed incapable of working on his own. As it was he wandered off during the day, played the piano in the evening, drank our home-brewed beer and generally got under our feet.

Christmas Day brought new tensions, as both Jen's and my parents joined us for the traditional lunch and present giving. Geoff and Anne-Marie had escaped to his brother's but there was no escape for us from the tension at Fisherground. Normally this was a merry meal with turkey and all the trimmings, but the brooding new presence at the table cast a blight on any hilarity. Eddie offered to wash up afterwards, and we set off for a walk, girls in papooses, grandparents rattled. This was the first time they had actually seen Eddie, and they didn't like what they saw. Mum and Dad simply saw him as a sponger, but Jen's parents, Norman and Marjorie, were anxious that he might be unhinged and possibly downright dangerous. They pointed out that come the Easter term I would be away all day and Jen and Anne-Marie, and the children, there alone.

When Geoff and Anne-Marie returned after their brief break the discussions were tense. None of us could justify kicking Eddie out: it offended against all we stood for. But none of us was happy about him staying, either, especially now that he was starting to talk about hearing voices in his head. Anne-Marie was the most affected: "Me, I will not have him upstairs when you are not here, Geoffrey. I just feel too trapped… there's no way out."

"I know what you mean, Anne-Marie, there's just something spooky about him, and if he turned on us when you two are at work…"

"OK, look, I can see he has to go, but it's nearly another week before I have to go back to school, can we just tell him, like, that he will have to go in a few days?"

"It'll have to be on your head, Ian, I have to go to work tomorrow. But let's give him to the end of the week and see what happens."

In the end the valley, and in particular the valley's policeman, came to our rescue. On his daily wanderings Eddie had taken to calling at houses offering to sharpen knives and axes for a small fee, and this soon brought him to the law's attention. Just after the New Year Eddie left in the back of a police car. We were unclear about just where he was being taken, and really just too relieved to be free of our moral crisis to want to know too much.

A brief phone call to the vicar who had wished Eddie on us established for all the clergy around that we weren't a commune and had no intention of being open for all and sundry to drop in. However, if not a commune, two families living as closely to each other as we were was at least a community, and we had set up our own small experiment in fellowship and partnership on New Testament lines. We agreed that all money earned from whatever source would be paid into the central Fisherground pot and that each family would be paid the same monthly allowance. All major bills - mortgage, cars, insurance, water, electricity and so on - would be paid out of the communal pot, leaving each family to pay for food, drink and whatever else we needed ourselves.

This worked quite well, with one important amendment after the first year. Anne-Marie started the negotiations.

"Me, I am finding the monthly allowance too small. We have to cross La Manche to see my parents and my family each year, and the ferry, she is expensive."

Perhaps she and Jen had had a private word beforehand, because Jen was straight in as back-up.

"Yes, we want to visit my uncle and aunt in Spain, but the airfare is far too much to save out of the allowance."

Geoff was defensive: " Well, yes, but if our family takes more money out I would feel we were robbing you - and for sure if you took more out I would feel you were robbing me!"

My turn, then… "OK Anne-Marie, have you got some sort of solution in mind. You're the bank manager's daughter."

"As it goes, well, yes, I talked to Papa about this problem, and him, he says it's easy. What we do is, each family it has what he calls a notional capital account, say a thousand pounds to start with, and we use it for the big buyings. At the end of the year we compare each capital account, and charge interest, say 10%, on the difference. So if you and Jen have spent £200 less than us, you get £20 added to your account. Easy, non?" One look at Jen's face told me it wasn't that easy, and I'd need to explain carefully, but yes, I could see it could work, and that either family could spend more without somehow defrauding the other.

*****

Of course 'practical Christianity' entailed going to church en masse each Sunday. Perhaps unexpectedly one element of the wider community came to be centred round the church, though most rural parishes by then had thin congregations, largely elderly women. There were enough of us simply from the farmhouse to provide a critical mass of young adults who could be depended on to be in church to encourage other young families to join, knowing they wouldn't be alone. It helped that both churches in the parish were small, so if you could get a dozen together it felt like a reasonable community, and we soon found there were at least that many, with other children too. Après church coffees and the occasional beer or glass of wine at someone's house made the whole Sunday morning a pleasant get-together, cementing the new-found friendships with Outward Bound staff.

There were two churches in Eskdale, the parish church of St. Catherine's and the newer St. Bega's, and their positions say much about the place of the church over the centuries. St. Catherine's is an ancient place, situated in just the right holistic location for those with a feeling for ley-lines: down by the river, away from any habitation, sheltered and hidden. Tradition says it was originally, in the sixth century, a monk's hermitage, with a holy well, St. Catherine's Well, which can still be seen nearby. St. Bega's on the other hand is in the middle of Eskdale Green village, built by the ubiquitous Lord Rea so his servants and staff could worship more easily. It always seemed that the two churches symbolised the different approaches to religion. St. Catherine's for spirituality at arm's length, meditative, contemplative; St. Bega's for religion involved in the community.

St. Bega's also featured a village hall under the church, which had been the village school until a brand new schoolroom was built. This had long been the centre of village life, with regular whist drives, the Women's Institute, the Amateur Dramatic Society and so on using it nearly every night of the week. They were no more, and there was only the occasional Mother-and-toddler meetings to fill the void. Anne-Marie soon threw herself into this group, organising children's games, wiping noses, changing nappies. It was the start of her long association with the Village Hall and with the valley children.

On our first visit to St. Catherine's I noticed, alongside the tasteful brass plaque to James Wharrier Hall, another commemorating a later incumbent, Revd. Gerald Ford, whose daughter Anna was brought up in the valley long before she found fame as a newsreader. The pews and pulpit were solidly made of pleasing pitch pine, burnished by generations of use to a soft, gentle patina. By contrast the lectern was oak, beautifully carved as an eagle with spread wings, holding a King James bible for the lesson readers. On one of the windowsills rested an old, cracked bell, the original tenor bell from a previous church on the site, extensively renewed in 1887.

In the graveyard was a magnificent tombstone featuring carved foxhounds, foxes, and the grinning face of Eskdale's greatest Master of the Hounds, Tommy Dobson.

The River Esk, gin-clear and in a hurry to get to the sea, runs by the churchyard, and if it is reasonably low, you can cross over a flight of stepping stones to the path that leads all the way down the left bank to the swing bridge that takes you back to Fisherground. If the river is in spate you have to go upstream 200 yards or so to cross by the girder bridge that used to take Ratty trains to the iron ore quarry. On our first trip over it was still just the twin girders, each about nine inches wide, and I terrified both children by doing trips, hoisting them on my shoulders and walking over with them aloft. I then scared Jen by holding her hand as we crossed each on our own girder. A few years later the National Trust planked it to make a proper bridge, which rather spoiled the fun of it.

Claire and Philip on the stepping stones over the River Esk beside St Catherine's

Walking down the path towards home we soon discovered Stanley Ghyll waterfalls, a real hidden gem with a 60 foot cataract plunging into a deep pool. Rhododendron grew all around and the whole atmosphere was that of a tropical rain forest, with thick lichen smothering the trees and rocks. Clambering up the winding path to the top of the fall we suddenly found ourselves on the brink of an immense drop, only to be properly appreciated by crawling forward on your belly to peer over. Jen decided her precious infants had

had quite enough excitement for one day and refused to let them anywhere near the edge.

A little further down we went through the ruins of an old farmstead and explored what was left. The base of the old farmhouse was clear, and looked very small by today's standards. The yard was still cobbled, and a gate led from it down to the river - doubtless the only source of water. Offering shelter from the west stood an ancient beech, with whorls and gashes on it suggesting a smiling face. The girls instantly christened it The Learning Tree, and were desolate when it fell in the 1987 storms. There was no road in now, and to look at what little was left of Red Bank you would have thought it had been derelict for centuries, but a little later we met an elderly lady who had been born and brought up there.

Chapter 9

Our other agricultural enterprise of significance that first year was an experiment in potato growing, a venture that really was worthy of the dreaded *'Good Life'* comparison. The 1976 drought had pushed the price of potatoes to unheard of heights, so much so that a bag of chips became cordon bleu. I thought it made sense to plant half an acre to provide our own in 1977, hopefully with some left over to sell. Lurking in the back of my mind was the country lore that potatoes should be planted on Good Friday and dug up on August Bank Holiday. Armed with such irrefutable scientific knowledge I insisted that Jen and I return a day early from our holiday so that we could 'do it by the book'. I was in the grip of some sort of wild holistic imaginings that went along the lines of 'Good Friday's date is determined by the moon and there's probably a connection that says this is the best time for planting'. It was that sort of decade; I was that sort of man.

Through his contacts at Sellafield Geoff had somehow tracked down a tractor driven rotavator, the exotically named 'Hayter potatervator'. It was a solid, robust machine, which was just as well as the field we chose to plant in hid a minefield of stones under its shiny green surface. The din as the flails hurled rocks left, right and centre was positively frightening. Inevitably bits broke off the Hayter potatervator and went whistling out from the back. Try saying that quickly! Everyone was by now taking cover to avoid being stoned to death in deepest Eskdale. Somehow we ended up more or less with rows of heaped earth: not pretty, but serviceable. Then in good old country style we 'mucked out' the milking parlour where the calves had been and Geoff and I went up and down the rows laboriously forking a heady mixture of cow muck and straw off the back of the trailer while Jen drove the tractor in crawler gear.

Next we planted eight hundredweight of very expensive seed potatoes, and then came the delicate art of driving along the top of the rows so the potatervator could cover the exposed rows of potatoes. This was all well and good in theory, less so in practice as the machine jumped and bucked every time it hit a cobble. Job eventually done we left it to nature to nurture and hoped not too many people went up the footpath and cast an eye over the dog-eared rows. Inevitably lots did, and lots commented, along the lines of "Why not start with an allotment?" All said with the sweetest of smiles.

Had it been 1976, the chosen field would have been good, as it never seemed to dry out. But this was 1977, and it was worryingly wet and soggy. We borrowed what was optimistically called a potato harvester to dig up our modest crop. This contraption had been horse drawn in its youth and consisted of a blade that was supposed to slip under the plants, as rotating metal arms nudged the potatoes gently out of the loamy mix and onto the surface, for easy picking. Had the soil indeed been a nice loamy mix all might have been well, but the stones soon broke the main wooden shaft and Geoff had to spend half a day replacing it. Jen and Anne-Marie resorted to digging the potatoes out by hand, and were winning hands down by the time the harvester was repaired. The half-acre lifted, we probably got more than the eight bags we'd put in - but not significantly so. In terms of time, effort and money put in the whole enterprise was a glorious failure. To make matters worse, the ideal potato growing conditions produced a glut and the price in the shops had plummeted. Bizarrely, though, the price of chips never came down.

Fortunately the last of the five ventures we embarked on in that first crazy year fared better; sadly – but significantly - it wasn't agricultural. After my time in Borrowdale with my parents I was well aware of the potential of tourism to improve incomes on these hill farms. One of the major problems Mum and Dad had on their tenanted farm was that the landlord wouldn't allow any camping or caravans. In common with most fell farms the previous tenants had taken guests on a Bed and Breakfast basis, and the farmhouse had six big bedrooms and so could hold a lot of guests. A dilapidated hut in the field nearest the house had been pressed into service every summer for the farmer and his wife and son to sleep in, freeing all six bedrooms to be filled with guests.

If you ever asked these worthy wives how well they did out of their B & B business, they would always answer that it was just for 'pin money'. But the truth was they were often making more than their menfolk - certainly if you discounted all the grants, subsidies and premiums that made up the larger part of a farm's income. When my parents took on Thorneythwaite in 1960 Mum was adamant she wasn't going to be a slave to the Aga and the washtub, nor was she prepared to sleep all summer in a leaky old shed, so, almost accidentally, they embarked on what was then a fairly new form of tourism: self-catering.

Thorneythwaite was, in some ways, ideally set up for this, as there were two kitchens and two sitting rooms. The only problem was that there was only one stairway, and more importantly only one bathroom and one loo. No-one seemed to mind too much, though, and for the full 15 years we were there we shared those simple provisions with up to ten visitors in the far end of the house. For the first three years there was no electricity either, for it was only installed in 1963, but that seemed to add to the whole slightly surreal experience for the new style holiday-makers. Reading by the light of a calor gas mantle before going to bed with a real candlestick was a novel form of what I was much later to learn to call a 'unique selling point'.

Clearly Fisherground farmhouse was already filled by our two families, so the same model couldn't apply, but there seemed no reason why we couldn't site a large caravan in the orchard for visitors to use as a self-catering unit. No reason, that is, except for the Lake District Planning Board. The board was set up in 1951 to protect the Lake District from unfettered development that might spoil the whole area, and the general opinion of all who lived there was that whatever you asked for, the answer was going to be 'No'. Having already got away with a primitive campsite open for double the allotted days we decided not to bother asking, and in order to save the Board the trouble of saying no, went ahead. We installed a large caravan, hidden as well as possible from outside view. We chose the site carefully. The north end of the orchard was hidden from the La'al Ratty by the Green Shed, and from the road by the 20 or so apple trees. The 'Dutch Barn' sheltered it from view from the farmhouse, and the site seemed as good as it could be. It was also just about the only place that was high enough for us to be able to lay drains in to carry waste to the farm's septic tank. You could hardly ask self-caterers to share the Elsan with the campers.

Buying a second hand 'mobile home', as they were known, was surprisingly easy. We found a 26 feet by10 feet two-bedroomed version that seemed perfect for the venture. It turned up on a lorry in early March and was unceremoniously dropped off in front of the Dutch Barn. This was where the fun began. The caravan was 10 feet wide, and the gap between the Dutch Barn and the garden wall that it would have to go through was 10 feet and 6 inches. Once through it had to negotiate a sharp bend. Saturday morning saw all four of us complete with the toddlers, in on the act. I hitched the Massey Ferguson 35 to the tow bar and began to inch forward, Anne-Marie keeping watch on one side, Jennifer on the other, and Geoff relaying instructions. Six inches spare isn't much over a length of 26 feet, and our less than mobile home soon became well and truly jammed in the gap. Geoff and I crawled about underneath with jacks and crowbars to straighten it up, while the womenfolk covered the children's ears to censor a steady stream of cursing and swearing. I was never at my best under pressure.

The caravan going in beside the Green Shed

Eventually we got it through, but it was nearly dark by the time we had it jacked up, levelled up and legs down in its chosen position. The children and their mothers had long since got bored with the entire operation. Once again my childhood friend, Maurice, came to our aid, with his state of the art digger attachment mounted on his tractor. He dug the channel for the sewage pipe, and I connected up to the septic tank and the house's electricity supply. Jen got the job of painting the caravan outside a delicate, some might say camouflaged, shade of green. Geoff built bunks for the tiny second bedroom, so we could advertise it as being 'four-berth', and Anne-Marie tended the children and fed her new-born Claire.

The 'deluxe mobile home' was open for business by Easter, advertised in one or two newspapers and the Farm Holiday Guide. There were very few 'holiday cottages' on the west side of the Lake District in those days, and almost none in Eskdale itself, and it was booked nearly every week that summer, right up to autumn half term. Of the five enterprises we had tried in our first year at Fisherground, only the two tourist based had succeeded. My determination to be a farmer remained undented, my confidence boundless.

At the end of our first year in paradise we held a party in the big barn to celebrate. Friends and neighbours were invited, the floor swept, music and electric light installed, hay bales artistically placed around for seating, and gallons of home-brewed beer poured into plastic bins. The more astute of our friends, having already sampled my home-brew, brought their own bottles and cans. Newer neighbours and other uninitiated friends manfully supped their first pint then slid off to the King George IV 400 yards down the road for alternatives. By eleven o'clock the party was in full swing, with whirling feet kicking up the dust of a hundred years from the barn floor. This was when the true genius of having friends from all walks of life showed itself, as a couple of doctor friends started dishing out little white pills to anyone who asked. No, not those little white pills - these were strong anti-histamines to counter the violent hay-fever attacking a number of the revellers. If only they'd also brought something to counter the after effects of my lethal home brew.

Chapter 10

Herdwick sheep, lawnmowers of the fells

Among our tentative, and generally unsuccessful farming ventures, there was one which carried on as it had for centuries - the whole basis of fell farming: Herdwick sheep. The Herdwick spend most of their time up on the hills, coming down only for special occasions - lambing, clipping, dipping and tupping. Herdwicks are the hardiest of all sheep, reputedly brought from Scandinavia by the Vikings in the 9th century, and bred ever since for their ability to live on the roughest of fells in the poorest of weather. Fisherground had a flock of around 250 Herdwick ewes plus the 60 hoggs, and they grazed a very poor but quite low fell at the western end of Eskdale Common.

Jen and I had had our first good look at the fell in the Easter holidays before we moved in, when Michael from next door helped us gather in the ewes for lambing time. The fell was devoid of pasturage or any decent areas of grass. There were lots of rocky outcrops surrounding boggy areas that might once have been good grazing, but which over the centuries had been denuded by peat-gathering and were now just wet, dangerous bogs where unwary sheep got trapped and drowned. Anything that wasn't bog or rock seemed to be covered in last year's dead bracken. Remarkably the old Herdwicks looked well enough on such hard tack.

Michael had three good dogs, while Jen was using her pet, Tess, who would bark but had been trained (up to then) *not* to chase sheep, and I had old Beaut, pressed into service once again just when she thought she could take it easy. At the fell gate the sheep scented bottom pastures and set off down the good track through the intake, and the three of us had a chance to chat as we followed in their wake.

"That'll be your peat hut theer", said Michael, as we passed a roofless stone shed. We stopped to admire: well, the stonework looked good.

"What's that for, then?" asked Jen, more willing to show her ignorance than me.

"Wey, storing peat, of course".

"Why would you store peat up here, Michael?" I kept quiet.

"Ah'm nut surprised you know nowt about it, Jenny, as far as ah know it's only Eskdale that has peat huts. Ah've allus thowt it's cos t'peat's a lang way up on t'fells in this valley. If you hed to cart it down in summer you wadn't hev time for mekking hay."

It was time I joined in. "What was the timetable, then, Michael? When did they cut the peat?"

"Hell, it was a lang while afore my time, but granddad allus used to say they cut it in May, straight after t'lambs were put out onto t'fell. They stacked it where it was cut to dry out till early July, just afore clipping time, then carted it down and filled t'peat huts. They could come up with a cart any time in winter to get a load for t'fire."

"Looking at this one it's the same system as the big bank barns," I realised, " Look, there's a ramp at the back and a high door to tip it in from the cart, then I suppose you shovelled it out from the bottom door onto the cart in winter."

"Aye, well, that's what ah've allus understood. We still have yan with t'roof still on, but ah don't suppose it'll last much langer."

The sheep reached the bottom of the intake and Jen opened the gates onto the La'al Ratty railway line and into the lane that led to the fields. Joyfully the Herdwicks got their heads down to some real grass and spread out over the field to do some serious mowing, while the humans did the same with sandwiches and coffee cobbled together in our illicit den in the farmhouse.

Jen and I slowly got the hang of fell gathering, which was just as well as we had to do it four or five times a year. I got a good dog, Moss, through a friend of Dad's who practically gave her to us. Moss had pups and we kept two, Nell and Fan. Eventually they became reasonable sheep-dogs, and Jen could move on from old Tess, who never knew what she was supposed to do, to Nell who had more idea. Michael often helped us, especially during the clipping time gather which was complicated by the young lambs that panicked when they lost touch with their mothers. In return Moss and I joined Michael on his biggest gather, right across the breast of Scafell, England's highest mountain.

On these particular gathers, all would go well till we got to the fell gate, where 250 ewes, nearly as many lambs, and all the delinquent hoggs milled about till Jen opened the gate. Most streamed through, except for the panicking lost lambs that shot off in every direction except downhill. Every time I ended up in hot pursuit, sweating, swearing, struggling to catch them with the crook. Dogs were useless in this situation, merely panicking the lambs further, and I wasn't much better. Normally a gentle sort of bloke I became a savage, cursing psychopath until eventually the last of them was caught and where we wanted them.

We did learn, in time, to leave all the gates open for this particular gather, to prevent the milling about that created all this commotion. The only problem with this approach was that there was no control over the leading sheep, and the crossing of the Ratty line went unsupervised for some time, the sheep and lambs at the mercy of passing trains. If these had been ordinary sheep this might well have been a recipe for disaster, but these independently minded Herdwicks had an instinct for survival.

Sheep and trains don't really mix

The sheep pens, that first year, were in a parlous state and it was one of Geoff's first jobs to weld a lot of metal gates while I built some block walls to make the job of handling so many sheep a lot easier. Sheep travel better uphill, and are easier to control in long, narrow pens, so we made good use of the lane that ran up to the old pens, with good stone walls on either side. Unfortunately this was also a public footpath so there were a lot of times when shepherds, walkers and sheep were inter-mingled, but no-one seemed to mind and it was a good excuse for a chat or for a walker to enquire why I was cutting half that lamb's ear off.

"It's called a lug mark, and it's only really the tip of its ear. This other ear just has a slit in it, like that." A quick slice with the shears.

"Ugh, that's horrible, why are you doing that?"

"Well, I have to know which are my sheep and which are neighbours' when we gather them in."

"I thought those marks on their backs told you that…"

"The smit marks? Yes, they do, but they can wear off. A lug mark's for life. Do you know why ears are called lugs?"

"Never thought about it – why?"

"It's a Viking word, lug, and we adopted it for log book, where you keep facts and stuff. They had a lug book, showing every farm's different lug marks. And this is ours, cropped near ear, ritted far ear." I could never resist showing off, so I picked up the elastrator before they moved on, slipped a rubber ring on, and asked, casually,

"What d'you reckon this is for?" Mystified faces, so I turned the long-suffering lamb on its backside, squeezed the handles to expand the ring, slipped it over the lamb's scrotum and prised the ring off into position. The men winced and moved off, the women laughed uproariously.

"Hey, can I borrow that for a minute?"

As they had said, the other identifying mark for each sheep and lamb was a sort of paint, called 'smit'. Eskdale has a good case for being the originator of this, as its haematite mines go back many centuries, and the smit was originally made by mixing up the red iron ore with various oils to produce a reddish marking material to rub into a fleece, giving a visible mark that would last a year. Smit has long been a proprietary product with no relation to haematite, but there are two other uses for the original recipe, now called 'rudd', presumably from the same root as ruddy. This dark red paste was often smeared on the tups' (rams') chests so that they would in turn mark any ewe they served, so the shepherd knew their state. The other use is to beautify tups and ewes ready for display at the various shows that take place over the summer in each of the Lakeland valleys. A more liquid rudd is brushed into the sheep's coat (possibly to cover small blemishes in colour) and the many pens full of impressive tups and blushing ewes at these shows make a fine sight. This is unique to Herdwicks: no other breed ever sees rudd.

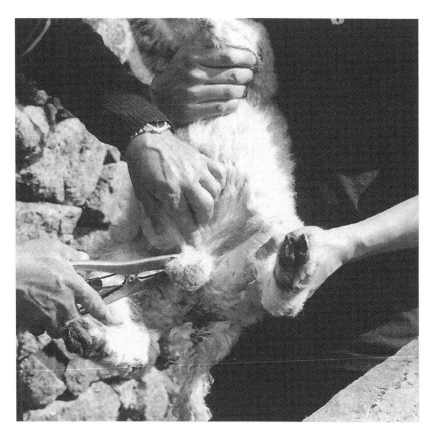

No wonder they winced! Applying a rubber ring

There were many reasons for having all the sheep in the pens, and that first year I seemed to spend every fine Saturday dipping, dosing, injecting, cutting out footrot or sorting them into different fields for various treatments. That first September, still working with the broken-down old pens, Jen and I struggled with the biggest job, dipping. Michael had helped us gather the fell, and the fields were full of ewes and lambs and those wilful hoggs that refused to 'follow like sheep'. But without the lane system, even getting them into the pens was a frustrating, time-consuming business, guaranteed to raise my blood pressure and press the trigger for the cursing and swearing that always accompanied my work with sheep and dogs. With the pen at last full we started to dip them all. With all that wool sheep are vulnerable to all sorts of parasites: lice, keds, ticks, and worst of all the maggots that blue-bottles lay, which can eat into their flesh. We couldn't understand why so much money had been spent on the superfluous Green Shed while the sheep pens, in use many times in a year, had been left so unfit for purpose. I had to catch each sheep I was going to put into the dipping tub, haul it to the narrow entrance then manhandle it through the gap and into the tub. This was a 12 foot long concrete bath, deep enough at the entrance to submerge the sheep completely, shallowing to exit steps at the far end and to a pair of draining pens, where the surplus water ran off them and back into the tub. Jen's job was to make sure every sheep got completely covered by pushing its head down with a curved metal rod. By the end of the day we were both thoroughly drenched and dipped.

It wasn't always so. High on Eskdale Common, as on all Lakeland fells, you come across broken down stone wall enclosures in odd places. These are the remains of sheep pens that were erected so all the sheep on the surrounding part of the fell could be gathered and inspected, clipped out and if necessary salved. Before the arrival of chemical dips there was no alternative to gathering the sheep regularly to rid them physically of any unwanted passengers. Not wanting to bring the sheep down to the pastures, where grass was being grown for the hay needed in winter, farmers did the job on the fell in these little high-level sheep-pens. By the time they'd cut peat as well they must have spent half the summer up on the fells.

Sheep pens and the dipping tub

After the First World War some fairly primitive chemicals started to be used, and sheep dipping started to take over from the labour intensive gathering into pens and hand salving of any fly-struck sheep. Cumbria, or Cumberland and Westmorland as it was then, was well placed to be in the forefront of this new technology: the basic constituent was arsenic, which was a by-product of the many lead mines in the county. So now farmers could dip a flock of sheep all day getting liberally soaked in a dilute arsenic solution, which was a great advance on spending half the summer on the fells tending the flock by hand. Except, of course, that it started to have a noticeably detrimental effect on these previously hale and hearty valley men. So much so that after the Second World War, when we had perfected much more sophisticated poisons, arsenic went out of fashion, only to be replaced by a product known as Dieldrin. This was introduced in 1955, only to be outlawed in 1971 as its cumulative effect on the farmers using it again became too obvious to ignore.

By the time we started dipping in 1976 technology had moved on to what were known as Organo-phosphate (OP) dips. It probably won't surprise you to learn that these were every bit as toxic to human beings, and the sort of soakings we were undergoing, though pleasantly cooling on a very hot day, weren't doing us or many other farmers any good in the long run, either. I always ended dipping days with a headache - but that might have been down to the effort and all that swearing and frustration. Either way, prolonged pickling in Organo-phosphates is not to be recommended.

Chapter 11

What's the Pig Idea?: 1977-8

Don't give up the day job. Good advice from both Michael and Maurice, both of them thinking a nice guaranteed salary for a few hours teaching must be well worth hanging on to. But I was adamant, and a 'few hours' teaching on top of all the tentative enterprises we'd tried in that first year at Fisherground was beginning to wear me down, and I seemed to have no time for the girls or Jen. Besides, Geoff had a well-paid, secure job at Sellafield, and the whole idea of moving to the farm had been to get off the teaching treadmill.

Nevertheless, it was a big step to take, and I looked for a way to lessen the impact. I had experience of building work through making our first house from a barn and felt confident I could build for money. When I heard that the local garage-owner had planning permission to build a new bungalow in the village it seemed a heaven-sent opportunity. Ronnie Postlethwaite's bungalow was going to be right beside his garage. He reckoned he could keep a close eye on the work and progress, so he took on this would-be builder and farmer, didn't- want- to- be teacher under his wing, at £3 per hour.

He looked on with quizzical amusement when I eschewed all the pegs, levels and strings that would normally mark out foundations to be dug, and asked instead for a five-gallon drum of old engine oil. When I applied this liberally all over the ground plan so that the JCB driver would know where to dig, he acknowledged that it might work, with only the quiet comment, "Oh, you're an oil painter on top of everything else, then?" Ronnie himself had worked for a builder for several years when younger, and he guided the digger driver through the maze of oily lines to produce trenches in the right places. He nodded encouragement when I went along all those trenches driving in wooden pegs to mark the required levels of concrete - although he would have much preferred to see a theodolite in evidence instead of a spirit level and a long length of timber. Ronnie ordered the concrete which came in huge mixers and helped me shovel and tamp it all down to the pegged levels. Then he left me to it, to see how I fared building concrete block walls up to ground level. After all, the end result would ultimately be hidden underground.

Ronnie watched with a mixture of respect and despair: the former for the sheer hard work I put in, the latter at the poor quality of my techniques. I was meticulous about time-keeping, even taking off the quarter hour I shared with them for coffee mid-morning and mid-afternoon, but although I was obviously trying to be quick the truth was that I was pedestrian compared to a qualified bricklayer. Still, credit where credit's due, I was trying my best, and there was no labourer to pay for pottering about doing very little. All in all, Ronnie reckoned he was getting value for money, and at the end of the day the outside walls would be covered in cement render, and the inside plastered, so the wavy lines weren't an issue.

The building inspector didn't agree. He'd been happy enough about the concrete foundations, but when he next dropped in the walls were about two feet above ground level. I wasn't there when the inspector called, but Ronnie relayed his basic message the next day. "He went bloody hatchy. Jumping up and down saying it's the worst bit of block work he's ever seen, and it has to be set straight. And he'll be back to make sure it has been."

I had to admit one of the walls seemed to have developed a bit of a bow, and perhaps the levels weren't perfect. Ronnie hired a theodolite to check it out, and we found one corner of the house was two inches higher than the opposite corner. I offered to take the worst wall back down to ground level and rebuild it in my own time, but Ronnie would have none of it, and showed me how to start to get the levels right with additional thicknesses of mortar, and how to be more precise with the string line. And, above all, not to go too fast.

Duly chastened, I worked on all through that winter, and eventually produced a full bungalow right up to roof level, with block work that, while far from professional, at least didn't cause the inspector apoplexy. By now Ronnie's wife, Audrey, was itching to move into bungalow heaven, and since it was clear it could take me years to complete on my own we parted amicably and a professional team completed the job in a few months. In truth I could probably have made my way as a jobbing builder, but it was farming that I really wanted. Besides, I'd had another idea.

Just as Mum and Dad had warned, without the 30 acres that Michael had bought Fisherground was unviable, and badly unbalanced as a farm. It had a fine set of buildings: the stable block, the huge barn, the milking parlour, the 'Lord Rea' building, the Dutch Barn and finally the immense new cattle kennels. But there were only 35 acres of poor grazing, plus the intakes and fell. There were two potential ways forward. Either we could buy or rent more land to keep enough stock to make full use of the buildings, or we could have an intensive enterprise that used the buildings but didn't need land. Actually, there was a third option, but we didn't realise this until later.

The trouble with more land was, as the Cumbrian motto goes is that 'they're not mekking it any more'. No-one was selling land in the valley, and in any case the reason we hadn't bought all that went with Fisherground was shortage of capital, and there was none available to rent. There was, however, an intensive farming activity that seemed to fit the bill: pigs. Geoff and I were sure we could convert the buildings to cover the whole pig life cycle. Farrowing pens where the sows could have their piglets safely would go in the stable block; the 'Lord Rea' block could hold sows or growing pigs; and the Green Shed could be converted to hold all the bigger pigs getting ready to go for pork.

I'm a great believer in fate, or to be more scientific about it, timing, and timing seemed to smile on the enterprise as Sellafield suddenly went on a mass strike, which was to continue for nearly three months. This meant Geoff was available to help with all the conversion work. Striking while the iron was hot, we bought eight 'in-pig' (pregnant) young sows from the famous Waberthwaite Cumberland Sausage farm, put them in Lord Rea's hulls, and set to work on the stable block to make sure there would be farrowing crates ready for them when needed - in two months' time.

Best advice from the Sausage Farm was that the crates should be raised a foot above floor level, for two reasons. Partly to create a space for the sow's effluence to drop out of the crate, and partly to produce a warm floor by trapping air under it. Geoff, with help from the three little girls, gathered stones from a field which had been ploughed and left rough, while I made the framework for the floors. In a couple of weeks we had the bases for seven farrowing crates, with a passageway along the front so the sows could be fed, and another along the back to barrow out all the muck.

Geoff came home with a powerful hydraulic pipe bender, capable of creating a graceful bend in pipes up to two inch diameter. We bought an electric welder and a pile of scaffolding pipe, and in the next few weeks he produced seven very professional looking farrowing crates, virtually for no outlay.

By the time the strike was over the first of the sows were in the crates, ready to farrow, and all four adults and the excited girls popped in and out incessantly to await the first arrivals. Anne-Marie, carrying Claire in her arms, was the lucky one, seeing the first piglet pop out into the world to take its first gasp of air. Remembering the pain and immensely long labour she had gone through with Claire she envied the ease with which one after another nine little piglets were, as she described it, 'squirted out'. Being tiny may make for an easy birth, but the piglets were very vulnerable to being squashed by their huge, fat mother, which is why she was in a farrowing crate. She could only stand or lie within her metal cage, while the piglets had their own warm nest under a heat lamp near her head. All nine of that first litter survived, and Geoff and I congratulated ourselves on a job well done.

Sow and piglets in Geoff's farrowing crate

Books weren't the only source of advice on the subject of pigs. Dad had raised pigs on a smallholding during a five-year interlude between farming in West Cumberland and our time in Borrowdale, and he rather hesitantly offered to show me the operations I would have to carry out on each new-born piglet. I could just remember as a ten-year-old being press-ganged into holding the piglets for him, so it wasn't entirely new. However, it's a lot harder being the one who actually has to cut sharp little teeth off with a special pair of pliers, and it's even worse being the one who has to slice the flesh behind the testicles with a razor blade, pull out the testicle, and cut it off. It was a lot more complex than the simple rubber band on lambs, and Dad had to show me the procedure several times before I got the knack and could guarantee efficient castration.

There was one more indignity to visit on each little piglet. When they were just a couple of days old each had to be injected with 1 cc of an iron preparation to prevent anaemia, as they were raised on concrete, as opposed to the more natural soil. Always on the lookout for more efficient ways of doing things I started to draw out 10 cc of the solution in a syringe; enough to inject 10 piglets without having to re-load. At the same time I was clipping the teeth so they didn't bite their mother and cause her to stand while they suckled. It all got a bit convoluted, so I would hold the plunger end of the syringe in my teeth to free both hands. The inevitable happened; one piglet bucked at the wrong moment pushing my left hand up and straight onto the needle, and 6 cc of 'pig iron' were injected into the back of my hand. An hour later it had swollen alarmingly and Jen took me off to the doctor's, offending bottle clutched in my good hand. After much head shaking the doctor couldn't find an antidote, and sent me off with painkillers and a stern warning not to be so daft again. There was no trace by next morning, and I've never suffered from anaemia, but I do have a tendency to ping when I go through airport scanners!

Chapter 12

The Great Pig Adventure: 1977-1984

There are lots of Blea Tarns in the Lake District, and Fisherground had its own up on the fell; a very lovely ten-acre mini-lake 600 feet above the valley floor, so close to the edge of the fell as almost to spill over. Directly below it, in the valley, was a large Victorian guest house that had gone to the expense of piping its water directly from the cool, clear depths of the tarn, but not to the expense of burying the pipe underground. Now that the valley was on mains water this long, galvanised pipe was redundant, lying there begging to be recycled.

Never ones to turn down beggars, Jen and I approached the owners the guest house offering to 'tidy up the fellside' for them by removing it, at no expense. Deal done, we returned next day with a brand-new hacksaw, several blades, and the tractor and trailer. It took us several days hacking and carrying, but at the end the fell was pristine once again, and there was a huge stack of perfect pipe for gates stacked ready for Geoff as soon as he had time. In the meantime I set about converting one half of the Green Shed into concrete block pens for fattening pigs as they were weaned off their mothers from the new farrowing pens.

This was becoming a much more serious attempt at intensive farming than previous ill-fated ventures in the shed, and we had to shell out serious money for materials alone, so it was as well we could do the building and welding ourselves. I revelled in the design and building; so much so that Michael observed on one of his 'progress visits', "Ah reckon thou's only happy when there's a trowel in yer hand". There was more than a grain of truth in this - especially on a job where there was no building inspector and the inhabitants weren't going to get precious about everything being level.

Michael contributed his bit to the recycling effort, giving us a field of very dead hay which made perfect insulated ceilings for the pig pens. Geoff kept pace with the production line of weaners coming from the new farrowing crates, and The Great Pig Adventure (TGPA) got under way. Twenty weeks on from the first farrowing the first set of porkers were ready to go. Since this was soon to be a weekly event, we invested in a proper Land Rover (old and second hand, of course) and a road trailer, and Jen and I set off for the abattoir at Ulverston with the first nine on board.

Porkers in the Green Shed: 1982

All in all, TGPA lasted seven years. Here are selected extracts from the diary I kept over that time, to give a flavour of how it went. (Extra explanations in brackets.)

April 15th, 1979: Jen insistent the in-pig sows should live out on the intakes. Made three pig arks from old Anderson Shelter curved corrugated iron sheets to put up there for them to shelter in. (We'd seen outdoor pigs on holiday in Cornwall. Bet you didn't know pigs had holidays!)

April 30th: All arks up, turned a dozen sows and a boar out to see how it goes. Glad we had gathered sheep in before they went out; I can imagine there will be a confrontation next time.

May 7th: Put up sign on intake gate saying 'Beware of the boar' after a visitor complained. (It's not a public footpath). A different visitor asked me to pose in front of it!

May 30th: Sows growing very hairy outside. Feeding them we were joined by two Roe deer who thought this easy pickings. Catherine and Sally wanted to ride a sow - put them on old Number one, she's very placid. They hung on by her hair, and she was still gentle.

June 18th: Getting sick of sleeping in the farrowing crates when a sow is due. (I had a camp bed and sleeping bag in the farrowing house so I could make sure no piglets were crushed when new-born).

July 29th: Jen and Hilary (the friend who'd accompanied her to the vets) went camping at Blea Tarn to get away from the stink of pigs for a night. Unrolled her sleeping bag and found she'd taken mine by mistake!!! Hilary refused to stay and they landed back home at 10 o'clock.

Sept 10th: Loading 15 porkers to take to Ulverston. For no obvious reason one suddenly leapt in the air and came down dead. Heart attack. Unloaded everything and barrowed it round to garage, hauled it up by the back legs and cut its throat. Blood gushed into buckets. Jen and kids melted away - except for Elizabeth (aged four) who brought a little stool and sat entranced as I cut it open. Seymour's book (see next chapter) open at the page on butchering pigs, I took all the offal out. Elizabeth full of questions, me very short on answers!

Sept 11th: Took what should have been yesterday's load this morning. Spent afternoon trying to cut pig up in Seymour approved fashion. Not easy to cut bones. Took all non-joints to nearby butcher to make into sausages.

Sept 13th: Freezer very full. Hope nothing else has a heart attack for a while.

April 7th 1980: Jen leading Napoleon (the boar) up the lane to the intake. He began to show more interest in Jen than food - she must give off strong pheromones! Usually you can slow him down by dropping a bit of food, and she had a bucketful. He got less and less interested in the food and more and more interested in her - to the point where she dropped the whole bucket and legged it up the lane with Napoleon in hot pursuit. She climbed the five barred gate onto the Ratty line double quick and left him huffing on the other side. Couldn't get back down the lane so she came for help by the fields, hoping no visitor would use the lane meantime. Had to have a brandy to settle - yep, Napoleon!

June 17th: Went to feed sows on intake, to find one missing. Eventually found her doing the doggy paddle in an underground tank of water I didn't know existed. She'd found the old water supply for the farm and fallen through the fragile lid. Went home for rope and reinforcements and we pulled her out apparently none the worse for wear.

November 7th: Used the rear loader to load the pig muck in the slurry pit. It gets hellishly wet and sloppy in a wet time, and runs all over the place. Spread it on the front left - daren't use that field in summer or the stink might upset the campers. Getting to hate the smell, it seems to get into my skin, however hard I shower.

Jan 1st , 1981: Bad start to a new year. Took bag of feed up to intake sows to be met on the Ratty line by four very cold, very pink piglets, mother going berserk trying to get to them. Don't know how I missed her due date. Got her down and into farrowing pen and gathered up six piglets to warm under the heat lamp, but I found another four dead from the cold.

March 7th 1981: Don't know whether to laugh or cry. Had too many porkers to fit into trailer, so Jen and I lifted three into the back of the Land Rover. Going over Birker Moor (the fell road) the pigs lifted the sneck on the back door (should have locked it, of course) and one fell out. Trailer ran over it and it lay on the side of the road squealing its life away. We were just outside Crosbythwaite (a lonely farm on the top of the fell road) so I dashed up and hammered on the door to ask for a sharp knife to cut its throat and put it out of its misery. I didn't know Mrs. Harrison, but I guess she recognised me - anyway she handed over her best carving knife with no questions, and I sprinted back and did the deed. The road looked as if there'd been a major accident for weeks after. Dashed back to ask if I could gut it in a shed, and again they lent me a wheelbarrow and a rope, and Jen & I hung it as quickly as possible and I cut it open and loaded its guts into the barrow. Started off with the whole family watching - ended up alone! Mr. Harrison said he'd let the guts go cold then feed them to the dogs. Back in the LR within the hour and on to Ulverston with the rest.

Mar 8th: Back up to Crosbythwaite to pick up porker and thank them again. Home to scald off the bristles with boiling water, then the dread job of cutting it up. Will try some hams this time, as it's cold out. Salting's a bloody awful job when you've got cuts on your hands.

June 20th 1982: Abandoned putting sows on the intakes. Old hands bully the younger sows who don't get enough to eat. (Geoff welded up 30 partitions and I made eight pens for four sows each so each could be fed individually in the rest of the Green Shed, which was now completely full of pigs).

May 9th 1984: Catherine has claimed the runt of a litter as a pet. She saw him limping along as I was ushering the newly weaned litter round to the Green Shed. He's always been arthritic - don't know why. She's called him Sam Pig after a character in an Alison Uttley story. She reads voraciously. She and Jen have made him a cosy pen in the garth, and the weather's good so he should be OK.

Aug 20th : Catherine distraught when I told her Sam Pig has to go to be killed today, but we can't afford a pet pig of all things, and he'll start to suffer as it gets colder. Took him with the rest but the abattoir wouldn't buy him, because of his arthritis. They killed him for us and Jen and I had to take him to the butcher to be cut up. He asked how many there were in the family and I thought he would be generous if I pleaded poverty, so I said nine, counting us all in.

Aug 22nd : Picked up cut up Sam Pig. The joints are huge - that's why he asked how many! Freezer full again.

Nov 5th : Norman (Jen's father) staying for a few days. Jen did roast pork and I happened to mention it was Sam Pig. Norman came over green and said he wasn't hungry.

Catherine swore she'd never eat meat again and would be a vegetarian for ever. I enjoyed Sam Pig enormously.

It was with very mixed emotions that we finally decided enough was enough. On the one hand it was clear that pigs and tourists don't really mix. The smell on a sultry evening crept into the campsite, and while no-one actually complained we felt embarrassed. I'd had enough of sleeping in the farrowing house, and was sick of the stench on my clothes and skin. But on the other hand it felt like a betrayal of my roots in farming, a meek submission to market forces that shouldn't be allowed to dictate how life should be lived. I was still fairly young and wet behind the ears, but I'd expended a lot of that youth on the enterprise and was bitter to see it go unrewarded.

The very end was a sad and embarrassing affair. The remaining sows and boar were getting old, somewhat poor on their feet, and in truth a sorry sight. They couldn't be taken to the normal abattoir, as it dealt only in prime meat, which these elderly ladies clearly weren't. So Jen and I loaded the lot into the trailer for the last time and took them to Carlisle Auction Mart, by now a very up-market market of gleaming stainless steel and polished wood. This was far enough away for us never to need to show our faces again, which was perhaps just as well. In such a venue, surrounded by prime beef and fat lambs, the sows looked positively Third World.

They made very little, of course, and God knows what sort of meat they went as, but they did all sell and we were spared the ultimate indignity of having to take some home again. We drove home in the enforced silence demanded by the rackety Land Rover, each wrapped in our own mixture of regret but relief.

Chapter 13

Self-sufficiency: 1976-1980

The first few years were a time of self-conscious self-sufficiency for Jen and me. This was partly in response to being very short of cash, but partly also it was a mind-set, not that unusual in the '70s. We had a book - *Self-sufficiency: the science and art of producing and preserving your own food,* by John and Sally Seymour - that became our constant companion as we valiantly learnt how to pluck and draw chickens and make cottage cheese from curdled milk. The garden was split in two by an old beech hedge, one half having been a kitchen garden at one time, though sadly overgrown and gone to waste by the time we arrived. An overgrown damson tree blotted out much of the sunlight. Cutting this down and opening up this valuable space was one of our first priorities - and the one which provoked the confrontation with my parents that overshadowed our first summer.

The damson down and cut up for logs for the fire, we were able to dig over this ancient kitchen garden and at least plant cabbages and Brussels Sprouts for winter use. Later came a strawberry patch and framework for raspberry canes, but in that first year Jen had to rely on Mother Nature for the fruit that the self-sufficiency book insisted were an integral part of the exercise. She had always delighted in picking brambles and Eskdale was full of suitable briar patches. To her delight she also discovered gooseberry bushes on the side of the La'al Ratty line, in a little triangle of land above the sheep pens. Goodness knows why some preceding generation had planted them there, unless it was the one small area safe from grazing sheep, but they produced well. Jen packed many a pound of gooseberries and blackberries into the freezer that year, and for many more to come.

The elderberry trees in the yard still had their flowers when we arrived and, following the book Jen stripped lots off to make elderflower champagne. This involved large plastic bins full of sugary water and, of course, the elder flowers themselves. There was a period of fermentation when they bubbled quietly to themselves in the corner by the Rayburn, and then came the bottling in old lemonade bottles that had to have screw tops to hold in the pressure as the last of the fermentation took place. Eventually she had at least 50 bottles filled with the promising 'taste of summer' all stored in the little half-cellar under the stairs on the slate sconces that went round the walls. This was always a cool spot, just as the Seymours advocated, and we looked forward to being able to slake a midday thirst when they were ready.

We were in the kitchen when the first one exploded, with a mighty bang. Mystified, we traced the sound to the cellar and discovered shattered glass all over the floor and a sweet, sticky substance underfoot. The cooling drink became a lottery. Who was brave enough to go down and bring up a bottle knowing it might explode in your hands before you could get the top off? But one of the aspects of self-sufficiency, at least in those days, was that you couldn't just give up. A lot of cost, sugar and time had gone into those bottles, and some amber nectar had to come out to make it worthwhile. I developed a system involving a blanket and a lot of faith. Those bottles which didn't self-destruct provided a very refreshing drink, but nobody ever went under the stairs unprotected, and all that summer long there was from time to time the sound of another Molotov cocktail exploding deep in the bowels of Fisherground.

With four adults and four young girls in the house we got through a lot of milk, so a house cow seemed a good idea, and we bought Daisy and her new-born calf Buttercup to fulfil the role of milk provider. The idea was to milk Daisy in the morning, drawing off enough for household use, then let Buttercup take all the rest. It worked fairly well, but the milk was very full cream and tended to have the odd bit of debris floating around in it. We did eventually get a primitive cooling system and sieved out all flotsam and for six months or so Daisy did us proud. There were three drawbacks. Firstly it was time-consuming, going out and milking her in the morning, cooling the milk and sieving it off. Secondly it was expensive, at least in the short-term, with barley to buy. Hopefully selling Buttercup would eventually make recompense, but cash flow continued to be a problem. Finally, and this was the most problematic, Daisy needed to be pregnant again if she was to carry on milking after Buttercup was a year old.

It's not that easy to tell when a cow is ready for the bull though there are tell-tale signs. Unsure of my ground I decided not to use the services of the Artificial Insemination Unit, who, for a fee, toured farms with 'straws' of prime bull semen to impregnate dairy cattle with the best of bloodstock. For one thing it was expensive; but more importantly I wasn't confident of hitting the optimum day for conception. The alternative was to walk her along to a neighbour's farm where a big fine Limousin bull would be more than happy to do the job. At that stage we had no Land-Rover or big trailer, so walking was the only way.

When I judged Daisy was ready, Jen and I walked her the short mile, without incident, for her romantic encounter with the bull, Henri. He was immense, with the powerful shoulders of a French prop-forward on steroids and the classic muscular rump that makes his breed so good for beef. Henri was completely uninterested in this rather plain, not to say dowdy, Friesian lass and his proud owner reckoned we were a couple of days too early. So, rather like the Grand old Duke of York, we marched her home and back again two days later. This time Henri swung into action, though with the vaguely disdainful air of a paid stud who finds it all rather beneath him, and we walked the presumably pregnant Daisy home. Jen thought she detected a satisfied bovine smile.

After about six months of the milk regime there was rebellion in the farmhouse. The girls found the milk far too creamy, Geoff didn't drink milk anyway, and even Jen, Anne-Marie and I were finding it a bit cloying. Buttercup was now big enough to be weaned and sold and Daisy was in calf. Reluctantly we agreed to abandon this particular form of self-sufficiency and I once more faced selling in Broughton Auction - with rather more success than I'd had with the bought-in calves.

Thinking that goat's milk might be more palatable Jen persuaded me, against my better judgement, to buy a female goat that she promised she would milk, pointing out that if the children wouldn't drink it we could use it to feed pet lambs in spring. This was a long-term project, as Emily, the goat, first had to have kids, and therefore had to be introduced to another neighbour's billy goat. Once again, female pheromones and all that, the billy, like Napoleon, was far more interested in Jen than he was in Emily. I had to rescue her and escort her well out of the way before Billy could be persuaded to turn his attentions to Emily, who might well have sniffed haughtily and demanded to be taken home - but that nature overcame her finer feelings.

Emily duly had her kids - two male, one female - in early April and we looked forward to her assistance with the pet lambs. She knew well where the bran she had each morning was stored and somehow forced her way in unnoticed and scoffed a huge helping. Next morning she was a very poorly goat, and the vet diagnosed alcoholic poisoning as the bran swelled and fermented inside her. He said there was nothing he could do, and she died a few hours later. So, instead of Emily feeding the pet lambs, Jen ended up feeding her kids as well. Self-sufficient was beginning to mean 'I've had enough'!

Jen, having plucked and drawn 40 hens

The other string on the self-sufficiency bow was all the things you can do with a pig (once it's dead). There are sausages, bacon and ham, as well as straight-forward pork, and we had a go at them all. Pork is the easiest: all you have to do is cut the carcase up in the correct places and you have leg, chops, belly pork and all the other cuts. The Seymours' book had diagrams of how and where to cut, and I did my best, though prising bones apart seemed surprisingly difficult. We gave up on trying to make sausages after one failed attempt with a table-top mincer, and took all the bits to the butcher for him to make them.

Bacon and ham were the trickiest and caused us a lot of trouble. Basically you need to rub as much salt as possible into a large joint - the rump- and then hang the joint up in a cool room for a long time, hoping it sets into ham rather than just going off. There was a genuine salting-room at Fisherground, on the cold north side of the house, with a tiny window, slate sconces all round the walls for salting, and hooks in the ceiling to hang hams and bacon from. Unfortunately, with two families in one house we needed all the rooms for more pressing needs, and one of my first jobs was to rip out all the slate slabs and enlarge the window to make a bedroom. The book insisted salting had to be done 'when there is an R in the month' which at first I thought was just another bit of esoteric folklore. Then I realised it means any time except summer, which is obvious when you think about it, with all the flies about and the increased likelihood of the meat going off.

The good book also insisted the job shouldn't be done by a woman, because of female hormones making it more likely to go off. Napoleon, Billy, and now this... Jen professed herself desolate not to be allowed to rub all that salt in.

We did eventually get about a dozen hams hanging from hooks, and none of them went off; but when we came to slice them up for bacon we found the skins to be far too hard for any knife and ended up more with crinkle-cut gammon than nice tender bacon. We even bought a cheap bacon slicer, but it baulked at the task as well. One way and another we got through all those sides of ham and bacon, but again at the end of it decided it was just too much effort for what wasn't particularly tasty meat.

And, I'm afraid, that was our verdict about most aspects of self-sufficiency. There is a lot of work involved in growing and preparing your own food - vegetable or animal - which is fine as long as you enjoy digging, weeding, gathering, blanching, killing, butchering, salting and preserving. Jen and I decided we didn't, particularly, and Anne-Marie and Geoff had never thought it seemed a great idea in the first place. So after a few years of the kitchen garden we ripped out the dividing hedge and turned it all over to lawn and flower beds, and enjoyed the splendid fruit, veg and meat to be had for a small fee from the supermarket. Jen did however retain her love of egg-laying hens and the gathering of wild fruit and mushrooms, where Mother Nature does most of the preparation for you.

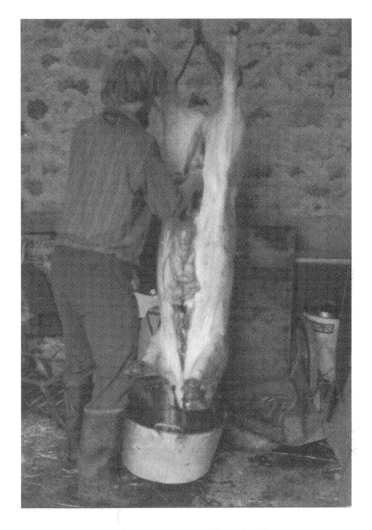

My first attempt at butchering

Chapter 14

JCB Joe and the caravans: 1978-9

Peter Dowling was the local National Farmers' Union officer, a man of great wisdom and practicality, and considerable girth. He was trying to help the Commoners' Association which represented all the farms with rights on Eskdale Common, in dealings with the European Economic Community. Fisherground was one such, so he visited to explain all the duties and requirements that would be a trade-off for receiving money via the EEC. He was in any case keen to get to know the four of us, and perhaps to judge for himself whether the rumours were true.

We proudly showed him round, especially the various building conversions we'd done for the pigs. As our insurer he was a bit dubious about free-range pigs on the intakes, but accepted my assurance that there was no public footpath, and that anyway the sows were very friendly. He was more sceptical about the closeness of the rowdy, smelly pigs in the Green Shed to the illicit caravan, and at the end of the tour chose to return to the issue and raise his concerns. Geoff and I explained the caravan had to be there in order to get 'fall' to the septic tank, and he mulled this over for a while till he came up with a radical, fundamental and far-sighted solution.

Basic premise: the caravan had to move. It was far from ideal to have visitors close to the smell and the noise of the pigs in the Green Shed. Basic problems: lack of septic tank and increasing visibility inviting National Park recriminations. Peter's solution: apply for proper planning permission, not for one, but for three caravans. That way economies of scale would justify a new septic tank, which could also serve the campsite, and the visitors could spread out into the lovely orchard and have an enjoyable holiday.

"Come on, Peter, the Planning Board will never give permission."

"No, you're wrong, Ian. I can make a very good case for the need for diversification. Fisherground is too small to survive on farming alone."

"Won't they just say the pigs are diversification?"

"Are you making much on pigs?"

"Well, no, but someday, maybe…"

"Face it, Ian, you'll never have enough to make a living on them. But they do show you're trying to make a go of it, and that'll count for a lot in the planners' eyes… give them a reason to allow you more diversification."

We were used to doing everything for ourselves - indeed I almost made a religion of self-sufficiency. So it was a new experience to have Peter put the resources of the NFU behind the plans, including drawings, cash-flow, and placing the application with his professional recommendation before the dreaded planners. It took a while, but early in September planning permission came through, and we had the winter to prepare for this new, exciting venture.

Obviously we would reposition the existing caravan, with all the fun of going back through the gap that had entailed, but we decided to go for much bigger units for the other two, now we had the planners' blessing. One was 36 feet long, and the last a monstrous 45 feet. But at least they didn't have to go through the gap. The new caravans were to arrive together one day in November, on two lorries, and Jen and Anne-Marie kept an anxious look-out for their arrival. They didn't arrive, but two fraught-looking lorry drivers did. A cup of tea and a slice of cake later, they were ready to tell their story. All had gone well till they reached the last seven, winding miles from the main road into the valley. They had met the school bus, in the narrowest of places, and had to inch their ten-foot wide cargoes past it. They had been overtaken on the only slightly wider stretch by the local boy-racer. They had caught a tree with the leading van, and a little TLC would be needed. And then they had got to the place where the narrow road really began - 400 yards down the road at the pub. There they had stopped, and there they were going to stop. They wouldn't be driving in with the hearty panache of the 26 foot van: they would be unloading on the wide section by my well-remembered railings and driving off into the sunset. From here on, the four of us were on our own.

Geoff and I went off to size up the problem - and to have a quiet pint in the pub. The drivers were right, these were caravans of a different order: the monster 45 footer even had two sets of wheels. This was going to be a tractor job, and it would need a bigger tractor than we had. It was obvious that neither van would go round the corner into the lane, so we would have to take down the wall on the corner. This was getting to be a big job. Fortunately, the next day was Saturday so Geoff wouldn't be at work.

We started early, throwing stones from the corner wall into the field. Jen, on the Fergie, pulled out the big foundation stones with a 'snigging chain'. It was coffee time before the wall was down, and the base roughly levelled. Time to give it a try, with the smaller caravan first. The cavalcade rolled into action: Anne-Marie in the Land Rover with all the kids, headlights on for full effect; me on Michael's tractor towing the 36' caravan between stone walls with only a couple of feet to spare; Geoff behind watching the back, and Jen relaying instructions. All went well until we reached the corner; 400 yards safely completed, only ten more till we were off the road.

The tractor turned in, the front corner of the caravan turned in - and the back corner hit the wall on the opposite side of the road. I manoeuvred, Geoff yelled instructions, Jen talked calmingly to the motorists trying to come down the valley, and Anne-Marie took the frightened girls home in the Land Rover. Out of nowhere Malcolm Watson, the village policeman turned up and talked to the drivers trying to go up the valley. No-one was going anywhere, because the caravan was completely stuck. We couldn't take down any more wall, because it was a hedge from there on. The only solution was to take down the wall on the other side of the lane, and drive onto the field instead.

45 feet of trouble on its way: 1979

Jen slipped away from the slowly growing line of cars, claiming she would be needed with her snigging chain again, and left it to Malcolm to placate the neighbours. Nobody could turn round in that narrow lane so nobody who was in the valley could get out and nobody who was out could get in. Suddenly the 'hippies in the commune' were less of a joke and more of a bloody nuisance. It had taken us two hours to take down the first wall, and it took nearly as long for the second. Motorists were spitting feathers. Eventually it was down. We made a makeshift ramp across the rough soil, and I prepared to pull the recalcitrant caravan into the field. I did get it in a few yards in before it became stuck in the mud: just far enough for the logjam of cars to start to unravel under Malcolm's careful direction. And we hadn't even started on the 45' monster yet.

All good things come to an end, and fortunately the same is true of all bad things. After another two days of taking more walls down, jacking up, backing up, swearing and heaving all three caravans were in place in the orchard. Now it was time to think about waste disposal, and a new septic tank and pipework to connect them all. Enter Joe, the gentle JCB driver. Gentle in all respects: Joe Gates could tickle a pussycat with a feather tied to the digging bucket of his JCB, and knew from experience everything there was to know about drainage. He was also able to share his know-how without belittling the new-comers. Joe was a gentleman. A chain-smoking, cigarillo chomping, overweight gentleman, to be sure, with his braces straining over massive shoulders, but definitely a gentleman.

He spent a productive hour with Geoff and me running a practised eye over levels, the stream, possible places for the septic tank, outflow from it etc. He suggested digging across to the water main so that water pipes could be laid in the same trenches. He asked about telephone cables (oops! Never thought of that) and existing water mains. He told us to get an oversized metal pipe to surround the sewer as it crossed the stream. In short, Joe was the project manager as well as the digger driver. Then he started to dig, quickly, methodically and accurately. He had me check the levels as he went along, but there was no real need, as he gave the required inch per metre fall almost by instinct.

The septic tank was huge, and all the gravel that came out had to be trailered away. Joe suggested it would make a great base for the new lane into the campsite. The whole job took two days, including the soakaway trench. As he said to me as I puffed over a little bit of spade-digging right beside a caravan: "Aye, it teks a good man to come a poor second to a JCB." He left, promising to return to backfill all the trenches when I'd laid the pipework and the water pipes. The three girls had watched our progress from a safe distance, and when he had gone Catherine had a request. Please could the big machine make the ford over the stream a lot bigger, so they could have a paddling pond? It could, and it did.

Again I started the sort of building I was good at - underground where no-one would see it. It took me several weeks to build the big three-chamber septic tank, six feet deep and twenty feet long. While I happily paddled away six feet down, trowel in hand, Jen and Anne-Marie got on with making the two new caravans fit for use as self-catering units. They had to paint the outsides the planning board's beloved drab green, but they could let themselves go on the insides, playing Wendy-houses for real. Joint enterprise is a great healer and that winter of working together to produce something so worthwhile eased away the strains of sharing the same house, the same space, even, in practice, the same kids. The looming deadline of Easter 1979, with guests booked in to all three caravans brought all four of us together for a final push to be ready, and the last couple of weeks were a whirlwind of activity. Geoff and I screwed together furniture, put up pictures and fixed water leaks. In the meantime Jen and Anne-Marie between them bought all the beds, bedding, tables, crockery and so on, and looked after four growing girls.

That Easter was a turning point in many respects. It was three years since the first breathless delight of having our offer accepted: three years of gruelling work for little return; three years of learning to live in a very different way. This new venture into tourism promised a decent income and was an enterprise involving us all. This was something that would need everyone's input every week, if it, unlike its predecessors, was going to work and balance the books.

Chapter 15

Black and White: 1979

Black and white: the theme for the night. It was Thursday May 3rd , 1979, and four of us were sitting in front of an old black and white television in Geoff and Anne-Marie's sitting room. The grainy picture had come down 200 yards of cable, leading up to the top of Stretcher Crag, the nearest place that got any signal from the distant repeater mast near the coast. Bob McKenzie was getting excited over his swingometer, which was beginning to predict a victory for the Tories, led by Margaret Thatcher, the archetypal black and white leader of her party. Actually, it was Friday 4th by now, and it was becoming clear she would win.

"Well, Geoffrey, man, what is happening to your socialists?" The voice was deep, and African. Gideon was a Zulu.

"Inevitable, Gideon, inevitable. You can't have 20% inflation and the winter of discontent and expect to win an election. Not our fault, though, too many wet Liberals and SNPs watering down every decision Sunny Jim tried to make."

So it was black and white on the sofa, too. Geoff, the white Labour man, defending the indefensible. Gideon, the black conservative, a consummate politician, fascinated by the immediacy of participating in history.

"Did you have to be elected to your, how do you call it…"

"Legislature, Anne-Marie, the KwaZulu Legislature. And yes indeed, it's very democratic."

"Are you ANC, then, Gideon?" It's the only South African party I'd heard of, and I was trying to stay on-board.

"No indeed, Ian, I represent the Inkatha Freedom Party, the conservative wing of the legislature. We are, if you like, the opposition to the ANC. Indeed, Chief Buthelezi hates their methods, their terrorism."

"And you must be well up in the church in Zululand, I guess, or you wouldn't be here."

"Oh yes, man, I am a reader in our church, and I lead the prayers at the start of each session of the Assembly."

Which begins to explain why this unlikely guest was with us. Carlisle Diocese had links to three other Anglican dioceses world-wide: Zululand, Madras in South India, and Stavanger in Norway. Anne-Marie had volunteered to have Gideon for a week while he learnt about the church in Cumbria, but he was much more interested in the political history being made this night.

By next morning the result was clear: Mrs. Thatcher had a 43 seat majority. Black and white politics was about to have its day, or decade. Gideon and Jen sat on the stairs by the telephone: he must phone his wife and recount the excitement of the night, and Jen must make the connection. Through the hiss and buzz of intercontinental connection she asks for... "Ceza 2: that's our number" Ceza 2, ye Gods, how many phones are there in Ceza, then? Clicks and whirrs, then suddenly a honeyed voice, in a language she doesn't understand. Hurriedly she handed the phone to Gideon and made to leave.

"You sit there, girl, and don't you move a muscle."

So she sat, obediently, and eavesdropped on her first and only conversation in Zulu.

Gideon's schedule was fairly light but included a visit to the local primary school, where he reduced the country children to an awe-struck silence simply by his presence, the first black man they'd ever seen. All except Catherine, of course, because she was now in the reception class at school and had had time to get used to him, so she proudly showed him round. The vicar was in charge of his schedule and entertained Gideon at the vicarage several times, trying without success to get him to join him on some of the lovely walks in the valley. Gideon confessed when he returned that in his country you only walked if you wanted to get somewhere, and there was no other way.

May 1979. Back row: Anne-Marie, Geoff, Gideon, Ian, Jen
Front row: Claire(2), Sally(3), Elizabeth(4) and Catherine(5)

There was one other major event that May, that was to affect the household much more than Mrs. Thatcher's election. Not long after Gideon's visit Jen's mother, Marjorie, became ill. Marjorie was a regular visitor for those first three years at Fisherground, for she loved children and took to all the

Fisherground girls with delight. She and Norman now lived a hundred miles away in Newcastle, but she stayed at the farm often and delighted in having Catherine and Sally back to stay in the big city. Catherine adored city life, and in particular city buses. Having taken her into town Marjorie found there was no way they were going to get off to go to the shops she had in mind, without suffering the indignity of trying to prise small fingers from every rail to be found on a bus. She gave in, and they spent the afternoon watching the city's sights from the top deck, till the child fell asleep and could be taken home.

It was the cruellest of ironies that one who lived for children should be struck down by a disease that so mimicked pregnancy. As Jen visited week after week that summer she watched her mother's belly swell, as the flesh slowly dropped from her face, arms and legs. Week after week she drove back to the farm, to children who were excitedly asking how Nana was, and when could they visit her. And to a husband who seemed to have nothing to offer in terms of sympathy or even simple understanding. Anne-Marie at least was some help, offering a shoulder to cry on. But she would insist on praying for healing, for a miracle Jen knew wasn't going to happen.

Everything about the end was so wrong. Marjorie's own doctor was on holiday and the locum seemed to know nothing about her history or, more importantly, about pain management. She was so thin, and her belly so swollen that Jen could hardly bear to look at a mother who looked, for all the world, like one of the horrendous pictures she remembered of the Biafran children in their terrible famine. So thin that even sitting on her bed was unbearable. So thin that even Jen's loving arm around her shoulders, while it brought the comfort of being loved also brought her pain. The only thing that felt remotely right to Jen was that at least she was there at the dreadful end to all this suffering: that her mother did die in her arms.

Marjorie's funeral was no better. Again, the minister who knew her well was on holiday, and the Reader who was standing in knew nothing of her history. What could he tell of the dashing young woman who, in the 1930s had been the toast of Chopwell; who had married on the eve of War and made a new life with her first-born girl in Alston, far up in the Cumbrian Pennines? How could he know of her love of children, her open house, her delight in the simple pleasures of life? How could he possibly honour and celebrate this life cut short? The doctor and the minister, however, had an excuse for their ineptitude. They didn't know Marjorie, and they didn't know Jen. I had no such excuse: even though we were just thirty, I had known Jen, and her mother, nearly twenty years. I should have known better.

It was a few weeks later when Jen's sister, Barbara, and her family brought Norman over to the farm for a break: weeks of smouldering discontent where I was completely unable to understand Jen's grief and sense of loss. Nothing in my past had prepared me for bereavement; I hadn't lost anyone close. And something in my make-up left a big hole where empathy should be, a hole I filled with busy-ness, with getting on with life. Black and white, no shades of grey. Perhaps it's part of being a mathematician: we look for elegant answers, irrefutable solutions, the QED triumphantly pencilled in at the successful end of a proof. Emotions, messy compromises, passions, grief, emptiness, insoluble tensions, perhaps indeed the whole business of being human, that whole spectrum of colour between the black and the white – it's not a mathematician's natural territory. Jen's grief was a foreign land to me, I didn't speak the language, and at thirty you're never going to gain fluency.

It came to a head that night. Everyone had gone to bed, the house straining at the seams. I was left alone in the sitting room wondering if the atmosphere would ever lighten, if normal service could be resumed as soon as possible, when Jen returned in her dressing gown, a strange and dangerous light in her eyes.

"Are you ever going to say sorry?"

"Sorry? Why should I say sorry? What have I done....
It's not my fault your mother has died."

"You just don't get it, do you... "

"What is there to get, Jen? Look, of course I'm sorry
Marjorie has died, but what can I do about it? People die, and
we move on. What do you want me to say?"

"Say? I want you to say sorry, I want you to realise how
it feels to lose your mother, someone you love, and to lose her
so horribly. I want you... oh God... I want you to be human,
to be real.. to be.. I don't know. I don't want you at all."

"So that's what this is all about. Well I want you to
grow up, to move on, to stop wallowing in grief, making the
most of it. Or maybe I don't want you either."

Jen threw her glass, full of water, full of bitterness, full
of pent-up frustration, wildly at me. Did I duck, or did it just
miss? It splintered into fragments against the fireplace.
Infinitely slowly the shards fell to the hearth, the sound
reverberating, beating off the walls. Infinitely slowly, with
infinite regret, I slapped her face – she was hysterical, I told
myself, at last finding my feelings. Just not the appropriate
feelings.

All hell broke loose, as Norman burst in, followed by
Jen's sister, Barbara. What sort of monster was I? Call myself a
Christian? Barbara took charge, shooed us all off to our
various beds, promised it would all look different in the
morning. Barbara took Jen to her own bed, as she had so many
times when they were young, and held her close. Why
couldn't I have done that?

Chapter 16

Travelling t'Entire: 1979-85

Old Tom Fisher owned ten acres of steeply sloping land five miles down the valley. He put the word out that it was for rent, and I heard about it on the grapevine in the pub. This could make a big difference to land-starved Fisherground, and I wasted no time in driving off to see both the land and Tom. My first impression of the land was that it would need a lot of fencing to hold our Herdwicks, and of Tom that he likewise would need a lot of fencing with, if I wasn't to be steamrollered by this larger-than-life character.

It turned out to be an appropriate metaphor, as Tom told me some of his history in that obligatory hour long circuitous chat before we got down to the serious business of how much the rent would be. In return, he filleted me, learning of my birth and early years just five miles away, my years in Borrowdale, and my more recent time as a teacher before the move to Fisherground. His own story was infinitely more colourful, and he told it well. He had for many years worked for the council mending and making the roads, and his job was to drive and maintain a huge steam roller. This meant getting up steam long before the rest of the gang were ready to start work, and they started at 7.30, so Tom would be setting in his fire and filling the water and generally greasing, tightening, oiling and cajoling this throwback to Victorian glory by 5.00 am.

As he was often working in remote areas of the county it wasn't worth going home each night, so he pulled a sort of gypsy caravan behind to sleep in during the week. When the county finally got rid of steam rollers in favour of the much more user-friendly diesel driven machines Tom gave up in disgust. There was no subtlety, no skill required, in such simple machines. What had been an art had become merely a tedious treadmill - at least that's how Tom saw it.

He moved on to what he called 'travelling t'entire'. My bafflement delighted him, further evidence of this nouveau pauper's lack of country lore. "Sorry, Tom, the entire what - county? West Cumbria?"

"Dus'ta nut know what an entire is, then?"

"Sorry, Tom, not a clue…"

"Well what dus'ta think it is. If a gelding's missing its balls, what dus'ta think an entire is?" The penny dropped:

"Oh, you mean a stallion!"

Tom, and the 'entire'
(Photo courtesy of the Fisher family)

Chuckling, he explained that in the days before the war, when every farm had a carthorse or two very few had a stallion, as they were difficult to control and not much use for farm work. That was generally done by mares or geldings. So when a farmer wanted his mare to be in foal he would watch for signs of her being in heat and send for Tom to walk his stallion to the farm as a stud.

Regularly, throughout this interview, if that is what it was, Tom would look his young interviewee directly in the eye, wag his finger at me and say, "Now listen, Mister, ah'm gonna tell you...." and proceed with my education. I learned more dialect and rural wisdom at Tom's kitchen table over the next few years than I had picked up in my entire life. This first seminar was on the delicate subject of pitching an offer for land rental. Direct as ever Tom demanded of me what I thought the land was worth to us. Unsure of my ground in the face of this master tactician I opted for my genuine offer, afraid to offend with an artificially low bid. Tom guffawed and I felt myself going red, afraid that I had indeed offended even with my best offer: but no, Tom stuck out his finger in my face and said,

"Now listen, Mister, Ah'm gonna tell you... diven't start ower high, or there's nae fun in it. Now offer me half that".

Obediently, and with a straight face, I complied, provoking a roar from Tom.

"Now listen, Mister, Ah'm gonna tell you... don't you come here thinking me a fool. Ah know what this land's worth, and thou's not getting it for less".

Contorting my face into what I hoped looked weasel wise, I hummed a bit, lapsed into my version of broad Cumbrian and said I "thowt ah could mebbe gan a bit higher. What mak o' figure had Tom in mind?" Tom smiled a bit, scratched his chin, and came in with a price a good bit higher than my first offer. Then looked challengingly across the table.

"Nae, give ower, Tom, tha knows it's nut worth owt like that. Tell you what, I'll gan as far as me first price, but that's me best offer." Tom stood up, towering over me seated at his table, arms akimbo, filling his half of the kitchen... then

114

broke into a broad grin, and stuck out a huge fist. "By God, you drive a hard bargain, mister, but right-oh. Thou's got a deal."

Having those ten acres meant the older Herdwick ewes didn't have to be sold off, generally for a pittance, when they came to the end of their ability to survive a winter on the fell. This was generally when they started to lose teeth. A sheep has upper and lower teeth at the back of its mouth, but only on the bottom jaw at the front. This is to help it chew off the grass, with those front incisors cutting onto a hard pad on the top jaw. Rather like children they lose first teeth and grow new ones in this front set, two at a time, symmetrically. This leads to a little confusion in names for sheep of various ages. No problem with lambs; we all agree. And pure Herdwick lambs are black. When they come off their mothers at about six months they become hoggs, and stay that way, turning brown. Towards the next winter the confusion creeps in: once clipped their next coat is grey, and they lose and regrow the front two teeth. Now they can be called shearlings, because they have been sheared; two-tooth because they have two adult teeth, or twinters, because they are entering and going through their second winter.

Michael-next-door explained this painstakingly to Anne-Marie after we'd been at Fisherground twelve years or so, when she looked puzzled as he observed of the four teenage girls in the house, "Aye, it's mebbe time to start clouting your twinters". Good opening line to a French lady who's done tremendously well with standard English, but knows nothing of the custom of sewing a cloth over the tail and nether regions of shearlings so the tup can't serve them. A sort of ovine chastity belt.

At three years old, the sheep have been sheared twice and have grown two new pair of teeth, so obviously are called either two-shears or four tooth ewes. This is the first time they have a lamb. Another year, another set of teeth and they're

The Fisherground 'Twinters', skating on the tarn.
l. to r Sally, Claire, Elizabeth and Catherine. 1990

'full mouthed'. Another couple of years and teeth are falling out. It's a hard life being a Herdwick: but now they could at least draw a pension for a couple of years on the ten new acres. Not bearing Herdwick lambs, though; if they were to be cosseted they had to have a better class of lambs, and the Fisherground sheep went for Suffolk crosses.

The plan was to feed these old ladies hay at home during the winter, then take them down to Tom's Fields in late March for them to lamb there in early April, as the grass grew green and sweet. It was a good plan, but it meant a lot of travelling as they lambed. I had to be there early, 6:30, unless I was prepared to be withered for lack of commitment, to look around the flock, help any ewe having trouble lambing and sort out any problems. The upside was that Tom would have porridge steaming on the table for me at 7:30, ready for my next induction into country ways. Many of them were along the lines of "Now listen, Mister, Ah'm gonna tell you… if thou can see Buckbarrow Fell frae t' yard, thou knows it's gonna rain. And if thou can't, it's already raining."

Another of his pearls was, "Sheep shouldn't hear the church bells twice running from the same field." Sound advice, especially in the days before there were drenches and doses against the various worms and parasites that sheep are prone to. However, it was clearly impractical to move these sheep every week or so, having no other fields near, so Jen and I went down regularly to pen them all up and dose them all against worms, cut out any foot-rot and clip the tails of any that were getting shitty. Sheep normally pass dottles and stay clean, but on good grass, or if they have worms, they can get very dirty, inviting a blow-fly strike. Tom brightened visibly whenever Jen was near. He must have been over seventy, and she just turned thirty, but he loved to flirt with her, and if there had been a while between her visits sent me home with a cabbage or a couple of pounds of carrots from his garden with instructions to "Tell her Ah's saying it wid vegetables." Old Tom bore only one testament to not always having been right. He had, in his youth, had a terrible accident with a circular saw, an accident that left him only the two main fingers on his right hand. Fingers he resolutely raised at the world.

By mid-June, though, it was time to take the flock back to Fisherground for a much needed change, to clip the ewes, and to dip everything against the various parasites. They had gone down in several trailer loads, but it wasn't possible to load ewes with lambs to go back the same way with the primitive/non-existent pens there. So, Jen, Geoff and I opted to drive them home the five miles along the road, leaving Anne-Marie again with the girls. So as not to cause disruption we decided on an early morning drive, starting at first light. Geoff was never at his best in the mornings anyway, and at 3:30 he was completely sullen and silent, so he got the job of driving ahead in the Land Rover making sure all gates were closed, turning them the right way at junctions, and generally minding the front of the cavalcade.

The problems started at the gate, before the sheep were even out of the field. Mothers got separated from their lambs, then caused mayhem turning and coming back to look for them, bleating piteously, and very loudly. As usual, under stress, I started to swear, quietly at first, so as not to wake the neighbours, but more and more loudly as I realised the front – runners were half a mile up the lane and turning onto the road, while Jen and I were still desperately trying to get the last of the stupid lambs through the gate. So much for minimum disruption, then. Once clear of the gate and onto the lane things improved, with returning mothers finding their progeny and the flock moving onwards.

It was a beautiful morning, and with the pressure off I cheered up easily and Jen and I began to relax into the almost biblical process of nomads leading (well, all right, following) their flock to pastures new. The dawn chorus was well advanced, God was in his heaven, and all was well with the world. Till we came to the village. Here there were too many open gardens for Geoff to man, too many openings for sheep to stray; and if a Herdwick can stray, it will for sure. Again, trying to be quiet as it was still just 5:30, we plied the dogs, evicted ewes who'd never tasted lupins, delphiniums and all the other exquisite desserts on offer before, and the noise level rose once more. Bedroom windows flew up, heads poked out, only to be shaken sadly at this latest example of the Fisherground Follies. But we didn't meet a single car, so at least there was no disruption.

Two years later we suddenly had the chance to spread out again, as twenty-two acres came up for sale near to Tom's Fields. With the caravans established and the campsite beginning to make real money the NFU was prepared to offer another mortgage, at more reasonable rates, so we drew a deep breath and took the plunge. Suddenly at least half of the grass-growing capacity of the farm was five miles away. There was going to be some serious travelling to be done, but I could at last feel like a real farmer, with some decent land to raise animals on.

That first year we didn't have enough animals to use it properly, so the obvious answer was to let it grow and make either hay or silage, probably to sell. This was in the early years of a new invention that completely revolutionised all grassland farming, but particularly in the Lakeland valleys. All through their time in Borrowdale my parents, Jim and Betty, had struggled to get forage for the winter. Sheep like hay, but in the wettest place in England getting that hay had sometimes gone into September, and the final bales were hardly worth gathering in. Many a time in winter the sheep, starving though they were, refused to eat the brown, burnt, smelly offering laid before them. They had tried silage, building an expensive clamp to compress the grass into, and the end product was certainly better than rotten hay, but still the sheep didn't take to it well, and had a tendency to pull their teeth out tearing the compacted wodges apart.

In the early Eighties someone had the brilliant idea of rolling up half a ton of slightly wilted grass, tying it tightly then putting a huge plastic bag over it to keep out the air. Voila! Instant silage, without the cost of a clamp, and without packing it too tightly for sheep to unpick. They called it big bale silage, and within five years of its invention there was hardly a fell farm not using it. No longer did we need a four fine day weather forecast, from a Met Office still far from dependable; two days would do nicely. More than two days were indeed forecast to be sunny and the summer was looking like a re-run of 1976, so, with the possibility of big bale silage as a backstop, I went ahead and mowed the entire twenty-two acres.

Haymaking is, more than any other farming activity, the one that is romanticised by those who don't have the responsibility, but hated by those who do. There are few things better than being in a hayfield with friends and family when the sun is beating down, the hay smells delicious, and you share the labour of gathering bales together, forking them onto the trailer, filling the barn and eventually sitting out in the garden with well-earned beers. Even though it has become mechanised our imaginations and folk memory hark back to a supposed golden era when teams of friends and neighbours would cut a meadow with scythes, turn the sweet meadow grasses with pitchfork and rake, and after four glorious sunny days would fork it onto a horse-drawn cart to take to the stackyard and mew into a neat rain-defying stack, dressed off with a thatch. I did actually just reach back to the end of that era, and have photos of my parents and grandfather mowing and making hay by horse power.

And this year was just such a year. Four days later the forecast was just as good, and the hay was ready for baling. All nine of us from the farmhouse, including the one-year old Philip, Anne-Marie's latest addition, turned out to be a part of it; along with Jim and Betty, past haytimes forgotten, and Jen's sister Barbara and her husband, Doug. There were over three thousand bales, and they all had to be stacked in groups of three hundred and sheeted over with a tarpaulin since there was no nearby barn to store them in. No matter how good the forecast, we weren't taking any chances. Everyone did what they could, ten-year-old girls and grandparents in their sixties, and the palpable camaraderie, the sharing of tea, sandwiches and the occasional beer washed over us all, confirming our best hopes for this living experiment.

Of course all that hay did have to come home, and as soon as possible. Geoff had to go back to work, and the work comprised loading 3,000 30 kilogramme bales onto a trailer, six high, driving them home, then unloading them into the big bank barn, up to ten high. Not a one man job. However, Geoff had a nephew, Jonathon, who seemed cut out to have a farm experience week. Just through A-levels, Jonathon jumped at

Haytime picnic. L. to r. Me, Geoff, Mum (Betty), Claire, Sally, Elizabeth.

the chance. All those pretty girls on the campsite, beers in the pub far from his parents, perhaps the chance of a few pounds in payment: perfect.

Jonathon had an immense mass of curly hair that haloed his face, which was irrelevant, and the muscles of an eighteen year old which was highly relevant. Because of the distances involved we pulled the trailer with the Land Rover, after the first trip with the International that took an hour on the road, and we got pretty slick at driving down, loading about a hundred bales, roping up, driving home and making the ever-heightening mews in the big barn. We could do five trips a day, which meant a full week on the job. An entire farm experience week that left Jonathon with weals and calluses on each palm from lifting bales by the strings. He had been magnificent, entirely voluntarily, and to mark his contribution and passage into manhood I awarded him a hand-written scroll proclaiming him a member of the grand Order of

Advanced Fishergrounders, OAF's for short. He felt it more than adequate recompense.

Jen, flexing her muscles!

Chapter 17

New skins for new wine: 1982-3

In 1982 the Eskdale group of parishes bade farewell to their vicar, Richmond Gurney, with the time-honoured knees-up in the village hall and the tearful last service in St. Catherine's church. Six months later it got its new vicar, another Michael, greeting him with the time-honoured knees-up… In between these linked events, Fisherground gained its last baby, a boy, Philip, something of a surprise to Anne-Marie and Geoff, but the perfect present for the four girls. Philip had no chance, poor boy.

The girls in 1983: Claire(6), Elizabeth(9), Sally(8), Catherine(10)

He was a living doll, swathed in swaddling clothes and laid in a manger, or a toy pram, or a toy cot. He was the girls' plaything, and how they loved it. Maternal adoration streamed from every pore - till they bored of him, or he started to cry.

Michael Smith first met Philip in church, appropriately, at his baptism in St. Catherine's. The church is built close to the site of the original hermit's well, re-excavated in the 1920s by Eskdale's great local historian, Mary Fair, and Anne-Marie brought water from this well and placed it in a cut glass bowl in the ancient font at the back of the church. She also brought a flotilla of family, her parents, a brother, a sister and her husband, and even an ancient grandfather from France. Geoff's family, Jen's family, Jim and Betty, friends from Outward Bound, and all the regular congregation: this was a baptism to rival a wedding, and the sun beamed down obligingly.

The service ended at lunch-time, and Anne-Marie had invited everyone to Fisherground for nibbles and drinks. The day being so perfect, Geoff set up a long table outside for the buffet, and willing hands brought out chairs, rugs to lay on the lawn and the food itself. And the piano. By now we were aware Michael was a pianist of distinction, and what could be a better background to the festivities than a few good old songs. There he sat, our brand new vicar, cheroot drooping out of the corner of his mouth, large glass of red wine on the piano lid, belting out Beatles, Beethoven and Blues in a merry medley.

Being by now well-versed in parties, Geoff and Anne-Marie had laid in plenty of wine and beer and soft drinks for the children and perhaps the older ladies from the congregation. But they hadn't reckoned with the French contingent, who brought magnums of champagne and a monster six-litre bottle of red wine. As the party progressed unusual things started to happen to the normally strait-laced older ladies and gentlemen. The elderly canon who had retired to the valley after a long and distinguished academic career as Professor of Theology at Durham went so far as to remove his dog-collar, remarking on the heat of the day. His wife, Constance, pillar of the Women's Institute, slipped lower and lower into the wicker chair: her hat became a little lopsided, and most remarkable of all her dress began to ride slowly up to reveal rather elegant pop-socks.

Michael, the new vicar, seated at the piano!

Michael played on, mingling French songs full of heartache and regret with rousing rounds of 'Frère Jacques', 'Alouette', and 'Sur le pont'. A cross channel battle developed with the old enemy. Who could sing the louder, the more raucously? The English easily topped the gentle 'Frère Jacques' with 'London's Burning'. Grand-père weighed in with an incomprehensible Breton song, aided and abetted by Anne-Marie and Bruno, her brother. The Cumbrians rallied with the help of good old John Peel but were finally trumped by the Marseillaise, skilfully blended into the Beatles' 'All you need is love'. At that point Anne-Marie called a draw to allow our new vicar time to mingle with his inebriated flock and get to know them all.

Next day one of the churchwardens, a very smart, well-groomed lady, confessed to Anne-Marie: "I don't know what came over me. When we got up this morning I found my clothes all over the stairs, and my knickers on the newel post!"

Before Michael and his wife Jane moved into the vicarage his father, always known respectfully just as Mr. Smith, moved in to modernise it slightly and give it a thorough going-over. He was well-qualified for the job, as a retired council project manager, and it was this particular skill that drew him to Fisherground. Geoff had volunteered to help him a bit at the vicarage, and had mentioned that I was beginning to build a new toilet block for the burgeoning campsite. Nothing would stop Mr. Smith coming down to cast an expert eye over the job. Embarrassing memories of Ronnie's bungalow still fresh in my memory, I would have preferred to be left alone to make my own mistakes, but he would have none of it.

This toilet block, much needed though it was, was an unexpected gearing-up of the campsite at Fisherground. Each year brought a bit more sophistication; from the rigours of the chemical toilet and simple standpipe for the first two years to the first single timber cubicle with a flushed loo emptying into the new septic tank for the caravans. Then on to the near luxury of a pair of cubicles - Ladies and Gents- each with a washbasin and cold water. Now, seven years on and flushed with its success, we were preparing to build a proper block: Ladies, Gents, hot water, showers, washing-up sinks, even a veranda.

After a lifetime of carefully keeping under the Planning Board's radar, and with the campsite taking all-comers from Easter till October, in direct contravention of the 28 day rule, one of its officers had actually approached us. When Pete, the officer, rang to ask if he could come to see us we thought the game was up. Someone must have informed the Board of our flagrancy, and that very useful source of tourism income would suddenly be cut short. Maybe we could even be fined. Cagily, nervously, I greeted Pete in the yard, after taking down the sign at the end of the lane, and turning away the would-be camper who came looking for a pitch on the morning Pete was due.

"Ian, nice to meet you at last. I've seen your name on quite a few, ah, documents, now, and it's good to put a face to a name."

"You too, Pete. I guess you mean planning applications?"

" Well, yes, them certainly. How many now? Three caravans and two cottages; quite a business you're building here... I'd love to look around – would you mind?"

So we took a wander round the orchard and he seemed suitably impressed by the drab outsides of the caravans, as only an officer of the planning board could be, and I showed him into Beckfoot Cottage, as it had no tenant that week. Fellside we just had to view from outside.

"Good, yes, good. They look well, Ian, a credit to you."

This was going better than I'd feared.

"Now, the campsite... could we take a look?" As we walked up the lane into the site he commented on the number of burnt patches where campers had had campfires. "Ah, yes, we like to let them have a fire, part of the joy of camping, don't you think?"

He didn't answer; instead "These documents... they haven't all been planning applications..."

"Oh?"

"No, not all. Actually, quite a few have been complaints." Here we go, my stomach, already keyed up, tightened a couple of notches. "Your neighbour writes fairly regularly to say that not only are there campers on both this field and that one towards the railway line, and that he can see fires late into the night, but also that it's going on all summer long."

Neighbour? Michael? Surely he wouldn't shop us?

"Can you tell me which neighbour, Pete?"

"Oh yes, he's quite open about it, indeed he wants you to know. Mr. Dobing, over there."

Ah, right, Ted. Lovely man, and we got on well, but he had warned me more than once he didn't like the campsite, and indeed that he had made several formal complaints. I had forgotten. And yet, strangely, Pete's eyes had a twinkle in them that belied his words. "So, what are you going to do about it?"

"You're the boss, Pete, what do you want us to do about it?"

"Apply for planning permission."

"What? Would you give it?" This was uncharted territory for me, the Planning Board allowing another campsite in the Lake District? As far as I knew all the existing sites had been there before the Board existed; I'd never heard of an official new one.

"Well, I can't say for sure... it would be up to the members of the Board. But as officer I would certainly recommend it. There are no official campsites in Eskdale, and what with the Ratty's popularity and more and more visitors getting over to the remoter valleys we do need more provision. The National Park Wardens keep having to move fly-campers on, and clear up their mess. It would be good to have an official campsite they could be directed to, and it would solve your problems with Mr. Dobing."

That evening we had the usual round-table discussion to plan the way ahead. It wasn't as straight forward as I expected. I'd asked Pete for an estimate of the likely cost of a toilet block, and had been a bit deflated by his, presumably educated, guess of at least £25,000. Current takings even with the site open April to October were only in the region of £2,000. Anne-Marie, the bank manager's daughter, played devil's advocate with the figures, and pointed out that unless we could charge a lot more and hope for more campers we might just be working for the bank. I countered that if we didn't go along with the planners' wishes then we could expect them to enforce the 28 day rule and virtually close the site down. In the end we compromised, again as usual. I would do all the construction to keep the cost of the toilet block as low as possible, and we'd try to find second hand partitions, which seemed to be the biggest single cost. In the meantime, we drew up the plans.

Time and tide were on our side. The National Park Planning Board agreed plans for a large new toilet block, and with impeccable timing a caravan site in Appleby advertised the entire second-hand stock of cubicle partitions for sale. We snapped them up. This, then, was the bungalow-sized building I was tackling when Mr. Smith came to see how I was doing. He watched me work as we chatted about his own progress with the vicarage - well in hand - for Michael and Jane to move into next month. I found it doubly disconcerting. I knew I was being assessed and it made me nervous. Worse still, Mr. Smith had a cyst the size of a pigeon's egg on his forehead that clearly didn't bother him at all, but I found my eyes continually drawn to it, no matter how hard I tried to look elsewhere. Eventually Mr. Smith pronounced, as he was to pronounce many times in the following days; "You are a funny man". No explanation, no excuses, no reason that I could divine. Just; "You are a funny man".

Slowly, point by point over the next few days, he gently showed me how it should be done; starting with the mixing of the mortar. He brought a bag of lime from the vicarage and insisted on adding a little to each mix. He made me use a lot more cement in the mix; sand is cheaper than cement and I was always trying to save a penny or two. He instructed me as I mixed it to a smooth, even, creamy consistency and told me to get it like that every time. Then he moved on to the trowel, showing how to load exactly the same amount each time, and to spread it an exact 18 inches. How to place each block, tap it with the trowel end to get it level and straight. How to use the trowel point on each finished joint to make smooth, even pointing as I went along. Given that I had by now built a large extension, a bungalow, a septic tank and innumerable pig pens I felt as if I were a Maths graduate being given lessons in elementary calculus - and then discovering that he'd never really understood differentiation after all.

Of course a new toilet block meant a new septic tank: this time a very large reinforced plastic version as there was no time to build it in brick. We were by now getting to know Joe Gates, the JCB driver, well, and we worked well together, Joe digging for Britain, me taking stuff away on the trailer. And what good 'stuff' it was, compact, solid and as hard as hell. Joe called it pinnle, but technically its name is boulder clay, the immensely hard-packed mix of gravel and clay that goes down many metres and is buried under only about a foot of soil. It is so hard-packed because it was scoured off the mountains by the glaciers of the last Ice Age and then compacted by the weight of up to a kilometre of ice grinding slowly over it.

Joe had a great many sayings, each encapsulating a little bit of wisdom. From him I learnt that you don't drain a wet area from the bottom as you might expect, but from the top, so as to prevent the water reaching it, and so to dry it out. This worked spectacularly well in one of the fields that had at least an acre of sieves in a boggy area before Joe applied his logic, and afterwards was capable of being mown for silage. He took a pride in his work, heavy and rough though it was, and handled his digger with the precision of an embroiderer. He also sat on it unmoved for the time it took to smoke one of his innumerable cigarillos, thinking about the next stage before rushing in.

Septic tank going in. Joe on the digger, Geoff watching on.

Again we used this windfall pinnle hoard to continue the hard track round the campsite, as we had with the first septic tank. The hole for the tank was an immense cube, but only provided about half the pinnle needed for the track. Since the JCB was on site, it seemed logical to dig another huge hole to get enough pinnle to complete the road, and then fill it with the accumulated rubbish of seven years. The next day Geoff and I gathered scrap metal, scrap wood, the occasional old bath, a primitive grass cutter that had never been much use, an old calor gas cylinder, and a pile of old hay and rubbish from the barn floor. Realising it would sink a long way later when the degradable stuff shrank, I poured on some diesel and set light to the lot. It burnt away amazingly well. Catherine found the fire fascinating and stood watching it from the side while I went off homewards. The explosion rocked the ground and the sound reverberated round the valley, and a very frightened but fortunately unhurt Catherine came running for comfort and a cuddle. Moral of the story: calor gas cylinders are never truly empty, and should never be anywhere near a fire. And perhaps ten year old girls shouldn't be left alone by a fire, or so Jen said, forcibly. And repeatedly.

Chapter 18

G-strings and J-cloths: 1986

The voice on the telephone was husky and low, and it took Jen some time to realise what was going on. She'd never had a 'heavy-breather' before, but as it dawned on her that this is what he was her heart started to pound and she felt the blood rushing to her head as adrenaline made her start to shake. Revulsion swept over her as she slammed the phone down; revulsion that quickly turned to anger at being subjected to what felt like mental rape. She found me and went over what had happened, the sheer perverse normality of it all. The pedestrian plastic phone, loosing that torrent of filth out of the blue. I tried to calm her, saying it would surely be a one-off, a stranger ringing numbers at random, but the next afternoon, about the same time, he rang again. Somewhat fore-warned she had the presence of mind to swear at him and tell him never to phone again, and hung up shaking every bit as badly as the day before.

Refusing to take her rejection seriously, or perhaps goaded by it, Alan, as he had called himself the second call, rang again the same time next day. This time, as it happened, he got Anne-Marie. We hadn't told her of the previous calls, not wanting to worry her, and she could make little out of his mutterings except the words G-String. Misunderstanding completely she asked him in all seriousness what he was doing wearing a J-cloth! She must have found the way to prevent such calls, as he never rang again.

In truth, a J-cloth really was more Anne-Marie's article of choice, along with nappies and hankies. She spent long hours cleaning the campsite toilets; and even longer with children, her own of course for many years, with Philip being six years younger than Claire, but also at the school, at the Mother and Toddler group, at nursery, at pre-school. She came from a big, French, Catholic family and being with children was natural to her. The run-up to any of the church's celebrations were very important to her, and she and whatever group of children she was working with responded accordingly. In Advent, with Christmas looming, the Toddlers made calendars to help with the count-down to the great day, and as the school term drew towards its close Anne-Marie was there with the older juniors making Christingles. A whole generation of children learnt of this slightly arcane symbolism, pinched apparently from the Moravian church, and they would join her in front of the congregation at St. Bega's to explain it all, as the decorated oranges were given out to everyone in church.

"The orange repre...repre..." *Represents*, sotto voce from the side. "The orange represents the whole world." The next would join her: "And the fruit on the four cocktail sticks reminds us.... reminds us..." *Of the seasons*, sotto voce again. "Of the seasons and of God's goodness." Gabbled, gratefully. The next is a boy, nine maybe, more confident: "And the red ribbon round the orange reminds us that Jesus died for us, it's his blood!" I think he invented that gory detail for himself. The last one up is Anne-Marie's most eloquent, but she's suddenly shy. "And the candles..."Anne-Marie prompts. *"And the candle in the middle.."* Confident again... "the candle in the middle reminds us Jesus is the Light of the World!" Anne-Marie beams at her protégés and stands to take over. "And now we're going to light our candles, turn off the electric lights and... yes, George, what is it?"

"Please, Anne-Marie, what's the tinfoil on the bottom of the candle for?"

"Good question, George, that doesn't remind us of anything – it's just to catch the wax from the candles. When they're all alight we'll quietly sing *Away in a manger* just in the candle-light."

The church-warden switches off the lights and the drama is played out again, for another year. Michael lights a Christingle from the altar candle and the confident girl shields its flame as she carefully carries it back to the front row of pews. She lights the end one, with the words "Jesus, the light of the world", and moves on to the second pew as the formula and the flame is spread along the pew. Soon, everyone has a lighted Christingle, and the organ quietly leads us in. Voices, old or young, tired or full of energy, cynical or full of promise, join together to celebrate the mystery once again.

Between Christmas and Easter is another opportunity for the children, the younger ones this time, to join in the service. Mothers' Day is the fourth Sunday in Lent, and the posies Anne-Marie and the children can make depend quite a lot on how early in the year this falls. In 1986 it's early, and Mothers' Day is on March 9th – the earliest it has been for a while – and it's a cold, frozen winter. February sees us all skating on the Outward Bound tarn, the girls excited, all decked out in skates that Jen has hoarded over the years for just such an occasion. Catherine is 12, very self-aware, trying hard to emulate the warden, Roger, with his effortless, graceful glissades, hands clasped firmly behind his back. The others, giggling, hold onto each other and fall about laughing, but gradually everyone gets the idea and starts to wobble uncertainly round the tarn. Philip, at only three, loves to be pushed around on a metal chair that might have been designed for skating, with runners connecting the front and back legs. Anne-Marie nobly volunteers to be his motor – it gives her something to hold onto.

Poor Geoff is at work, missing out on all the fun, as Jen and I re-learn skills first used properly in the winter of 1963 in the very early years of our school romance, when Derwentwater was frozen over for weeks on end. Jen is graceful, showing off her ability to skate backwards, to dance, to pirouette. Unsurprisingly I am agricultural, rough, untutored, but effective. The tarn is a mass of skaters, sliders, mothers with babies, toddlers, and teenagers. Suddenly there is a cry from the far side of the tarn, the part Roger warned us is always the thinnest, the part we must keep away from. Anne-Marie is nearest and rushes over, Philip clinging on to his chair. Catherine stands up to her neck in the freezing water, fortunately in the shallowest part of the tarn, howling from shock and cold. Tipping Philip off onto the cold ice, no time for niceties, Anne-Marie lies down at full-stretch and pushes the chair towards her for her to grab. Somehow, in desperation, Catherine manages to haul herself hand over hand up the metal leg and gets her hands onto the slatted seat, her knee onto the ice, and with a seal-like flop is out, gasping on the ice, alive but cold, oh, so cold. By then Jen was across too, and cautiously they make their way back to safety, and then more hurriedly home, to a warm bath, and bed.

This then was the season Anne-Marie had to find flowers for posies, for the children to give to their mothers, and to all the ladies in church on Mothers' Day. Given the freedom of the Outward Bound, she and Jen went foraging through the grounds. Primroses were a good month away, but at least the snowdrops were in profusion, and in a sheltered corner the first daffodils were in bud, though none was in full flower. They came home with a basket-full and stood the daffs in pots beside the Rayburn, the snowdrops under the stairs in the cool of the cellar, and next morning had a gorgeous collection of yellow and white for the toddlers to help make the posies.

Michael takes the service, and St. Bega's is full. The older ladies look on indulgently as the mothers struggle to contain their bundles of energy who would much rather run up and down the aisle than sit quietly. Anne-Marie takes them all to the back to sit and draw, colouring in the books she has brought for them, while Michael hurries through the early part of the service. We all sing the hymns lustily, to drown out the occasional wails from the back as George discovers Philip has the red crayon he needs, and isn't giving it up. Eventually

136

the moment they have all been waiting for is here, and Michael invites Anne-Marie to bring the children up to the front, with the baskets of posies.

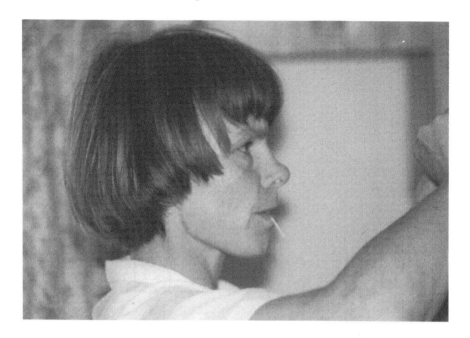

Anne-Marie in '83, a study in determination

Anne-Marie goes into her prepared patter. She does it every year, but it still takes her hours to think it out, write it down, and learn it well enough not to have to read it. The older ladies have heard it often, but it's new to some of the young mums.

" This is Mothers' Day, but we're building on a long tradition, and the children are going to help us remind ourselves where it all began. Many years ago it is that all these parishes were under the leadership of what they called the Mother Church. What is it that our Mother Church was called, Susan?" Susan has been well primed, and pipes up shrilly, "Saint Bees, Anne-Marie".

"Very good, Susan, and this church, St. Bega's, it is named after her too. So way back in the 1700s lots of people

137

from Eskdale made the long journey to St. Bees to worship in the Mother church. How far is that, George?"

"It's 20 miles, Anne-Marie."

"20 miles, that was a long way then, how do you think they travelled, Peter?"

"They had horses, Miss, and carts." Peter is in the Reception class at school. "Even so, it must have taken all day to get there and back.... Yes, George?"

"Maybe they stayed overnight!"

"Yes, quite right, maybe it is that some did. Anyway, it was the big thing to visit Mother Church."

It's time to move on, the kids are getting restless. "Then later on, in the last century, Mothering Sunday became something else... what is it that happened then, Susan?"

"All the serving girls were allowed a day off, Miss." Susan is also in Reception, and has realised 'Miss' sounds more grown-up.

"Yes, quite right Susan, and where did they go, do you think?" She beams at the small class and conducts their answer as they chorus, "To see their mummies!"

"Yes, and on the way, they picked the wild flowers, the snowdrops, and the daffodils, to give to their mamas. Now we'll do the same..."

There is a shuffling as the children stand, there are grateful smiles on every female face as once again the burden and the joy, the responsibility and the heartache of motherhood are recognised, saluted and celebrated in wildflowers.

Chapter 19

Trouble at t'mill: 1983-86

Jen and I sat in the vicarage kitchen chatting to Jane, waiting for Michael to return. He'd popped out for some ciggies, three-quarters of an hour ago, down to the village shop, all of a mile away. I was impatient; it isn't in my nature to hang about and I hate being late. Jane was philosophical, having seen it all before, many times. "He'll have met a parishioner and he'll just be chatting. It drives me crazy, but what can you do?"

"Fine, but why did he have to go in the first place, they do stock cigarettes at the pictures"

We were on our way, or rather we were supposed to be on our way, to the nearest cinema, sixteen miles away in Ambleside. 'Octopussy' had been out a while, but it was still big box-office there, and it started at 7:30. Ambleside was theoretically our nearest town, but it was over two of the steepest, twistiest passes in the country, Hard Knott and Wrynose, and it was already quarter to seven.

The journey over was magnificent, as ever. Locals said you should never go over Hard Knott in summer, because it was single track and full of visitors in Chelsea tractors who hadn't a clue how wide they were. Or even worse, real tractors pulling trailer loads of sheep at 15 miles an hour. Farmers tended to think that since they were working and the visitors just on holiday there was no need to make life easy for them. And obviously you should never venture on the passes in winter because they are either closed by snow or covered in ice and highly dangerous. However, 7:15 on a late summer's evening was as close to the perfect time as you could get, with very little traffic and the low sun lighting up the fells with a warm wash.

As we went Jen, sitting in the front seat beside Michael, filled the newcomers in with the local history. "And now, ladies and gentlemen, on your left you will see the magnificent Hard Knott Roman Fort."

"Very impressive," Michael concurred, "those walls must be six feet high."

"What's the smaller building at the front, Jen?"

"That, Madam, is the bath-house. Fundamental to Roman hygiene and pleasure, with a sophisticated underfloor heating system. The first, perhaps still the only, under floor heating in Eskdale." She had in mind the rather primitive electric storage heaters that were Fisherground's token gesture to central heating.

"And what's it called, this paragon of Roman architecture, halfway up a hill in wildest Cumbria?"

"Mediobogdum!" I declaimed, with maximum dramatic effect.

Jane burst out laughing, and then, more soberly... "They must have frozen in the winter. Imagine being transferred from guard duty in the middle of Rome to this, this, I don't know, hellhole halfway up a mountain. It's nice enough on a summer's evening, but what's it like in winter?"

"Often full of snow. This is where we come to sledge."

I piped up with my bit of lore: a theory that you could know which Lakeland valley you were in just by the form of the gateposts. In Borrowdale on my parents' farm some of the gates were still wooden rails slotted into upright slate slabs with holes in, because there was so much slate quarrying there. Here in Eskdale the old classic method copied the Roman example at the fort: a big stone flat in the ground held a spike sticking down from the bottom of the gate, while a huge stone laid on the top of the wall had another hole fitting a top spike. It was an ingenious method and, I claimed, unique to Eskdale and the nearby valleys, where the Romans had been.

The Romans had marched the road we were now taking between the fort at Ambleside, Galava, and the port at Ravenglass (Glannoventa). Michael already knew that the Victorians had obliterated the fort in Ravenglass when they drove the railway through, but the bath-house still stood there, up to twelve feet high, the highest in the land. He learnt fast, and Ravenglass was one of his new parishes.

It was nearly eight o'clock before we got parked and into the cinema, but the adverts and trailers for coming attractions were still playing. Michael looked smug and sat back in his seat, lighting up two cigarettes - one for Jane. We sat in companionable silence for a couple of hours as Roger Moore plied his trade, then sought a pub for a drink – shaken, not stirred - to fortify us for the return journey in the dark. This time the discussion turned on the relative merits of Moore over Connery, the men favouring Roger, the women the more urbane Sean. Back at the vicarage the babysitter reported all well, with Adam, Rachel and Ben fast asleep. We of course had our resident babysitters and had no qualms over Catherine and Sally. They probably hadn't even noticed we weren't there.

Over the next couple of years this became the pattern, though we didn't all go out together very frequently, as babysitters weren't too easy to find for Michael and Jane. Instead we learnt card games - Canasta and poor man's Bridge - or the recent and popular Trivial Pursuit, played in the vicarage. Often Michael, Jen, and I would start the evening in the pub in Boot village where we coached our new friend in the finer skills of playing pool while Jane put her children to bed, Anne-Marie doing the same for ours.

The backlash crept up slowly. Geoff was making a new bedroom for Elizabeth now that they had three children, and it was becoming important for Philip to have his own bedroom. This new room could only go in the attic, and required a staircase to replace the steep loft ladder.

"Would you like a hand, Geoff?"

"Well, I know what I'm doing, got it all planned out, but if you think you have time... Are you not up at the vicarage tonight?"

"No, no, night off for good behaviour, you know."

"Hmm, thought perhaps your behaviour was bad up there."

What? I didn't rise to the bait. "Where's this staircase going, then?"

"There's only one place it can go, isn't there... so tight on space in this flat... It has to be in this bedroom, even though it means Elizabeth coming through it every time she goes to bed. You're bloody lucky downstairs, able to build on for Sally's bedroom."

Again, I didn't rise, or point out that being downstairs meant everybody trailed through *our* 'flat' every time they came in or out.

"Which wall's it going beside, then?"

"For God's sake, it can only go on the far side. I've had a good look in the attic, worked out how the beams go. Perhaps you'd like it right up the middle – take out all the space in the room?"

"No, no, I just thought it could maybe do a bend and lead up from the door: that way you could actually partition it off..."

"Ian, just piss off and leave me to it. While you've been gallivanting up to the vicarage three times a week Anne-Marie and I have been dealing with your kids, dealing with Philip bawling and waking Elizabeth up, and planning how to make it better. Now you think you can muscle in and change what's taken us a lot of time to plan just like that. You really are the most conceited, self-centred bloody man I've ever known. Just piss off back to the vicarage." Once again I backed off baffled, not recognising the description.

Geoff and Anne-Marie in '84

At the same time Jen noticed Anne-Marie no longer joined her for coffee, and the times the three of us met as we always had dried up almost to none. As Jen and I grew closer to Michael and Jane, so it seemed we opened a gap in the close relationship that had led us to Fisherground in the first place. Anne-Marie made her own friends, a couple in Ravenglass whose fervent Christianity mirrored her own. They formed a prayer group and she was often with them for prayer and meditation. Geoff had always had his own circle of friends from work. Slowly, imperceptibly almost, the gap widened; both couples asserting their right to independence, but both avoiding the honest confrontation we should have been having.

The malaise spread to the children. Catherine found her comprehensive school impersonal and rather overwhelming after the rural idyll of the 40 pupil Eskdale Primary School, and, seduced by her reading of lots of public school children's books, began to talk wistfully of leaving her 'sisters' for the delights of the dorm. We couldn't have afforded the fees, but my mother, Betty, who had read her own fair share of the previous generation's *'Anne of Green Gables'* offered to bail Catherine out if she was adamant. There followed a term of angst for us all, with Catherine sitting and passing scholarship exams for Giggleswick School, some sixty miles away, till at the last moment she opted for the status quo and the comfort of the family nest. Ironically her decision may have been influenced by her first boyfriend, Adam: Michael and Jane's eldest son.

Sally too was having her own complications. She and Rachel - Michael and Jane's daughter - were best friends also, and due to leave Eskdale School to follow in Catherine's footsteps. This friendship excluded Elizabeth, her lifetime companion. While almost all of that year's leavers were put in the same class at the new school, Rachel and Sally were separated. Sally, and therefore Jen, was desolate. Jen the more so when Michael refused to challenge the decision and back her in a fight to re-unite the two. Sally and Elizabeth, coming from the same household, were of course put in the same class together.

It was time for a change, almost any change, to reduce the strains on the crucial friendship that kept us working at our unconventional partnership. The change came from an unexpected direction. I had, from childhood, always had an inkling to be a priest, or a vicar… something in the church. This seemed unlikely ever to be fulfilled, though, since I had already made the big move out of teaching. I had become a church-warden in Eskdale, but that seemed to be the practical limit.

It was Michael who alerted me to an unforeseen possibility, telling me Carlisle Diocese ran a sort of 'Open University' course to train people to become what were called

Non-stipendiary ministers. The joke ran that proper ministers are paid to be good, but NSMs are good for nothing. This seemed custom made for me. I could do the training while continuing with the farm and tourism, and when ordained would be able to help Michael by taking services in the local churches. The Church of England by 1985 had lost much of its former glory and been forced into its own compromises. Where once there had been four vicars serving the parishes of Eskdale, Irton, Muncaster and Waberthwaite they now had to share just one. In population terms Michael still had well below the average, with just around a thousand people in all four parishes; but in terms of plant and administration he was stretched with six churches (Eskdale and Muncaster each had two) and four Parochial Church Councils. If ordained I would be able to take two services each Sunday ensuring each parish had a weekly service.

Obviously the training regime would put a strain on everyone at Fisherground. There would apparently be 12 essays to be written, weekly tutorials with various theologians, six weekends away with all the other students and a week-long summer school each year for three years. Geoff, Anne-Marie and Jen were very supportive and encouraged me to apply for the course. I was very keen, ready to study again after 15 years since Oxford. They assured me they were happy to feed the sheep, collect the campers' money, clean the toilets and deal with whatever else was thrown up if I wasn't there. Apparently I wasn't indispensable. On the contrary, perhaps they were keen to see the back of me!

I was interviewed by Alan Smithson, the Director of the Training Institute. Jen was very amused by his subsequent report which contained the line 'Mr. Hall is a bright, intelligent and extremely forceful candidate, who must be quite difficult to live with'. Bravely, he accepted me on the course, and I spent a very happy three years studying Old and New Testaments, Ethics and so on, but very little time on how to visit old ladies, ill people in hospital, or most importantly people recently bereaved. Maybe you can't teach that sort of thing, but there must be some ground rules that weren't ever covered on the course, and it's not really the sort of skill to learn on the job.

Towards the end of the first year the Church of England assessed whether we were suitable candidates for ordination. The body entrusted with selection was called the Advisory Council for the Church's Ministry, (ACCM), and they met in Chester.

I travelled down together with another student, John Hine. We'd become good friends on the course and were generally required to share a bedroom on the study weekends, as I was the only one who slept deeply enough not to be disturbed by his stentorian snoring. The selection process was to take a full weekend, so once again I ended up sharing the snoring.

The process was a mixture of individual interviews, group role play and dynamics, a short essay and a group preparation of a service. Part of the group work was a quick-fire 'think on your feet' exercise where you drew a piece of paper from a hat and had to speak on the subject written there. I drew the phrase 'When I am Bishop...' and got a laugh from fellow students when I ad-libbed 'my first task will be to scrap the selection boards'. John and I were both accepted as ordinands, and so started the next year's course knowing there was a point to all this study.

I found it quite odd to be a student again, especially as I'd never had to write essays when studying Maths, and it took a while to learn how they were supposed to be structured. My first were for a very local tutor, Canon Turner, he who had removed his dog collar at Philip's baptism. He had retired from Durham with his wife Constance to live in Eskdale. His initials were HEW and he was universally known in academe as Hugh, but respectfully in the valley as The Canon. Writing essays and having tutorials meant visiting the Turners' home on the banks of the mill-pond that had served the water wheel in yet another of Lord Rea's enterprises: the sawmill in Miterdale.

This home in many respects seemed split in two. The kitchen was clearly Constance's domain but the Canon had his study, a book-lined retreat from the world, wreathed in smoke from the pipe he kept lit throughout tutorials, looking out over the mill-pond, which would have been lovely but that it was unfortunately breached, permanently empty and muddy-bottomed. The sitting room was where their worlds met, and again it was clear who sat where with his chair surrounded by his books and debris, hers neat and tidy with a handy tray for nibbles and drinks.

In the same way it seemed that their car, a large dark Ford, had its different areas. Constance always drove, somewhat erratically, while the Canon sat in the back left seat rather regally. He was obliged, by Constance, to take a constitutional each morning to the village shop for his papers and anything else required, a round trip of about a mile and a half. As far as I could tell he had no interests outside the church and theology, but Constance was a stalwart of the Women's Institute and a member of their darts team. They were both on the PCC and much deferred to by the rest of the Council. Canon Turner continued to take services from time to time, with erudite sermons not entirely appropriate for the country parish.

My first attempts at essays drew rather sardonic comments from the Canon - much gentler perhaps than they would have been for a callow undergrad at Durham - but he confided to Michael, who couldn't resist passing on to me, that whilst I might or might not have been a passable mathematician I had absolutely no idea of how to go about constructing an essay. Slowly, with help from both the Canon and Jen, who had written essays all through her undergraduate years, I got the idea, and by the time I moved on to the next tutor could at least get a pass.

Canon Turner died some ten years later and the then vicar, Malcolm, visited Constance to offer his condolences and arrange the funeral only to be told, quite sternly, "You must understand, Malcolm, that Hugh and I were only ever loosely affiliated". Somehow I wasn't particularly surprised.

Chapter 20

The railroad runs through the middle of the farm: 1977

I had my first introduction to the Ravenglass and Eskdale miniature railway, t'La'al Ratty, in 1950, aged just two, on the same occasion that Mum and Dad's friends took the photo of the three of us beside those railings outside the pub. In those days the pub had been universally known as Tatie Garth, presumably because of a potato field nearby. Nowadays it was known by what had, in 1950, been its Sunday name, The King George IV, having had to change from The King of Prussia on the outbreak of the first World War. As we travelled up from Ravenglass to the terminus in Eskdale, I must have passed the back of Fisherground, as the line runs between the back fields and the intakes, just 100 yards from the farmhouse. I was to get to know this stretch of line very well.

The line was built in 1875 to haul valuable iron ore from the rich seams above Boot Village down to the main line at Ravenglass. It took passengers virtually from the word go - anything to turn a profit - but was very vulnerable to the price of iron and steel. It was declared bankrupt in 1897 but continued nonetheless to haul iron ore till 1913, when it closed for lack of use. In those days it was called 'Owd Ratty' (Old Ratty) and had a three foot wide track. Somehow, in the middle of the Great War, it was resurrected but on a smaller scale - hence the new name La'al (Little) Ratty - and started its new existence hauling granite from the quarry near Boot. With the quarry's closure in 1953 it ran out of steam and was due to be sold off for scrap in 1960.

Fortunately by this time tourists had spread across the Lake District to the western fringes and it was saved from the scrap yard by a consortium of business-men and a hastily cobbled together Preservation Society. From then on it went from strength to strength, becoming a real tourist attraction in its own right for those sampling this more hidden side of the Lakes.

Fisherground itself played a part in this development. As the campsite became a permanent feature the Ratty drivers were more and more frequently asked to drop passengers off at the nearest point, just across the field from the tents. They were actually often stopping there anyway as there was a large water tank beside the line where the steam engines took on fresh water, and it was a natural progression to designate it an official halt. It was a proud day for the four of us when the maroon sign went up proclaiming FISHERGROUND in bold capitals. We had arrived.

The new sign for the campsite station

The intakes above Fisherground bore the scars of two separate enterprises by the Ratty owners, one more successful than the other, but both ultimately doomed by changing markets. Jen discovered the first when gathering the sheep from the furthest intake the first winter we were there when the bracken was dead and the ground easily seen, and she insisted Anne-Marie and I join her to see what she had found. At the top of the intake was a cave, obviously man-made. The mouth had been filled in long ago, but the plug had worn away over the years and you could get in with a bit of a squeeze. The problem was it was full of water up to the level of the barrier. We promised ourselves we'd come back with a canoe and explore another day.

Anne-Marie looked around and said, "What's this mound we're standing on, then?" Jen and I looked down and, yes, she was right. Jen kicked at the ground with her boot. "It's made of iron ore rock, by the colour of it. Why should there be a mound here?"

"It's not just a mound" I said, looking down the hill "Look, it's built up for a long way down the intake." We moved on down, exploring as we went. "It's the same width, look, all the way, about five yards."

"And here, here it is not a mound, it's cut into the ground, what is it you call it…"

"A cutting! Yes, you're right Anne-Marie, it's a track of some sort, made level."

"Well, hardly level Jen, it must be nearly a 45 degree slope."

"Pedant! You know what I mean… the slope's the same all the way, it's been cut out or built up to keep it level."

"Yes, and look, here it widens, it is, how you say, broader, for a few yards." We were about halfway down the hill by now, and Anne-Marie was right, there was a wider section. Suddenly I recognised what it was. "I know, there used to be one of these in Whitehaven when I was young. It carried coal down to the valley bottom from Haig Pit… I think we called it a Brake. There was a railway line on it and the heavy wagon going down, full of coal, pulled an empty wagon up for them to fill at the top, with a passing place in the middle, like this."

"A funicular!" We have them in France."

"And we have them in Scarborough. My parents used to take us on it when I was little. There wasn't a passing place though, there were two tracks." Jen's parents came from the North-East.

"I suppose this is much longer, and it would be a lot more expensive to put two tracks in. Must be quite complicated at the passing place, though."

Piece by piece we worked it all out. At the top of the intake, just out on the fell, there was a huge depression in the ground, and asking about in the village we were told there had been an iron ore mine there, but that it had collapsed suddenly and fallen in, leaving the hole we'd seen. By the best of luck it had happened on a Sunday when no-one was working. Anne-Marie claimed another miracle. So the cave would have been an 'adit', a horizontal shaft dug to drain the mine workings, and the iron ore dug out would be loaded onto the down wagon till it pulled the other wagon up, coming to a halt by the Ratty line.

The second enterprise had been staring us in the face for years before we realised its existence. We always called the crag behind the farm, on the first intake, Stretcher Crag, because that's what our friends from the Outward Bound Centre called it, as they used it for mountain rescue training in lowering stretchers down the cliff face. At the foot of the crag was a huge boulder that the children loved to visit because they could climb to the top up a route at the back, but from the front it looked impregnable. Also it made a great place for dens. They called it the Animal Rock: the adults never discovered why.

Jen and I passed this rock often - every time we went up the fell, and every day when I was feeding pigs on the intake, and we had long ago spotted that it had come out of Stretcher Crag, leaving an obvious hole. We never queried why such a huge lump of rock should come away, until we had to rescue a sheep that had got trapped on the crag. Hilary's husband, Tony, an OB instructor, had given us a rope that had passed its sell-by date, and Jen nervously belayed me from the rowan tree growing at the top of the crag while I gingerly made my way down to the crag-fast ewe. Climbing down past the hole left by the departed Animal Rock I could clearly see a semi-circular groove running three feet down the back. Suddenly it all clicked into place.

The Animal Rock had been blasted out. Stretcher Crag had been intended as a stone quarry, much as the vast quarry further up the valley had been carved into that piece of fell, but for some reason there had only been that one blast, and the resulting rock had just been left to lie. Looking down from my vantage point high on the crag I could make out another raised track: something more to explore if I ever got this damned sheep off the crag alive and lived to tell the tale. Shouting up to Jen to take special care I inched my way across the face until I came to the narrow shelf it must have jumped down to, tempted by the juicy grass where no sheep had been before. Nervously the ewe stamped her foot, barking that strange warning note I have only ever heard from a Herdwick, and backed away to the furthest limit of the shelf. What would happen if I tried to catch hold of it? Would it stand and let me? Would it jump over the edge, to fall maybe 40 feet straight down to the rocks below? Or would it charge me, knocking me off too. Could my diminutive wife hold me on the rope?

Anxiously I shouted up to Jen, unable to see me over the lip of the crag, and warned her there might be a large weight to hold in a moment or two. Making soothing noises I inched towards the ewe. In return I got threatening barks as she backed away to the very edge. I lunged, grabbed at wool, and held on for dear life as the ewe tried to rush past. The rope tightened comfortingly as Jen took the strain and gasping from the effort and the nerves I found my feet and stood up, the ewe suddenly quiescent in my hold.

Now what? The only realistic way I could see to get the sheep off the crag was to lower it down the rock face on the rope. Jen was less than enthusiastic, but I insisted everything would be fine as long as she let the rowan take most of the strain.

Turning the sheep onto its backside, into clipping position, I held it with my left hand while I undid the bowline knot with my right. Then I tied it tightly round the ewe's chest, just behind her front legs, hoping she wouldn't slip out, before yelling up to Jen to lower her off. It all went remarkably well, with the sheep bumping her way down the rock face till she stood, somehow comically, at the bottom. That's when I realised the next problem. Sheep and rowan were attached to one another by the rope I would prefer to have on as I retraced my shaky steps around to the hole, and then up to the top.

Jen realised the problem at the same time, and shouted down for instruction. Should she let the rope go, allowing the ewe to run off with it attached, or go round the back and down to untie the damned thing? We decided she'd better untie it, so I had some protection and the sheep didn't go for miles with the rope. Muttering mutiny Jen tied the rope off to the tree, went all the way down, cursed over the tightness of the knot I'd tied, and climbed all the way back up to belay me again. Relating the story to Hilary that night, over a glass of wine, she was taken aback by Hilary's protest: "Oh, you should have given us a ring. Outward Bound loves to do this sort of thing. Good practice, and it puts us in a good light with the farmers."

*****

Not long before we moved into the farm the Railway Company put new systems in place to cope with the increasing traffic, including building a new passing place just behind the farmstead - Fisherground Loop. Campers and visitors took pleasure (and lots of photographs) in watching this cross-over of trains. It was fortunate that this loop was just a hundred yards above where the lane onto the intakes crossed the line, as it meant that trains coming down the track hadn't picked up much speed and could theoretically stop if a flock of sheep were crossing. We tried hard not to cross when a train was coming, but there was a big bend between the crossing and the loop and occasionally we were taken by surprise.

Only once did a train fail to stop and it ploughed right through the middle of the flock in mid-crossing to Jen's consternation, as she imagined dozens of bodies, but these were Herdwicks, bred to look after themselves, and they leapt nimbly this way and that and the train passed through the middle of them like the Israelites through the parting Red Sea. Jen was left trembling and furious that the driver had made no effort to stop and immediately telephoned the station in Ravenglass to complain. It turned out that this particular train hadn't needed to wait at the loop as there was nothing coming up the line, and so was travelling much faster and the driver simply couldn't stop when he came round the corner and saw the sheep crossing. Nevertheless a new 5 mph sign went up the next week.

The other major brush with the trains, on the other hand, was entirely my fault. I had 30 or so hoggs to dip and didn't want to mix up a full expensive tub of sheep dip for such a small number, so I rang Michael-next-door to ask if I could use the remains of his as he had also been dipping that day. It seemed sensible to drive them up the railway line - by far the easiest way with fences each side to keep these unruly teenagers on the straight and narrow. I set off after 5 pm when I thought all trains had finished for the night. I was wrong. Halfway up I heard the unwelcome sound of a train coming down the line. At the time I had two dogs with me: old Moss whom I'd had from the start, and young Shep just beginning his training. Moss easily herded the hoggs well to the side for the train to pass, and was standing beside me when she inexplicably leapt across the line just as the train arrived and was caught by the front buffers. I watched in horror as she was literally torn to shreds as she fell under the engine and wheel after wheel sliced through her. Shep gave an anguished howl, leapt the fence, and set off for home pursued by every canine demon ever devised, while I burst into tears in front of the equally distraught driver. He relieved his distress by swearing at me for my stupidity. In front of a train full of equally horrified passengers I gathered together the still warm separate bits of the only dog I ever had that was any good, and numbly carried them home for burial.

Chapter 21

The appliance of science: 1986

"Ah'm gonna call you Zanussi from here on."

"Why's that then John, do I look Italian?

"Nah, you know, Zanussi, the appliance of science". I nodded and smiled ruefully. The catchphrase from the advert. I knew what John was on about, but actually he was wrong. John had brought the dozen stirks from the farm to Broughton Auction for me, in the lorry that was part of his farm diversification plan. Nine years of selling in Broughton hadn't made me any less nervous about auctions, and any stock I brought still did that trick of shrinking to three-quarters of their previous size when they got into the pens, and only half size when I had to follow them into the ring.

This time I'd come within a whisker of passing them out, knowing that the price bid didn't even cover our costs, and I'd indicated that to the auctioneer. Piqued, one of the dealers had bid again, and another, and eventually the stirks were £10 more each. The appliance of science.

The extra 22 acres of land we had bought five miles down the valley had tempted us back into raising cattle. We still didn't have enough land to run a herd of sucklers - cows having calves on the farm. You need a lot of land for that, and a bull to run with them, and a cow can eat a hell of a lot of silage in a winter. So we compromised and bought calves in at six months and kept them on for a year. With the new-fangled big bale silage we could make enough fodder to feed both the sheep and these growing stirks - especially with the 3,000 bales of hay stored away in the barn. We even went so far, in that first cattle year, as to rent a further 15 acres way out near where Mum and Dad were living, 14 miles away, to feed another dozen cattle through the summer. Dad was happy to look over them each day to make sure all was well, and I was happy to let him.

Besides, now that the pigs were gone, wintering the stirks inside made good use of the Green Shed. Once again Geoff got out his welding rods, this time to make a feeding alley right down the middle. I took a sledge hammer to all the redundant pig pens and Jen made a huge bonfire of all the smelly old hay bales that had formed the insulated roofs for so long. She got bitten all over from the various mites and lice that made their home there, but she was always at her happiest playing with fire, just as I delighted in forever redesigning the insides of the Green Shed. This was its third or fourth reincarnation: would it make a profit this time round?

Wintering stirks in the Green Shed: 1986

All the land had to be fertilized twice a year, and I felt very much the real deal loading up the trailer with three tons of fertiliser, the old drill for applying it, and driving off down the five miles on our 'new' tractor. Gone was the old Massey Ferguson 35 that was such a bugger to start. In its place a gleaming white David Brown bought from a neighbour and only five years old when we got it. Of course it didn't have a front loader; somehow we could never justify the expense on what was still just a smallholding. So the tons of fertilizer came in hundredweight bags, and I got used to unloading them from the lorry that brought them, stacking them, loading them onto the trailer, then loading them from the trailer into the spreader. It wasn't efficient, but it was good exercise.

Old Tom's fields were steep. "Now Ah'm gonna tell you, Mister, you tek care with that greet daft tractor. Thoo's top heavy with half a ton of fertiliser on." Old Tom, Mr. Smith, Dad… why did they all think they knew best? Going down the steepest bank with a full load, the spreader whizzing fertilizer out both sides, I went through the mental checklist. 'On no account put your foot on the clutch or you'll start speeding up and the brakes won't hold it. The brakes are only on the back wheels, and it's easy to start sliding on a greasy steep field. Power back on the hand throttle so your engine slows you down.' I knew it all - hell, I'd been driving tractors since I was eleven. And yet, still, that hedge was coming up fast, and nothing I could do was slowing me down. At the last moment I turned, hoping for the best but fearing the worst, and the tractor went up on the two lower wheels. If they had been of equal sizes I might have made it, but the front wheels were tiny - car sized, and the back were big - lorry sized and the rest.

With a sickening crunch we went over, the drill spinning futilely, fertiliser spilling out over the sides instead. The tool box opened, raining spanners, bolts, and a bottle opener on my head. The engine revved manically, oil spilling from the filler cap. Thanking my lucky stars that this was the new David Brown, with a reinforced cab, and not the old unprotected Fergie, I hurriedly pulled out the fuel stop to kill the racing engine, and climbed out of what was now the top, pushing the door up. Sitting on the ground, surveying the damage, I began to shiver uncontrollably.

It took a few minutes to pull myself together, then I got up and sneaked round Tom's house and out onto the lane. The last thing I needed now was "Ah'm gonna tell you". He had, and he'd bloody well been right again. The farms down on this coastal strip are big, and the tractors correspondingly so, and Fred was very happy to come to my assistance. It would make a good tale in the pub that night, the latest chapter in the college boy's story. Fred brought a huge snigging chain with him, hooked it over the David Brown's tank-like cab, and simply pulled it back right way up in no time.

"Give it a try, then, Ian".

"It's lost a lot of oil, do you think it'll be OK?".

"Yeah, the oil filler was on the top side. It hasn't lost hardly any".

To my amazement the tractor fired first time, and sat there chugging happily. Fred had brought a shovel as well as the chain, and sat on his tractor puffing on a cigarette while I shovelled what fertilizer I could back into the drill.

Fred drove off with a friendly wave, and I looked at my watch. The entire incident had only taken just over an hour from start to finish. It felt like a month. Next time I came down the slope it was in bottom gear, and I turned without any problem. Nothing broken, nothing damaged - except my pride. Oh, and I couldn't find the bottle opener.

The appliance of science? More like basic arithmetic. Two years of buying in store cattle, feeding them through a winter in the Green Shed and a summer down on the 22 acres was enough to show the enterprise would never make any serious money. In fact, if you took into account the diesel needed to go down each day to check them, the price of the fertilizer, the mortgage interest on the money borrowed to buy the land, there was nothing in it at all. Compared to the ever-burgeoning campsite and the self-catering it was a complete mug's game; at least the way we were playing it.

It was my own off the cuff response to Tony's question that finally opened my eyes to the obvious discrepancy. Tony Warburton was a TV celebrity, at least in Cumbria, and was doing a walkabout programme through the valleys visiting various enterprises and interviewing their owners, liberally interspersing his own acerbic views on many of the developments along the way. Tony's overwhelming passion was for owls, and he ran what he called the World Owl Trust, with its catchy acronym WOT, from Muncaster Castle, down the valley near Ravenglass. Arriving at Fisherground with his cameraman he interviewed me against a backdrop of blossoming apple trees and the stream in the orchard.

"So, tell me Ian, are the campsite and these caravans just incidental to the main farm, or critical to your survival?"

I thought for a moment then responded, "Let me put it this way, with the visitors we probably make about £5 an hour for our work: with the farm we probably work five hours to make a pound".

And that just about summed it up. The main problem, I comforted myself, was with the grant and subsidy system, and nothing to do with my poor husbandry or farming methods. There were various EU schemes: the Common Agricultural Policy; Hill Livestock Allowance; Environmentally Sensitive Areas and so on, and most of them favoured breeding. Ewes and lambs, cows with calves, goats and kids even, all these attracted big subsidies that made them worthwhile. Pigs, fattening wether hoggs, fattening stirks - all the enterprises we had tried - attracted no subsidies whatsoever. I assured the others that was the problem, and that I had, at last, the solution. More ewes and lambs.

Instead of selling off the old Herdwick ewes when they started losing teeth, I reckoned we could keep them another year or two, building on our experience on Old Tom's land, putting them to the Suffolk tup and running them on the 22 acres. We could modify the Green Shed again as a lambing shed, lamb the old ladies inside then take them off in groups of ten or so in the trailer the five miles to the better land. The lambs would grow well, as they had at Old Tom's, and there would be a nice fat subsidy cheque each year. And the green shed would at last come into its own. "Oh goody" said Geoff. A little sarcastically, I thought.

There were two slight problems, when we put this plan into practice. The first became clear in June. When we were only using Tom's ten acres we were only driving 60 ewes plus their lambs up the road home. With a total of 32 acres it was over 150. The annual droving morning became a fixed point on the village calendar. People booked holidays away to coincide with it. The second problem was more subtle, the sort that you just don't see coming, and in any case can't do anything about. Having lots more lambs meant selling lots more lambs, and suddenly, because of a major nuclear disaster in a distant land, selling lambs became a lot more complicated.

May 4th 1986 was a momentous day for every livestock farmer in Britain, and more especially in any mountainous parts of Britain. In Eskdale, just ten miles from the Sellafield nuclear plant it seemed ironic in the extreme to be suffering radioactive rainfall from a plant 2000 miles away at Chernobyl, in the Ukraine. Overnight a heavy, hard rain fell, over two inches on the fells, and with it fell Caesium 137 and Strontium 90, radioactive isotopes that anything grazing the grass ingested, and promptly gave out beta rays that registered on a Geiger counter.

Everything ground to a halt. Nothing could be sold, pet lambs in Farm Parks couldn't be stroked. Perhaps you shouldn't even walk on the Lakeland fells for fear of getting radiation on your skin. In the King George IV that evening everyone was an expert.

"Bloody hell! When father was farming in '57 and Sellafield blew nobody cared. All they had to do was pour t'milk away for a month. Nobody stopped you selling lambs then, and it must have been ten times worse. And they got paid for t'milk. Father said cows were suddenly giving twice as much milk as usual!"

"Bastard papers. All they want to do is print scare stories to sell more papers. They don't give a bugger about our livelihood. Ah've 50 wether hoggs ready to go fat. What am Ah supposed to do with them? Stick 'em in t'freezer?"

"They were saying on the news that people shouldn't walk on t'fells in case they pick up radiation. You'd think they were gonna glow in t'dark, the way they tell it."

"Aye, we had a group ring to give back word. Should have been stopping in t'B & B for a week. Ah bet there's no compensation for us."

"It's not just local, though, like it was in '57. Dealer Ah know says it's all about t'export trade now. Bloody France will use any excuse to boycott our lamb. They missed out on t'mushroom cloud. If we can't prove t'lambs aren't radioactive they won't buy, and if they don't buy there'll be a glut."

And that was the nub of the matter. The Ministry of Agriculture, Fisheries and Food (MAFF) needed to find a way of demonstrating that anything sold wasn't radioactive. Every time we wanted to sell, either Herdwick wether hoggs or Suffolk cross fat lambs, I had to phone MAFF so an official could come and monitor the stock. 'Monitor' became the buzz-word. 'Monitor' meant someone with a Geiger counter pressed against a lamb for a minute, counting beta particles. 'Monitor' came to mean Davida and her colleague Carol, and that wasn't so bad, because they were young and pretty.

"Do you want them to pass or fail, Ian?"

"What d'you mean? Are you going to cheat?"

"No need for that. It just depends where I monitor them. If you hold them right beside the wall like that, they'll fail. The granite gives out more particles than the Strontium, so if you want them to pass you'd better bring them to this side of the pen. Look, I'll show you."

Davida was right. Monitored beside the wall a hogg registered twice as much in a minute on the counter. One hogg registered far too much anyway, and she pronounced, knowledgeably: "You've just brought that one off the fell, haven't you?"

"How the hell d'you know that, then, Davida?"

"Simple, the grass in their belly's all that's giving off radiation. The radiation on the fells is lasting a lot longer than it does down here. We think it must be the peat and the moss that's holding it. Once a sheep's been on the bottom grass for three days it's passed the fell grass out of its system, and the radiation drops right down."

Regardless of this, MAFF had to keep on monitoring, presumably for PR. As soon as I got used to the hassle I didn't mind. The Ministry paid £1.30 per sheep monitored, and for a Herdwick hogg making less than £10 in Broughton Auction it was a useful dividend. At Fisherground, as in most of the Lakes, monitoring went on for nine years, until not a single sheep could be found over the limit. In one or two places it went on for 25 years. The price paid was never increased.

There was one more unexpected bonus. Davida's day job was as a graphic designer.

"Ian, how do you manage to get anyone to camp here with that crappy sign at the end of the lane?" I was quite proud of the sign, actually. Clear white letters painted on a rectangle of thick black plastic board. Never rotted. *'Fisherground Campsite. Full facilities.'* What was wrong with that?

"Sixty quid, I'll do you a beauty, one that mentions the self-catering as well. Double sided - what d'you say?"

It was, it did, and it lasted a lot longer than the nine years of monitoring.

Chapter 22

Graham and the Deanery do: 1986

June 21st, 1986: mid-summer's day. A special Ratty train drew into Fisherground Station with a celebratory blast on its steam whistle. A large crowd of church people from all the surrounding parishes - the Deanery - were there to greet the honoured guests with garlands of flowers to put round their necks. Michael, the vicar, gave a welcoming speech extolling the merits of the Carlisle Diocesan links, not this time with Zululand, but with Madras, in the south of India. Their leader responded with his own compliments, seasoned only by the comment that trains in south India were considerably bigger, and had covered carriages.

Greeting the Madras visitors off the Ratty special.

Faced with the task of entertaining ten visitors for a couple of days Michael had asked if the church could use the campsite at Fisherground as a venue for a 'Fun Day' for the Deanery to entertain the visitors. It was after all ideally placed. There was a fine big field they could organise games in for all the kids, the campsite itself was a natural amphitheatre where the band could play, and then there was the Ratty which would make a great introduction for the Indian delegation. There was also a nice new toilet block!

Anne-Marie was a prime mover in all this - her church connections reached out far and wide - and I of course was now heavily involved with my theology course under way. It did mean shutting the campsite for the weekend, but surprisingly few campers came in June anyway.

So the Fun Day was now a reality, and out on the field dozens of kids were grouped around a large parachute. A jolly, red-faced man in Rohan shorts shouted instructions, as the kids hoisted the parachute high up into the air, allowing it to settle back down again slowly. "All the people with a birthday in May!", and a scurrying, giggling gaggle shot off under the raised 'chute, trying to reach the other side before it descended on them. This was Graham, plying his trade and earning his keep. Graham Young was the Methodist Church's roving youth officer for the north of England, and he'd taken to staying at Fisherground for a couple of days whenever his roving brought him to West Cumbria. He soon fell in love with the farm and the lifestyle, and it wasn't long before his visits were for a few days so that he could help with whatever project was on at the time. I enjoyed the challenging discussions on all aspects of politics, the church, the meaning of life and all that was happening in the big world out there. Graham enjoyed having his beers provided as payment for his labours, and the crack in the local pubs.

One of the projects he had worked on was the Adventure Playground we'd constructed for children camping on the site. Joe and his JCB had dug out another large pond and there were a couple of rafts to sail across to the island, or to the playground itself. It was in a copse of oak trees that we used as the anchor posts for the monkey bars, the wobble-board, swinging tyres, and best of all a pirate's castle tree-house only to be reached by swarming up a rope net or climbing a slippery pole. Absolute pride of place, though, went to the awesome zip wire, powered by scream. The kids climbed up a ladder to the launching platform, grabbed the hanging chain and leap onto the tiny seat as they took off down the 40 yard wire. Once they got here all Graham had to do was organise an orderly queue.

The Fun Day unfolded, the ice-cream van did a roaring trade, and it seemed no time before the cling film came off all the goodies that the ladies of the various parishes had prepared, and the trestle tables were loaded to capacity. Bales of straw made do as seating and the band struck up on its makeshift stage, the farm's trailer, still attached to the David Brown.

Back at the farmhouse when everyone had left the four of us and Graham enjoyed the late sunshine in the garden, each with our own favourite tipple. After a long hard day fuelled only by tea we three men were soon cracking open the cans of lager and Jen reckoned she deserved a G & T. Only Anne-Marie stuck carefully to a cup of herbal tea. She let down the whole French wine-drinking nation, with a head very easily turned by any alcohol at all. She was delighted by the air of camaraderie shown on the campsite that day, with friendships struck up between people from different churches and backgrounds. Slowly, we savoured the day, enjoying Fisherground's ability to host such a major event.

"Let's have a bonfire" announced Jen our resident pyromaniac, never happier than when looking after a fire. There was a permanent fire site in the garth, where she often burned a few boxes, old bits of wood, a branch or two, and this was where she insisted we move to now it was getting chillier. Graham and I were dispatched on a wood gathering expedition, Geoff down to the pub for some more cans (she wasn't going to risk letting Graham and me down there), and she and Anne-Marie went in to get a few sausages, potatoes, some salad stuff. And the kids, dragging them away from the telly to enjoy themselves properly, like in the old days. "But we've been doing that all day, Muuuum".

It wasn't really a bonfire, more a camp fire, and we brought a load of cut branches that I was storing to cut into logs for the winter, so we were well set for the evening. Jen brought out firelighters and sticks, much to Graham's scorn.

"Come on, that's cheating. You have to rub two boy scouts together till they spontaneously combust."

"Possibly, but we haven't got all night. We need to get these potatoes in to start cooking so the kids can have some supper."

The campfire:
l to r: Anne-Marie, Philip, Catherine, Sally, Elizabeth, Geoff

Ten minutes later she had a cheerful blaze going, Geoff was back with the beers, Anne-Marie had set up a table with all sort of goodies. Jen had hauled out the cast iron frying pan that went with the Rayburn and there were, to Graham's delight, sausages and bacon sizzling happily balanced on a couple of glowing logs. I cut some lengths of stiff wire and the kids were toasting marshmallows to their hearts' content. As we sat in the warmth of the blaze the slowly setting sun bathed the whole scene in a mellow, pink light.

There was a long swing hanging from a high branch of a nearby beech tree, and Sally swung and gyrated while Elizabeth pushed and made her spin. Claire sat dreamily with the three year old Philip on her lap, contentedly sucking her index finger. Catherine brought out her new flute, which she was just learning to play, and Jen accompanied her on the old guitar as they played some simple Beatles tunes, Anne-Marie singing along. Graham and Geoff were deep into politics and arguing like pundits. Mrs. Thatcher: Graham was staunchly Labour and appalled by the way she had out-manoeuvred Arthur Scargill and broken the unions. Geoff could well have made the same case, but never could resist an argument, so he passionately defended the Iron Lady, saying Scargill brought it all on himself by refusing to ballot the miners.

I sat back contentedly with my beer, musing on the fact that it was virtually ten years to the day since we'd all moved in. I was nearly 38 now, and I remembered JCB Joe saying a man needed to be settled by the time he was 40. Needed to have got his life sorted, his business set up and working. Well, the campsite was doing well, and even had planning permission. We had converted two of the farm buildings into self-catering cottages; and also had the three caravans. Even the farming activity was at last managing to make a small profit - mostly due to the Common Agricultural Policy. And in two years' time, if I could keep on course with the essays, I should be an ordained minister, able to help out with a different kind of flock. Yes, we were getting our lives settled.

An hour later we chased the girls off to bed, a lot later than their usual bedtime, and Anne-Marie stood up with the fast-asleep Philip in her arms and went off to put him in his cot. Jen stayed out with us, all huddling closer to the fire for its warmth now the sun had long been set, and we poured ourselves another drink. Graham, mellowing along with the evening, became expansive; almost embarrassingly so.

"Today was amazing, you know. You guys don't even realise what you give out to people. Where else could they have got a place so welcoming, where kids could have such a great time, and where the Indians could arrive in such style?"

"Um, I'm not sure they thought much of spending half an hour crammed together on little seats getting frozen."

"Geoff, bring out your whisky. I need to get through to you lot just what it means to people like me to be able to come to a place like this and be made so welcome."

"Ah, well, you're a bit of a special case. How many others do you see sitting round our camp fire?"

"But that's my point. OK, they're not sitting round your camp fire, but all those campers who come, you let them make their own camp fires, and they sit round just like us."

"Not drinking my whisky, they don't!"

"Stop it, take this seriously, you need to be told once in a while just how much pleasure you guys give to people who spend most of their lives in concrete with wrap-around TV. You let them come and, I tell you, they, we, I, find a peace here that's really special."

"Oooh, I like that, - we could use it as a strap line. *Fisherground - a little peace of Lakeland.* Oh yes, that's definitely got possibilities."

"Oh piss off, you're impossible."

The evening became the night, the beer cans were traded for the whisky glasses, and the chat was passed from one to the other. Who knows how many of the world's problems we solved that night? And away up at the top of the valley a full moon rose over Hard Knott and the Roman Fort.

Impossibly big, against its mountain backdrop, it hung there almost a luminous yellow, and smiled down on the valley below.

Chapter 23

Carnage: 1987

It was in February 1987, a crisp, blue beautiful winter's day. The telephone rang.

"Hello, Fisherground." I'd learnt this response in Borrowdale, where Dad always answered "Thorneythwaite". It had always seemed a cool way to answer, if your farm had a mellifluous name.

"Ian? Francis here…"

"Francis?"

"Francis from the shop,"

"Oh, sorry Francis, didn't recognise your voice. What can I do for you?"

"Well, it's a bit tricky, really. We've just had a walker in babbling about there being a lot of dead sheep on the fell. From his description it sounded like your Low Fell."

This wasn't immediately alarming. 'A lot' is pretty imprecise. Five? Ten? Where on the fell? If there were ten dead sheep in different places on the fell it wouldn't be unusual at that time of year. The fells were heavily overstocked and it was one of those global situations where no-one could unilaterally lower his stocking rate or his neighbours' sheep would simply move onto his fell. Besides, all the subsidies were based on the total number of sheep you ran, so numbers had to be kept high. Everyone just accepted that a significant number wouldn't make it through the winter, and the fells produced a number of carcasses each year. These were never buried - who was going to take pick and shovel up to try to bury a sheep among the rock and bracken. They were picked over by the foxes, buzzards and carrion crows. It was all part of the natural order; distressing, expensive, but just the way things were.

"Did he say where, Francis? Are they all over, or what?"

"Well, you see, that's the thing, he said there's a pile of them, by the fence at the top of the intakes. Look, I'm sorry to be the bearer of bad tidings, Ian, and I'm not sure whether they're yours or Michael's. He was a bit hard to pin down as to just where...."

"Well, there's only one way to find out. I'd better go and take a look. And thanks for ringing, Francis."

"Yes, well, I hope everything's OK, Ian... you know these townies, they're easily upset..."

It was with a queasy feeling that I said goodbye and set off up to see for myself how big 'a lot' was. I'd gone from a rather blasé assumption that this was just another easily upset townie to a dread heavy gut feeling that this was a genuine disaster.

As I laboured up the fell track conflicting emotions jockeyed for attention. It was hard to imagine this was just going to be townie over-reaction, distress over the sort of small dramas you had to get used to in farming. This robust approach often required softening for visitors, and we'd all learnt to appear to be as upset as them when they came to announce a death or a weakly sheep or lamb, making empty promises to investigate and if necessary bury.

As the fell gate came into view, so the scale of the carnage started to unfold. At first just a few bodies spread out, but then the horror of a pile, a large pile squashed into the corner between the fence and the wall, a huge pile of precious ewes, eyes bulging, tongues lolling, piled three deep in their desperate attempts to get over the fence and away from whatever it had been that had harried them. Dogs, it had to be. Some had long wounds in their sides, their throats, where they had been torn and worried, but most had simply either died of fright or else been suffocated by the pressure of bodies piling onto them.

Farmers get used to death. They even get used to inflicting death on unwanted creatures. I'd never liked the brutality of a fox hunt, but when I picked up the remains of a lamb that had simply had its throat ripped out almost for fun by a fox that hadn't taken it off to eat I could understand the venom some felt towards the fox. When I looked at the bleeding, empty eye sockets of a sick but still living ewe I could wish I had a 12-bore to despatch the carrion crow that could inflict such pain. I had even, before we had enough money to have our bitches spayed, unwillingly drowned litters of pups, weighting a jute sack with a brick to make it sink.

But death on this scale? Slowly I turned and walked back down the peat track, away from the carnage, home. When I got in Jen and Sally were in the kitchen, and could tell from my face that it was bad. Wordlessly Jen gave me a hug and put the kettle on as I slumped in the armchair. Sally crept onto my lap, and suddenly the floodgates opened and I wept, long, bitter tears: tears not just for all those dead sheep, but for the end of the dream, the end of any attempt to be a farmer. I knew, with a sudden dreadful intensity, that I would never be a real farmer, never actually make a living from the land, and the knowledge broke something, something I had treasured ever since the first day my parents moved into Thorneythwaite when as an 11-year-old I told Dad that I wanted to be his farm lad, and didn't want him taking on any older lad from the valley.

Still on auto-pilot, not really thinking, I rang Edmond Porter, the local huntsman. He would take the odd dead sheep or calf to boil in his vats for dog feed, as he had 40 hounds to feed. Ed could tell from my voice how upset I was, and agreed to take what would be a trailer-load, though he couldn't possibly use them all. I just wanted rid of them, and Ed had enough insight and humanity to help out. With Jen I took the tractor and trailer up to the fell gate, camera to hand to record the massacre for any possible insurance claim, and began the horror of throwing them on the trailer. There were 42 in the pile. 42 out of a flock of perhaps 250 on the fell. 42 ewes in lamb with what should have been this year's replacement gimmers and some wethers to sell.

Loading the 42 mauled sheep on the trailer: 1987

The trailer was piled high and the load wobbled horribly and precariously as we drove slowly down. I couldn't bear to have them anywhere near and drove straight round to the foxhounds' kennels. Edmond helped throw them off, in silence. There are no words that make any sense in that situation, and he wisely kept his counsel. I thanked him, gravely, and drove slowly home, the iron sliding soundlessly into my soul as I came to terms with the end of the dream.

The story came out, piece by piece. The dogs were farm dogs, and had been seen by others on the fell, gathering the sheep downwards on their own, gradually tightening the net on them as they reached the fell fence and the end of places to run. From the descriptions it became obvious they were Maurice's dogs. Maurice, my childhood friend, Maurice who had shepherded me to school at Waberthwaite. Maurice, who had made us welcome, who had clipped our flock that first year at Fisherground. Maurice, who suffered himself as he shot his three best dogs. We never talked about it. His insurance paid, probably handsomely, but there was no payment could take that iron from my soul, that knowledge that I never was and never would truly be a farmer.

One thing I'd learnt, and this episode helped to reinforce: every end is also a beginning. It sounds trite, a truism, but that's only because it is so right, so true. Again we met around the table, the four of us, to pick up the pieces. Geoff and Anne-Marie, coming in from outside as it were, were sympathetic. "Bloody hell, Ian, I am sorry. That must have been a horrible sight."

"Ah oui, forty two, all lying dead. That's awful."

"You say you took photos, Jen – must have made your stomach turn. I'm not sure I could…" "Well, there might be insurance, we might have to prove how many… but yes, it was the worst thing I've ever seen." I wanted to move on, not dwell on it, the horror. The horror was all too real. "Yes, well, the question is, what now?"

Geoff looked at me quizzically, "How do you mean, Ian, what now. I thought Edmond took them all…"

"I don't mean what now with the dead sheep, I mean what now with life."

"How do you mean, what now with life?" Anne-Marie cocked her head, appraisingly, as she glimpsed a flash of the cold iron within.

"Ian, what is it that has happened? Is this more than just this terrible thing?"

"Yes, I think it is. I think it's time to stop pissing around, to stop fooling myself that Fisherground is any sort of real farm."

" Hang on, Ian, surely this is just the shock talking. Fisherground is more of a farm now, with all that land in Irton, than any time since 1970. You can't let a setback set you, em, set you back." I almost laughed. Almost. "I know you're right, Geoff, in abstract. But this isn't abstract, I think it's just the last straw." Jen, after an afternoon of talking it through with me, came to my rescue. "I think what Ian's trying to say is that we're making all our money from tourism – the campsite and the caravans – that all the work on animals, all that driving down to Old Tom's, it's just starting to seem pointless."

"Yes, in a nutshell, that's it, love. Thanks. I know we could get over this, build the fell ewes up in a couple of years, but somehow now it just feels like a hobby. We make all our living from tourism –"

"And Sellafield, don't forget the steady wage!"

"Yeah, sorry Geoff, I mean all the living that Jen and I contribute to, we make it all from tourism, and this has just, I don't know... well, if it's just a hobby it's not what I want." Anne-Marie got it: "Of course, it is that you have another hobby now, with all the study for to be a priest."

I hadn't got that far in my own mind, but she was right. From here on, tourism was work, working towards being an NSM my main hobby, and we'd just keep the fell sheep and forget any doubtful projects like pigs, calves, store cattle and so on. If tourism was to be our main suit, it was time we started to do it properly. We bought a second-hand ride-on mower and the orchard became a neat, mown, pleasant place for visitors in the caravans. The gate went from its entrance: no more would there be sheep mixing with the visitors. Far more radically we agreed to improve the visitor experience all round; specifically to apply to the planning board for permission to upgrade the caravans to proper log cabins, suitable for use all year round, and much easier to let out week by week, at a better price than we could get for a caravan. By the end of April, just two months after the sheep catastrophe, our plans were in front of the Planning Board, and on the 18th September they were approved.

We were assured by Pete, the officer who had first approached us regarding the campsite, that there was unlikely to be any significant opposition to replacing caravans with more robust and better looking lodges, so we began finding out all we could about the bewildering array of lodges on the market. They ranged from little more than wooden caravans on fragile wheels to heavily insulated Norwegian lodges with two storeys that you would have been pleased to live in permanently. The prices ranged similarly, and it became clear that we would need funds to make this all a reality. Having already recognised that I'd never be a farmer it was no problem to sell off the twenty-two acres we had bought five miles away: in fact it was a relief. In my new mode I realised I was actually happy to lose the responsibility of care for animals so far from home, and we gave up the rented ten acres willingly too. My only regret was losing the contact with Old Tom.

Selling the land was another lesson in the tangled web of rural life. We were advised to offer it for auction in the Ulverston auction room of the local auctioneers, who also ran the weekly sheep and cattle auction there. All the local farmers used that auction, and could be depended on to attend and possibly even to bid for the land, which we'd bought four years previously at £1,000 per acre. I picked up in the pub that there was a bit of a ring at work, and that the farm nearest to the land wanted to buy and had made it clear to the neighbours that they didn't expect any serious opposition to their bid. The Fisherground four weren't 'local' and, according to this story-line deserved no favours, whereas they were and went back generations.

There didn't seem to be anything we could do about this, so it was with a feeling of foreboding that the four of us entered the auction room with our solicitor, and nervously took our seats at the front, beside the auctioneer, facing what now felt like a hostile crowd. Our nerves weren't helped by the dismal surroundings. The auction room was more used to furniture sales than land, and was half full of either next week's hopeful bric-a-brac or the accumulation of several previous failures to sell. Some neighbours were sitting on old tables, others on a pile of mattresses, a few lucky ones actually had chairs, and the rest stood around the back of the room. This might have been a good sign if it meant they intended to bid unseen by competitors, but looked more likely to be as a result of lack of horizontal surfaces to perch on. An old grandfather clock in the corner insisted it was quarter past two for the duration.

The auctioneer read out the particulars of the sale and stressed that there was a reserve price (the only defensive action we could take), that the land was well-watered, in good heart, and well-fenced. He asked for bids of £20,000 to a stony silence, and reduced in steps till eventually the farm next door opened the bidding at £15,000 fully £7,000 less than we had paid for it. My heart sank, but all was not lost; there was a bid of £16,000, followed immediately by a rather sour £17,000 from the neighbour, who looked round meaningfully to see who had had the temerity to cross the picket line. I could see who it was, and recognised his family features but not him individually. He bid £18,000. The auctioneer, taking his courage in both hands, asked for 20, and got it rather grudgingly. And so it went, back and forward, to £28,000 - against the farmer who was so keen on it, and who seemed unwilling to improve his bid.

Sagely the auctioneer announced we would withdraw while he took advice from his clients. In the back room he took out a hip-flask and swallowed a generous mouthful, flashed us a grin, and said he'd give them a minute to stew. He did confirm with us that we were selling (the reserve had been a modest £20,000), and a few moments later we all trooped back in, sitting a little more comfortably, while he announced the land had reached its reserve and consequently was for sale. He invited further bids, and with a furious glower the neighbour offered £30,000, only to be rebuffed almost immediately by another bid of £32,000. After a lot of head scratching and harrumphing the farm next door came up with £33,000, making it clear this would be the last time, and his opponent let it go. It was twice what he had hoped to pay, and half as much again as we had bought it for. Profit that would be a great help in buying high standard lodges that would stand the test of time.

Chapter 24

Without change, there would be no butterflies: 1987-8

"Em, Jane and I are leaving, this September." Straight out with it, just like that.

Jen did a double take. "What do you mean, Michael, you're leaving? Where are you going?"

"We're leaving Eskdale, Jen. I've got a new job…"

"Leaving! You've only just got here. Hell, you've only been here four years - you can't just go and leave us. The parish needs you; we need you; friends are hard to come by!"

"Well, I'm sorry, but we are. We think it's for the best. Rachel has just started secondary school; if we don't move on now we'll have to stay till she's done GCSEs, and then I'll be too old to get anywhere."

Jen sat back, absorbing this bombshell. Michael and Jane, our bosom friends, card players, pool partners, vicar, choirmaster… leaving.

"Where are you going? Will you still be vicaring?"

"In a sense, yes. I've been appointed chaplain to Uppingham School. It's a public school, in Rutland. I'll have to teach RE and take services in the chapel. It's a great opportunity. And Jane's got a job as Matron. We'll be much better paid."

Jen broke the news to us all that evening. At first I was devastated. I didn't have many close friends, and Michael was certainly one of the few. I was going to miss them, but I could see that five more years would make a move difficult. Geoff was his usual robust self: "Michael, teaching? They'll eat him alive. Can you see him in front of a class of boys?"

"I don't know... me, I've seen him lose the temper often enough in Deanery meetings. He can be, how you say, intimidating" said Anne-Marie.

"I bet it'll be months, if not years, till we get another vicar. Diocese likes to claw back a bit of cash with a vacancy. They won't let us leave off paying the quota, though, you can guarantee." Geoff was the parish treasurer.

As it happened, he was wrong, in this case at least.

I was supervising the emptying out of the campsite septic tank, and the tanker driver was new to the job. I'd watched it being emptied once before, so felt I had some insight, so to speak. This lad opened the cast iron top, dropped the suction tube in and started the machinery to suck out the contents. It didn't take long, and he made to gather the pipes up and leave.

"What're you doing?"

"What do you think I'm doing. That's it."

"Are you kidding? That's just the clean water out of the top. See that big white ball: you have to push that down and get your pipes in to the bottom section, - that's where all the shit is. That's what that long metal proddy thing on the wagon is for."

Muttering, the driver did as bid, but the ball was a floating sphere of polystyrene, and not very willing to submerge. I held it down while the driver fed in the pipes.

"OK, you can start to suck now."

So far, so good, but it soon became obvious that the tanker had sucked out all the water, but left all the solids. A huge sticky mass, filling the bottom half of the lower chamber.

"What now then?..." 'Clever clogs' hung in the air, not quite said aloud.

"Well, you have to blow all the water back, twisting the pipe around to break up the shit, then suck out what you've got. Then do it again if the shit's still sticking."

With palpable bad grace the driver scratched his head over the various levers, selected one and pulled it down hard, the engine still on full revs. The length of pipe surged into life, snaking like a wild thing, and bucked up and out of the tank, spraying shitty water all around, jerking uncontrollably. Quickly, the driver pushed the lever back up, and the pipe came to rest. His face was a picture of conflicting emotions. Fear for his job struggled with hidden mirth as he faced a customer completely covered in shit.

My face conveyed at least as many layers. Strangely, not anger. I was a man reduced to swearing and cursing by the smallest setbacks, but somehow the big ones left me stoically placid. No, my face reflected some quick calculation. Obviously I needed to go, change and have a bath. Could I trust this plonker to do the job right if I wasn't there to oversee? What were the right words to make sure he did? "I'm off for a bath. When I come back I'll have a torch and I'll peer deep into this tank. If it isn't spotless, I'll be on the phone to your boss. If it is, I'll forget about it. OK?"

One more calculation buzzed in my head. Peter and Sue were due in an hour, and I really wanted to get off on the right foot, because this relationship was going to be important. From my experience with pigs I knew even a bath wasn't going to make me smell all that good, and yet I hated wearing deodorant sprays.

Peter and Sue Ashby. What did I know about them? Very little, yet, except that they were going to be the next couple in the vicarage. The Bishop had insisted, and had short-circuited the normal long-winded procedures that Geoff had predicted. To the extent that Michael and Jane's dust was virtually settling on Sue's new furniture. Not that they would have a lot of furniture, because they were newly arrived back from a long period of ministry in Zimbabwe. Also that, like Michael and Jane, they had three children, the oldest the same age as Sally, so presumably they would be roughly our contemporaries.

Jen took one look at me as I came into the yard, mucky water still dripping, hair plastered with some truly horrible stuff, and stinking to the highest heaven. Naturally, she burst out laughing. She insisted I stood there in the yard while she turned the hosepipe on me. Then she made me strip down to my underpants while she continued to spray me. Then, and only then, I could go inside and have a bath. She used a stick to put the clothes in the bin. There really was no way we couldn't confess to Peter and Sue just why I stank like a whore's boudoir, and why it was better than the alternative. Peter looked horrified: Sue guffawed. Jen and Sue were going to get on well.

Busy weekend on the campsite: septic tank well used!

I was two-thirds of the way through the Ministry course by now, 24 essays behind me, just 12 to go. I should be ordained next July, and then would be Peter's curate, not Michael's, as I'd expected and looked forward to. It would be a difficult curacy, inevitably. I was used to being self-employed, my own boss. How would I take to learning on the job, with someone marginally younger than me telling me what to do? Geoff foresaw problems, with a certain glee.

The high point of each year's training for the ministry was the week-long summer school held in August, when the entire Institute took over a site for intensive training and fellowship. Of the two I had attended one was in St. John's College, Durham, and the other at Edinburgh University. Durham felt like a re-run of Oxford, with the college on Cathedral Hill, close by the shadows of that magnificent and ancient edifice, and the whole week was suffused by the aura of the church throughout the centuries; powerful, with magnificent buildings and an unquestioning belief of most of the population in the literal truth of its message of Heaven and Hell, and its power over souls.

As we students sat and drank, late into the nights, discussing and debating, I couldn't help a twinge of nostalgia for my three-year stint studying Maths. I'd found the study almost impossibly difficult but I had enjoyed enormously the social aspect, rekindled on this summer school. I recalled the delights of punting on the Cherwell. I forgot the long hours of intricate study trying to fathom Schrödinger's equation and remembered instead the good friends made there, the evenings drinking in the pubs of downtown Oxford.

Maths is a subject unlike any other, in that everyone eventually hits a ceiling where they simply can't take the next flight of fantasy needed to keep on understanding. If you're lucky it happens just before O level, or its equivalent, so that you get the necessary qualification then give up before it is too late. If you're very unlucky you hit your ceiling in the first year of a degree course. I was unlucky. I struggled through those three years, going religiously to two lectures a day, five days a week, but never quite knowing what to do with the results. I took detailed notes of all that the lecturer wrote on the board, but it was so fast I couldn't at the same time understand the logic behind it all.

But at Durham it was entirely different. This was a self-indulgent week. I revelled in the camaraderie of mature students excitedly unravelling a Bible they had thought they knew. We were led by Durham's finest theologians through form criticism, source criticism, and given at least a taste of current theological thinking and exhorted to re-examine our simple acceptance of the New Testament as 'gospel truth'. I found all this immensely energising and took to this new liberal theology with the same zeal I had previously lavished on more traditional Christianity. At the same time I did wonder how this new message would fare in our quiet backwater.

Edinburgh presented a challenge of an entirely different order: not this time to my theology, but to my understanding of how some people lived. Here we were shown some of the horrors of inner city life: the barrenness of the tower blocks; the ravages of drug abuse; the sheer despair of many lives. This was not a challenge I could rise to. I recognised from the very start of that week that I had nothing to offer in these places. There was simply too big a gulf between my gentle, protected upbringing and the way these children grew up; between the beauty of the valleys I'd always known and the ugliness of the stark concrete and litter-strewn landscape they called home. The only evening that came close to my world was when we all climbed Arthur's Seat to share a simple service of Compline under the stars.

I came home to the beauties of Eskdale and the delights of family life at Fisherground with fresh eyes. To a wife whose ideas of fun were wholesome, not dependent on needles and booze; who could take a group of kids onto the intake and have a wonderful afternoon building a den, making a fire, cooking sausages. Or down to the riverside to watch the brave ones leap from Forge Bridge into the clear, clean, crisp waters of the Esk and help the more timid learn to swim in the shallows. I came home to daughters who could lose themselves for an afternoon engrossed in a book, but could still be child enough to play 'Izzy whizzy, let's get dizzy' outside my bedroom door. To partners who shared a vision of a life of co-operation, of giving rather than taking. I was infinitely sad for the broken lives I glimpsed in Edinburgh, and the more determined to enjoy the beauty that I was fortunate enough to be surrounded by in our lovely valley.

Chapter 25

Out with the old, in with the new: 1987-8

The pick went straight through the pipe, and the water shot up in a plume and came down soaking me, as I was carefully trying to find just where the main was. Jen and Geoff bent double in laughter as I swore violently and scrambled out of the exploratory trench I was digging. It probably wouldn't have been so bad if I'd just hit it accidentally, but to be actively looking for it and then put a pick right through made me feel a complete idiot, and their laughter wasn't helping. I might as well have left it for Joe to dig up - he could hardly have made more of a mess of it.

JCB Joe was due the next day, to dig foundations for our venture into quality self-catering: the new pine lodges. We'd all spent a couple of days marking out where those foundations were to go, exactly; the artistic director, the engineer and the mathematician.

"One *has* to go here, beside the stream. It's just perfect."

"Well, yes, but it's really sloping ground. We'll have to build the front up a lot."

"What, four more rounds of blocks? That adds at least another £200 to the job."

"Don't care, it still has to be here."

Eventually, with Anne-Marie as final arbiter, we agreed each site, making best use of the remaining apple trees, the lovely row of beeches on the boundary of the orchard, and as far as possible having each lodge facing South to make the most of the sunshine. The only problem was the water main that we knew went through one of the sites. Still, that wasn't a problem now, we knew where it was. Just had to repair it. Fortunately, facing south also meant facing away from the old

189

and rather ugly Dutch Barn and the new and very ugly Green Shed.

The discussion as to where to put the lodges was mild compared to the discussion on when to aim at for the opening date: when to start the booking calendar. The caravans were booked till the end of the October half-term, and I was adamant that we needed to open for Easter the next season, so as to maximise income. Geoff and Anne-Marie were all for putting it off till the May half-term, and the discussion became as near an argument as the four of us ever allowed anything to become. We agreed to take advice. The lodges were to be the modern equivalent of log cabins - cleverly shaped and jointed five inch thick logs that piled on top of each other in true wild west fashion, and the manufacturers had recommended a Northumbrian firm who had put some up on Kielder Water to do the actual building. We all agreed that we would do all the rest ourselves, as usual, to save money.

I rang David, the owner of the chosen firm, to ask how long it would take his team to put up three lodges, if the foundations were ready for them.

" Two weeks each lodge - six weeks in total", replied David.

"Promise?"

"Definitely, we've done enough now to know."

Assuming Jen and I could get the foundations in before Christmas - another six-week spell - then the lodges should be up by the middle of February, leaving yet another six weeks to put in water, electricity, carpets and fit them out. Tight, but eminently do-able, I insisted. Against their better judgement Geoff and Anne-Marie went along with the schedule, muttering darkly. I knew I'd better get this one right: immense self-confidence meant nothing if it didn't deliver.

Southern Ireland had an insatiable appetite for used mobile homes in the late '80s, and we easily found a willing buyer who would take all three and be responsible for transporting them to Liverpool Docks. All we had to do was put the wheels back on, lower the legs, and have them ready for loading onto three lorries that would arrive two day after the last guests departed. Sounds easy... but some of the tyres were perished and most of the legs had to be hacksawed off as they were rusted solid. Nevertheless, they were all 'mobile' once again and lined up ready when the lorries arrived. I couldn't help contrasting the smooth professionalism of the drivers with their winches and loading ramps with the rank amateurism of our attempts to get them in seven years previously, and a mere two hours later we were waving goodbye to caravans that had repaid their costs many times over – a lot different from our early forays into animal husbandry.

Time for foundations, yet again. Memories of Ronnie and Audrey's bungalow resurfaced as I directed JCB Joe through the ground plan of three new lodges, carefully skirting the newly repaired water pipe. Memories that were reinforced as I pegged out levels, still using a plank and spirit level instead of a theodolite. Some people never learn. One thing I did learn, though: never stand behind a lorry load of concrete blocks and open the tailgate. The pressure on the release lever jerked it out of my hand and it struck my forehead a mighty blow, felling me to the ground. As the tailgate swung free a score of blocks tumbled out of the back, landing on me, quickly making me forget the pain in my forehead as I scrambled to my feet and out of the way. From the cab came a cheery voice, "Okay to start tipping?"

Jen and I were busy laying these foundation blocks, with me taking care to follow Mr. Smith's instructions as per the campsite lessons, when our new vicar Peter came to visit and see how his curate-to-be was progressing.

"How's it going, then, Ian... happy in your work?"

"Hi Peter, yeah, it's going OK. Nice not to have a building inspector breathing down my neck..." and I told him the tale of Ronnie's bungalow and the wonky foundations.

"Maybe I shouldn't tell you this, then... Out in Zimbabwe where I was archdeacon of a large diocese I had the responsibility of inspecting any church building work, any new halls or mission rooms. I'm a pretty good building inspector by now. They called me Hawkeye, after that character in M.A.S.H. Did you know that corner's a good inch out of true?" I could see that being Peter's curate was going to be interesting!

We finished the foundations by early December, and the logs for the new lodges were booked to arrive just a fortnight before Christmas. The builder, David, and his team of two came and stayed overnight in what were to be their winter quarters, Beckfoot Cottage, carefully kept clear of any bookings except Christmas and New Year – when builders never work, and cottage prices are high. The phone rang at 10 pm; JCB Joe to say two 45 foot articulated lorries had just trundled through his village and would likely be with us in half an hour. With memories of the previous lane end misery etched in our minds Geoff and I dashed off down the road to ambush them outside the King George IV and to warn them not to try the last 400 yards in the dark. The drivers were more than happy to be bought a couple of beers and then kip down in their cabs ready for the morning.

They turned up for breakfast after walking up to inspect the dreaded lane entrance. The good news was that they were confident of getting in, and the day went from strength to strength as David's professionalism showed itself. Even the weather cooperated. A hard frost over the previous week meant the ground was rock hard and the fork lift he'd ordered in quickly and efficiently dispersed piles of 20' logs to their allotted lodges, ready for sheeting over to keep out the inevitable Christmas rain. The lorries were unloaded and gone before the early dark set in, though I doubt they were back in Aberdeen before midnight.

True to building tradition the world over the team then downed tools for their fortnight's break, leaving a rather forlorn orchard sporting naked foundation walls and tarpaulins rippling in the wind over truly vast mounds of Douglas Fir logs. The frost broke nicely in time for Christmas, the rains returned replenished, and the orchard began to resemble the Somme after a hard day's shelling. In three months' time, to the day, the first visitors were booked in for their promised week in a luxury pine lodge on a traditional Lakeland Fell Farm. Well, we had the tarpaulins, at least, and Jen was always good at making dens.

I needn't have panicked. True to his word David returned fresh from Hogmanay and the team got stuck in. They set up arc lights so they could start early in the morning and carry on late into the evening, and Eskdale in mid-winter had few diversions to woo them from their task. Second in command was Big Steve, a 'dead ringer' for the American singer Meatloaf with long, lank hair and a 44 inch waist. It was no surprise to hear the iconic album playing at full volume, and it was a great relief to see the team work so hard and the lodges spiral upwards 'Like a Bat out of Hell'. Spiral is the right word, for the men worked round and round laying grooved log on log, ever up till they reached roof level. All the way Big Steve belted them down with a huge rubber mall, but even so David warned me the lodges would shrink and settle at least two inches in the next couple of years, and that I would have to tighten up the nuts and bolts periodically.

By early February three shiny new lodges graced the orchard, shingle roofs glinting in the pale, wintry sun. We were lucky; that pale sun shone nearly every day and allowed Jen, Anne-Marie and the five-year old Philip to stain and varnish the outsides while I got on with the gruesome job of applying several coats of fire-proofing varnish to the inner walls. Half an hour breathing in the heavy solvents left me high as a kite and I emerged each time grinning inanely and whistling badly out of tune. Geoff brought home a Sellafield gas-mask which preserved my sanity, but at the expense of sweating copiously.

Lodge 1 on its way up.

A week before D-Day things were getting tense. Geoff and Anne-Marie were muttering darkly at my rash confidence, and even I was beginning to wonder how on earth we would get everything finished, when there were still major jobs like the bathrooms still to complete, before we could begin on carpets, curtains and the like. Mum and Dad rallied to the cause; a friend from Outward Bound spent a day putting plugs on what seemed like a hundred different electrical appliances; Jen returned from Carlisle with the car weighed down with kitchen ware, bedding, electric fires, dustbins – all the thousand and one things we take for granted will be there in our holiday cottage. Seized by a sort of siege mentality Geoff and I worked on longer and longer each evening as Saturday loomed.

We finally put up the last picture, hung the last curtain, hoovered the last floor, at lunch-time on Saturday 26th March, 1988. The first guests arrived at 3 pm. Told you we would make it!

The finished product, Field End Lodge.
Anne-Marie and Meg testing the raft.

Chapter 26

The Big Four-Oh: 1988

Summer 1988. Anne-Marie, Jen and I were all coming up to the big 40. We sat around the table, one coffee time, in ruminative mood. Jen set the tone:

"Well, Ian, 40... are you going to do a repeat run of when you were 30? Deep depressions, beating of breast, Oh my God, forty, how can I be 40?"

"Ah mais oui, just think, in just ten years you'll be fifty!"

"You needn't talk. You'll be first to 40 - 'cept for Geoff of course"

"He didn't mind, and anyway, me, I gave him the great present. Philip! What could be better at 40 than to be Papa again?"

Jen struck a more serious note. " You're getting a great present as well, Ian - you'll be ordained by then, a vicar! Can you believe it?"

I wouldn't actually be a vicar, of course. For a year I'd be a deacon, allowed to take any service except Communion. Able to conduct marriages, funerals and baptisms. Scary, really, but I was very keen to start this new phase of life. I often thought how so many church services signify new stages of life, but are in another sense just the high point of a change that has been welling up for years. Marriage is the obvious example: a particular day, moment even, when you embark on something completely new. The day itself celebrates a loving and continuing relationship, but it adds to that relationship in a special, precious way.

Getting carried away on this train of thought, I wondered if you could say the same of a funeral. For the bereaved and their friends it could perhaps mark an end, but an end which had been coming for years in some cases. For the person who had died was it the crystallisation of a relationship with God that had gone on for years? I would like to think so, and that particular thought was often in my mind when I was asked to take funerals.

But for me, and the twelve others who I'd trained alongside, the service was to be Ordination. Again, a special moment setting the seal on the three years of training, and a lifetime of Christian faith and a calling to serve our neighbours in this particular way. Funny, really: I could remember being an eleven-year-old and Dad asking what I wanted to be when I grew up. Without any hesitation I'd piped up, "A farmer. And a builder. And a vicar." Not surprising, actually, since Dad was a farmer, his best friend a builder, and his brother a vicar. Still, in a sense I would be all three, in an amateur way.

The service was to be in Carlisle Cathedral, that strange, unfinished sandstone bastion nestling near the castle in a border town which had seen so much fighting over the last three hundred years. If it wasn't Bonnie Prince Charlie and the Jacobites then it was the Border Reivers rustling, raping and murdering across the 'debateable lands', the marshes and rough country in a sort of no-man's land between England and Scotland. Even the Romans had decided Carlisle was the end of the civilised world and built Hadrian's Wall to keep a sort of order. The cathedral was unfinished because most of the nave was pulled down by the Scottish Presbyterian Army in the Civil War to provide stone to fortify the castle. So there was only the top end available - which was going to mean an almighty squash when thirteen ordinands brought all their friends and relations.

Traditionally ordination takes place on the Sunday nearest St. Peter's Day, 3rd July, Peter being the apostle Jesus charged with continuing the church. This year it actually fell on the Sunday, which I felt augured well. Certainly the

197

weather that morning was beautiful, and I woke to a cloudless sky and the feeling I had last had on our wedding day - that today was special in a way I could reach out to, but not quite touch. The parish had laid on a bus to take all who wanted the 50 miles to the cathedral, and the extended family gathered at the end of the lane to wait for it. The new vicar, Peter, and Sue his wife, were the only ones already on, as the bus had started only a mile up the valley, where the little one charabanc business William Sim had started back in the Thirties had mushroomed to a major hire company with nearly a dozen coaches fanning out daily to various contracts throughout Cumbria. Most valleys had had a community bus for the decades before many people had a car, but most had succumbed to market forces as cars became ubiquitous. Not Sim's buses: they had moved with the times and prospered. It was a strange place to park a dozen buses, however, and many a visitor had had a close shave meeting a large coach on a small country lane, with granite walls on each side of the road.

Jen and I were delighted to have Michael, our former vicar, staying with us for the weekend, and Anne-Marie had her parents and a niece. As the coach made its tortuous journey picking up parishioners from all four parishes it became clear there was a lot of goodwill, at least among the church people, for this home grown ministry, and it was a full 57 seater that finally reached the main road. Most of Geoff's extended family came from the North-East and were joining us in Carlisle, as were Mum and Dad, Norman, Jen's sister Barbara and family, and a few other friends. To my amazement I had about a hundred well-wishers for my big day. I was whisked away to robe and prepare in the ancient Fratry, leaving friends and family to find what seats they could.

Led by the Bishop, Dean and other cathedral worthies, the 13 of us processed in through the magnificent carved main entrance and up the aisle between the choir stalls. Senses sharpened by the seriousness of the day, like a bride at her wedding I took it all in greedily. On the right I saw, for the first time, the replica of the ancient Celtic cross at Bewcastle, uncle Tom's parish for so many years. I smiled at the serendipity, glad to take on Tom's mantle. Looking up, as we entered the choir area from under the mighty organ, the ceiling was deep azure blue, with a painted star in each gilded panel; somehow reminiscent of the Alhambra Palace Jen and I had visited with the girls the previous year. The great East window ahead was rich in biblical scenes, but I had no time to linger over it as the service began. The cathedral was packed, and the hymns were sung with a gusto that would have made Charles Wesley proud, particularly the first, his great 'Love Divine, all loves excelling'. A firm favourite for weddings, it felt entirely appropriate to the mysteries of ordination too.

The service itself was complex and we ordinands were left in no doubt of the gravity of the promises we made: to be diligent in prayer; to seek out and help the poor, the sick, the lonely and the disadvantaged; to proclaim the gospel; and to respect the discipline of the church. One question in particular made me smile ruefully: "Will you endeavour to fashion your own life and that of your household according to the way of Christ, that you may be a pattern and example to Christ's people?" "Except when I'm bellowing swearwords at sheep and dogs" I added silently, as I joined in the prescribed reply "By the help of God I will."

One strand of the Bishop's sermon particularly appealed to me, and remained as I moved about the parishes later. It was the charge he laid on the parishioners who had come to support each of the thirteen being ordained: his insistence that they needed to support their priest and deacons just as much as to expect to be supported. Ministry, the Bishop maintained, was a partnership between priest and congregation, and the wider parish. It was not the sole responsibility of those being ordained today, but the shared responsibility of the whole church. For someone born in the parishes I was to serve in, working alongside old friends and neighbours, this struck a chord that continued to resonate.

All too soon it was over, and with pomp and ceremony we newly ordained men and women processed out and back to the Fratry, where drinks and canapés were laid out for all to share. All our well-wishers gathered in the grounds, chatting, renewing old friendships, and congratulating the candidates. The parishes had booked lunch for everyone at a hotel part of the way home, and soon the bus was ready for the off, held up, inevitably, by Michael who had yet again found himself out of cigarettes.

Ordained! Catherine, me, Jen and Sally: 3rd July, 1988
in front of the porch at Fisherground

Chapter 27

Keep the campfires burning: 1988

Looking back I could see pattern and reason in what had seemed, living through them, to be random, unrelated events. The massacre on the fell; the drawing back from farming; the new pine lodges in place of the rather tatty old caravans; and now my new role as non-stipendiary minister were all linked by perfect, but accidental, timing. Now that I was ordained I wanted to throw myself into the role with my usual enthusiasm, and that was only possible because I suddenly had so much more time to spare. There had been a lot of truth in my reply to Tony the Owl Man's question. Farming for five hours to make a pound practically made it a hobby. Now the new-found security of the pine lodges and the burgeoning campsite gave me the freedom to pursue another course.

Except for Sunday mornings, that is. There were four parishes and Peter wanted each to have a service every week, which was only possible if he took two on Sunday morning, and I took the other two, so I was always due in one church or another at 9.30 am. At the same time the campsite was becoming very popular, particularly at weekends when a number of local young 20 somethings swelled the ranks of more traditional campers and their families. Most summer weekends now we opened the second field, and if the weather was good there were often well over 100 tents on site, with over 200 at Bank Holidays.

This always led to tension, as happy-go-lucky young men and women sat around their campfire playing a ghetto-blaster, arguing, and drinking for hour after hour. Towards 11 pm two differing points of view collided. The families had had enough of the increasing volume, both of the unwanted music and the foul language. They had children who needed to be asleep. The twenty-somethings had work to go to on Monday, but Saturday night was made for freedom under the stars.

It led to tension in the house too. Geoff and Anne-Marie made their position clear: they were happy to be the main cleaners at the toilet block, spending a couple of hours there at lunchtime, if necessary, and on the busiest weekends Geoff would get up and clean the toilet block at 8.00 too. Anne-Marie was happy to come out at 8 am to help collect camping fees. But if I wanted to open more fields, have lots of tents at a weekend and virtually invite the sort of impasse that happened every Saturday night, then I would have to bear responsibility. Jen was frightened by the sheer numbers of people descending on Fisherground each weekend, and certainly wasn't going to be able to confront any night-time problems.

It all came to a head the last weekend in July, just three weeks after my ordination. School holidays had started and both fields were open. The accountants insisted we should keep a record of the number of tents each morning so as to be able to demonstrate to Her Majesty's Revenue and Customs that we had truthfully declared the total income from camping - almost all in cash, of course. Both Anne-Marie and I were collecting fees, and I had counted 168 tents. It was going to be a rush to collect the money and be ready to take the service in St. Bega's at 9.30.

Alf was a regular, a solitary guy in his fifties who often camped with us, and this morning he was angry. Not 'Alf.

"It's no good, Ian, you got to get a hold of this. The bastards over there were at it till three o'clock this morning, and everybody's completely fed up."

"Well, I don't know what to do, Alf, we've got a big sign as you come in saying what the rules are..."

"It's no bloody good having rules if you don't enforce them. Us campers can't do it. I went across to them last night

202

at midnight and asked them nicely to turn the music off and they just told me to… well, you know."

" What can I do, Alf? I can't monitor everybody coming in to see if they're suitable."

"You know what you can do! You have to be the one who comes here at 11 o'clock and makes sure all the fires are out, all the music off. I'm telling you this, if you don't you're going to lose all the families. Word will get round and nobody with kids will come, that's for sure."

Alf was right, of course, something had to be done. We went through the options. Partly the campfires were the problem, but we were all adamant we wanted people to be able to have them. Jen argued that it was all part of camping, and we were well aware it was a big draw. Partly the sheer numbers were a problem, but we liked the income, and anyway, unless you had a gate system and someone on it full-time how could you stop people coming? I ran out of arguments. "OK, I'll just have to be there each Friday and Saturday night, about 11 o'clock, and enforce the bloody rules."

I soon found it was easier said than done. I took a big torch, and Mick, our biggest dog, a bearded collie. Soft as putty, really, but he looked big and fierce, and I hoped he would add an air of authority. There were three fires still going, and I could hear the music from the beginning of the lane into the site.

"Right, lads, let's be having this fire out and the music off, please."

"Who the hell are you, creeping up in the middle of the night?"

"I'm your landlord. This is my site, and those were my rules you drove past on the way in. And they say there's to be quiet and no fires after 10.30. It's 11 o'clock, so put your fire out, please."

"Bloody pervert, creeping around like that, spying on us out in the dark."

"No, come on Jack, fair play, let's just call it a night," came a more moderate voice. It was strange, there always seemed to be someone in the party who would be reasonable, and I soon learnt to pick them out and get them onside. I also learnt, quickly, not to swear, and not to be too confrontational.

I went off home to bed at quarter to twelve, thinking I had done my job, and it wasn't too bad. Next morning Alf had bad news for me.

"Nice try, lad, but you'd only been gone half an hour when they started up again. At least they didn't have the fire, but the language was appalling. And the music started up again as well."

There was nothing else for it, I had to be a visible presence on site for as long as it took on Friday and Saturday nights. That meant doing the rounds at 10.30, getting all the fires out and trouble-makers at least aware I was there, and then hanging around for a couple of hours till I was sure all was quiet. I ended up taking my sleeping bag and kipping out in the van with the back doors open, so I would hear if there was trouble. I parked in the light from the toilet block so they all knew I was there, and even if there was trouble, as there often was, at least the families knew I was trying. But it meant I often didn't get to bed on a Friday or Saturday night till well after 2 am.

I soon found I was incapable of writing a sermon early in the week, for the Sunday services I now took. For one thing, life had a lot of deadlines, and anything without one tended to get put back. Even if I did manage to write in the week, what I'd written always seemed hackneyed and stilted when reviewed. The only way was to write the sermon on Sunday morning, trusting that there would be some inspiration. The big advantages were that I couldn't afford to mess around, had to write something, and there was no time for review. I comforted myself with the thought that, after a lifetime of hearing sermons every week, I couldn't remember anything specific from any of them, and that no doubt no-one was expecting any better from me. There was also the consolation, important to me, that even if it wasn't the greatest sermon in the world it was pretty damned good considering the time constraints I had to work under. Simple, but effective, psychology.

Walking on water on the campsite pond. Easy, compared to keeping order on the campsite at 11 pm.

This regime meant I had to be up by 6 am on Sunday morning, write whatever came to me by quarter to eight, and then get out onto the campsite to collect money and help Anne-Marie clean the worst of the mess in the toilet block. I had to be back in the house by 9 o'clock to change and get to the service by 9.30. It was a punishing schedule, but in practice there were only the main Saturday nights in high season when it was at its worst. I got to hoping for a wet night on a Saturday. There was nothing like a good rain for putting out the fires and persuading campers to go to bed.

The campsite was by now a major part of our income, and an immensely popular destination for families and walkers alike. The second, unregistered, field was in use every Bank Holiday and every school holiday from Easter till the end of August, and we even opened a third field on sunny Bank Holidays, with up to 300 tents jammed into every conceivable pitch. There were the inevitable tensions, but as long as the sun shone everyone seemed content just to chill out in the beautiful surroundings.

The campsite was a great source of contradiction and tension, and of many a discussion for the four of us. The obvious friction between those who wanted to party the night away and those who wanted to sleep was just one of the tensions.

"It's not just this night-time problem, you know. What do you think the people in the lodges think about having so many people just a hundred yards away? I know I find it threatening."

"Mais oui, but you're right, Jen. You advertise 'a little peace of Lakeland', Ian, how do you think it is that visitors feel when there's so much noise? That zip wire is going all day long, and the kids are yelling and shouting."

"Fine, but we all like the income, don't we. And not just us, the people in the village shop were saying just yesterday how important campers' shopping is to them. I don't think it could carry on if it wasn't for us and the campsite."

"True enough," agreed Geoff, "and I bet the Ratty is pleased with all the extra passengers. They wouldn't have made a special station for us unless it was well worth while."

Jen tried again: "Personally, I'm worried about opening other fields. Why don't we just stick to the official campsite?"

As usual, I was robust. "What would we do then about all the people who come and can't get on? We'd have to be up there all day turning people away, or they'd just go on the other field anyway."

"Surely if we put up a sign saying Campsite Full nobody would come in?"

"Well, maybe, but where are they gonna go then? There aren't any other places. I think we have a responsibility to provide for those with less money. They love it here just as much as people who can afford a lodge."

Geoff, with the crunch argument: "And anyway, let's face it, we all like the extra money. It's been hard enough for a long time."

Chapter 28

I danced with a girl with a hole in her stocking: 1988-9

From the moment of my ordination in July 1988 my life changed considerably - and my clothing even more so. Or rather, I found myself changing my clothing frequently, as I moved from being a campsite fee-collector in the early morning to a clerical hospital visitor a little later, with perhaps a session of sheep worming in the afternoon and a Parochial Church Council meeting in the evening. There were days when I seemed to change four or five times. What I wore also affected how I behaved, and of course how others reacted to me.

I'd first noticed this as a trainee teacher doing my Post Graduate Certificate in Education at Leeds University, the year after Oxford. I spent a full term in a minor public school in Wakefield, living in and feeling rather miserable. My lessons were a shambles as I tried and failed to get the boys onside. I needed to do something. The something turned out to be terribly simple: I started to wear my Oxford gown for lessons, and found two things happened. First, and most importantly, I began to feel like a teacher, with a badge of office confirming that I knew a lot more than the pupils did, and was there to impart this knowledge. Secondly they responded to the outward sign of authority and started treating me as a teacher.

It was the same with a dog collar. I put it on, wore smart trousers and a jacket, and I was welcome in any house I visited, as someone with an acknowledged role, a job to do. Likewise in hospital: in those days a priest could wander unchallenged through the wards at any time of day or night, ask to look through the admittance records to see which of his parishioners were there, and stop at any bedside to exchange a few words. It wasn't just that people treated me with respect, I found that, in uniform, I also treated the role itself with a greater sense of dignity.

Taking services was the same. Dressing up in a simple cassock, stole and preaching scarf gave me a legitimacy that was as essential to me as it was to a congregation. It says much for the uniform and for the generosity of spirit of our neighbours that they could accept both roles, ordained priest and hot-headed farmer, in the one person.

My first service; Waberthwaite Church where my uncle had ministered 35 years previously

My new role introduced me to far more people in the surrounding parishes than I could have hoped to have met in any other way. The only difficulty was that I had problems in recognising faces and remembering the names to go with them that bordered on a clinical condition, prosopagnosia, or 'face blindness'. I found I had to see someone and have access to their name at least four separate times before I was reasonably confident who they were. This was a significant disability for a priest, especially as I became more known to the large congregations attending some of the funerals. Time after time I found myself conducting quite deep conversations with people who appeared to know me well, but whom I had no memory of ever having met before. It was very embarrassing, and I never learnt how to deal with it properly.

My first funeral in the crematorium, some 25 miles away, was for a man I had only met briefly in hospital, recognising from the records that he was a parishioner. His name was Ernie Lamb, and his wife Sybil and daughter Pat were at his bedside. One look at his ashen face was enough to see he was gravely ill, having had a severe heart attack. Pat drew me aside to talk and confirmed that his chances of recovery were slim, and that her mother would be distraught if he died, after over 50 years of marriage. They had never been church-people, Pat confided, but when he died would I be able to take his funeral? I tried the positive approach, saying it might not come to that and Ernie would probably have lots of years left - after all, medical science was amazing now, and the doctors could almost perform miracles. Pat brushed this aside. She had been told, and Ernie's pallor confirmed, that it was just a matter of time. His heart was fatally flawed, and at 82 nothing could be done to help, except for pain relief. She took my phone number and promised to ring...

Pat rang two days later with the sad but inevitable news that Ernie had died, and I arranged to visit her and Sybil that evening. This would be my first 'solo' funeral, and Jen's warning not to be either crass or flippant rang in my ears. She was, frankly, perplexed as to how a man who had shown such a complete lack of empathy when her mother had died, nine years previously, could be let loose on such an important task. At this moment, so was I. Sybil lived in one of the new houses in Ravenglass, where the ancient village was growing along the railway embankment. Pat lived in the old part of the village, but would of course be with her mother this evening and no doubt for some time to come while she came to terms with bereavement.

Pat led me in to a sitting room that felt more like a shrine: a room brim-full of keepsakes and knickknacks. Every shelf had its mementoes of holidays they had shared - shells from a beach in Torbay, a tartan calendar proclaiming itself 'a souvenir of bonny Scotland', a photo of the two of them with a much younger Pat in Blackpool - the tower growing proudly out of Ernie's head. The walls too were festooned with photos, giving hints of their earlier life together, life in the Wirral where Ernie had worked in the gigantic Lever Brothers' factory at Port Sunlight. All these memories on display were a godsend in prompting Sybil in what she wanted to do most - remember her beloved Ernie - and it was all much less daunting than I had feared. We had, too, the practical details of the funeral to provide a framework to our talk. They were happy enough for me to use the standard Church of England service, and we went through its form together. They had their own thoughts on music - no hymns, but a particular favourite of Ernie's, The New World Symphony, to play in the background as we came in, and left, the crematorium chapel. Pat lent me the vinyl LP to take to the officials there.

This was the first hiccup in the proceedings. I wanted to check out the crematorium before the service and took the record along to give to George, who I discovered was in charge of what in a theatre would be 'front of house'. As my visit continued the metaphor seemed more and more justified. Seating was just that, individual seats rather than pews, making the congregation look, and feel, more like an audience. There was what seemed to me almost a proscenium arch, a curtained area at the front where what was beginning to feel like a drama would be played out, with the final act drawing a curtain on a life. There was a podium, subtly different from a pulpit, where the narrator – me – would stand and conduct proceedings. And there was a backstage where George would twiddle the knobs to fade lights and play music to set the mood. I much preferred the amateur but sacred atmosphere of a church, needing no such dramatics. The hiccup was that, among all this technology, there was no record deck. George could play any cassette, but no vinyl. I would have to record the New World onto the New Technology, and deliver it when I came for the service itself.

I was, of course, ridiculously early for the service, due to begin at 11.00. I delivered my cassette to George, spent time in the back office getting to know the two administrators, then a lot more time in the vestry, dressing up in cassock, alb and stole, nervously going through the service book for the umpteenth time, checking my notes on the address I was to give, and generally working myself up into a nervous wreck. I was never as early for a service again. At ten to 11 I went out to await mourners and the cortege, aware as I stood in the imposing entrance of the previous half-hour's slot coming to its climax behind the oak-panelled doors into the theatre. No doubt in much more capable hands.

That service over, George joined me at the door, assuring me more than once that the cassette was in and ready to go. A steady flow of Ravenglass villagers came to support Sybil and Pat, but virtually no other family members. It seemed they were the last twigs on a far branch of the family tree. We gathered to await the hearse followed by Sybil and Pat in the black limo. There was a brief hiatus as the undertaker got Ernie's coffin transferred to the gleaming bier, in which George disappeared backstage. At the undertaker's nod we began to process: me in the lead, followed by the coffin, Pat and Sybil, and the villagers.

The music started…

But not the *New World Symphony*. Instead a track I instantly recognised as being by a band Jen and I were particularly fond of, Chameleon. In truth, it was reasonably appropriate music, a gentle instrumental track with nothing to jar the procession - except for Pat and Sybil, of course, expecting the haunting largo from the New World. In panic, as I solemnly led the procession, I realised what must have happened. I had recorded Pat's LP on the B side of our Chameleon tape, and George was now playing side A. I also realised that the next track, far from being 'reasonably appropriate' was a raucous version of the old favourite '*I danced with a girl with a hole in her stocking*'.

I quickened my pace and the congregation shuffled into their places, and blessedly the music faded, still on the gentle track.

Relief made me gabble the first bits of the service, but I settled into it, gave a halfway decent eulogy, using all the material Pat and Sybil had provided. Solemnly we all stood for the committal, and I spoke what are generally the last words over a coffin: *We have entrusted our brother to God's merciful keeping and we now commit his body to be cremated...* No sonorous, mellifluous *Earth to earth, ashes to ashes, dust to dust* in this modern, chromed, sanitised theatre. I announced the end of the service, and stood to lead the congregation out - not of course by the way we'd come in. Another performance was due in ten minutes, and it would never do to mix the two.

As we started to process the music faded back in: the same track, from where it had left off. Again I quickened my pace, eager to leave both theatre and music behind, but as we turned the last corner I heard it move onto the dreaded 'Girl with the hole in her stocking'. As I stood at the rear exit to shake hands there were masked grins from some of the villagers, and frank amazement from Pat. I could do nothing but confess. She asked for a copy of the CD, and I promised to make one for her when I returned her vinyl.

This first funeral was not unlike my whole experience of ministry: a mixture of grief, merriment, high drama and low farce. And the long gentle day-to-day visiting of the sick, the lonely, and the slowly fading away. Throughout it all, no-one ever requested, for funeral music, 'I danced with a girl with a hole in her stocking'.

Chapter 29

The Boxing Day Meet: 1988

The run-up to Christmas in 1988, as every year, was manic. Jen and Anne-Marie were members of the joint parishes choir, 'The Amethyst Singers', organised, lubricated and bullied into shape by the indefatigable Kate Goodwin and her generous, urbane husband Vic. Kate insisted that all four parishes, most of the pubs, and a couple of old peoples' homes had to have their share of carol-singing, so for four nights in the week before Christmas we piled into various cars and Vic's long wheel-base Land Rover to charm the night. Wednesday 21st December was Irton and Ravenglass night. Irton was well spread out and required much hilarity as we bundled in and out of the Land Rover. Anne-Marie's parents were with us for Christmas, and Papy was having great fun 'helping' the ladies in and out. Tradition held that money be demanded at each door by the youngest member present – this year six-year-old Philip did the honours.

We pulled up in Ravenglass main street (well, all right, Ravenglass only street) and started from the heavy steel flood-gate, shut to keep out the expected high tide. In contrast to far-flung Irton, here the choir could stand in the middle of the road, singing lustily, while Philip, aided by Anne-Marie whom he christened his elf for the evening, knocked cheerily and shook their 'Children's Society' money box. The news started to seep out, bit by bit, as we progressed up the street: at first just a news-flash reported by a house watching TV. By the top of the street, Ravenglass, the whole country, the Western world, had heard the news. Pan-Am Flight 103 had exploded in mid-air, almost certainly the victim of a terrorist bomb, and had come down in pieces over Lockerbie, just 75 miles north of us. We sang no more that night.

The Boxing Day Meet is one of fox-hunting's great traditions, and all the pubs in Eskdale had large photos of the red-coated huntsman surrounded by his baying hounds, taking a goodly glass of whisky outside their particular establishment. Fisherground had its own 'Boxing Day Meet', which became every bit as much a tradition for many years, dreaded, so they said, by the kids, but actually one of those cords that bound our families together. In our case, the extended double family that we had become. Jen and Geoff were first cousins, and they shared a valuable gene: a gift for, and a love of, music. They shared it, too, with their siblings and those siblings' children, and Boxing Day was one of the red letter days on the calendar when everyone came to Fisherground, and music came to the fore.

Jen's sister Barbara was the first to arrive, with Douglas and their children Louise and Ian, always known as 'little Ian' to distinguish him from me – even after he outgrew me. Ian's instrument was in a mighty case, befitting the gravity of a bassoon, and he soon opened it up to give us his newest piece 'L'après-midi d'un dinosaur': skittishly named, but quite fiendish to play. By contrast, Louise took out her piccolo! Doug had played the drums way back in our Keswick School days, and had borrowed a kit specially for tonight's soirée. Barbara was our musical director, a very competent pianist, violinist and recorder player, with the skill and perseverance to transpose the 20-odd pieces that we would perform together this evening.

"Now, Sally, here's your portfolio." Sally giggled – what was a portfolio?

"It's all in E flat, for your saxophone."

Jen cut in, hesitantly, "Actually, Sis, she's taken up the cello now, and I thought it would be good for her to have an outing with it. And it would beef up the bass line."

"Well, whatever, perhaps she'll play the sax for some pieces. And here's the pieces in B flat for Elizabeth's clarinet... unless she's taken up the Tuba?"

"No, no, Elizabeth is still clarinet." As Jen knew well, a certain amount of tact went a long way on these occasions.

"At least you and Catherine are easy, why can't every instrument play in C like the flute? Speaking of which, here's your recorder music, Claire."

Geoff's brother, Brian, another Wake of course, was next to arrive, with a car full. Full of presents for the time-shifted Christmas that this Boxing Day represented, and full of family to boost our numbers. Brian and Gill's music had gone down the singing route, and they were talented members of several choirs in Yarm, over in the North-East. They could be depended on for harmony and to hold the less capable of us (my side of the family) on key. Jonathon had his trusty trumpet by his side, while his brother Simon stood out, even in this exalted company, as the pianist who would provide the intros and chords. Ivy, Brian and Geoff's mother, was last out of the car, tutting a little about the state of the roads, and Brian's driving. She would get her moment on the piano this evening, too.

Last to arrive, with the shortest journey, were Mum and Dad. They and I would be the audience. We knew our place! Well, someone had to sing the carols while the rest of them were playing. They had been with us for Christmas, but preferred to go home to sleep – and in any case the house was full, with Anne-Marie's parents and Jen's father, Norman also with us. In keeping with that strong Wake gene he had also played several instruments in a long life, but tonight he just had his mouth-organ. He wouldn't need music, he could do it on auto-pilot.

As usual, Jen and Anne-Marie had rustled up a superb buffet supper in our kitchen, and after the second-stage present giving friends and family went into huddles all over the place catching up on all the comings and goings. It was

217

one of those special moments in a family's history, when three generations are all active and interested in each other's lives. The grandparents were all in their 70s, still fit and capable: our generation in our 40s or thereabout, with full, abundant lives; and the children nearly all in their teens, bursting with vitality and promise.

The orchestra

After supper everyone piled into our, fortunately large, living room. Six grand-parents, eight parents, eight teenagers. And Philip. And assorted instruments. I was designated photographer, and as I stood on a chair to get a view of everyone concentrating on their individual parts in *Silent Night* I had one of those strange out-of-body experiences where my viewpoint slipped further away and I felt as if I looked in from a distance at some almost religious gathering. Each had a part to play, a part which on its own was thin, reedy, scarcely recognisable: and yet, put together they became a haunting music, with the power to move me to tears.

Two evenings previously, on Christmas Eve, I had officiated at my first Midnight Mass, the lovely service that ushers in Christmas Day. Vic Goodwin (of the choir) and his team in Irton Church had decked it in candles for the service. Each of the three huge chandeliers, long converted to electricity, was returned for the evening to its original purpose. Every window-sill sported its candelabrum, every pew end its candle on a wand. By 10.45 pm all was ready, all the candles lit, and Vic turned off the lights as the bell-ringers gathered in the tower. Mighty peals rang out over the frost-covered countryside, urging late-comers in. In the vestry I nervously went over my notes, adjusted my stole over my shiny new alb, and checked my watch. On the stroke of 11 pm I walked, more confidently than I felt, out into a church filled with people, filled with the glorious warm light of a hundred candles, filled with love.

Buoyed up by the response, the strength of the carol-singing led by Kate and her choir, I too played my part, holding the space for the secret magic of Christmas to make its place in every heart. Each of us making our contribution, just like the original shepherds and kings, we joined in something greater than the sum of its parts. The service ended not long after midnight and the bell-ringers welcomed in Christmas Day as that huge congregation gathered to chat and share the mulled wine and mince pies the church-wardens had provided. Every face was wreathed in smiles, every heart seemed touched by the Spirit of Christmas.

Now, as I stood on my chair, camera in hand to capture Fisherground at play, these three events of Christmas fused together in my mind's eye. The aeroplane ripped apart over Lockerbie, with so many lives snuffed out: the candles in church each burning itself away to give light to a service I had found so uplifting: and now these 24 people I loved most, gathered together each burning with their own light, each playing a part in a glorious whole. Truly, each of us has a part to play, and each chooses whether it is for good or ill, and the result is a greater good, or a greater evil, than the sum of all the parts.

Chapter 30

The folly of youth: 1989-90

Anne-Marie was in thoughtful mood, regaining her composure after seeing off her parents on the long journey back to France. She found their visits wearing, but nevertheless was always in tears when they left.

"You know the top loft, where you and Geoff had the workshop?" Upstairs from the farrowing crates, in the old Stables.

"Yeees, what about it?"

"Well, I was thinking; now you have made a new workshop and, how do you call it, the maintenance bay, it's not really used except to store the tools and the rubbish. Could we not make it into a small flat where Mamy and Papy could go for a while when they come to stay?"

Anne-Marie's parents came over probably twice a year, for a fortnight each time, and she found it quite tiring always being with them in her part of the house with the added pressure from teenage girls and the energetic Philip. We all talked it over and agreed that the 'top loft' was indeed underused now, and would make a really useful addition to the house. It was after all the nearest building, just ten yards from the front door, and the house was bursting at the seams. Anne-Marie had obviously given it lots of thought, as she piped up, "And let's call it The Annexe. I find top loft hard to say!"

Anne-Marie's timing was perfect. I had been ordained and had had my birthday, but Jen's was still to come. Where better for a great 40th birthday party, if it had a new floor? Next day Jen enthusiastically started to destroy the old floor, deputing to me the humbler task of removing all the old tools and rubbish. The floor didn't put up much resistance: it had been there since the 16th century and was rotten and full of woodworm. As she worked her way from the door Jen simply dropped what was left of the boards through to the defunct farrowing crates below. This was definitely a building crying out for a new role. When she reached the far wall the flaw in her enthusiasm struck her.

"Iaaaaan!" It's a small name usually, but in extremis she could make it huge. I came running, fearing the worst.

"I'm trapped!" I couldn't help but laugh. Jen sat on the last bit of floor, her back to the wall. At least paint will dry if you paint yourself into a corner.

"Um, you're one plank short of a dance floor, then?"

Since the floor was gone, we decided to do the job properly and raise it by eighteen inches, so the farrowing house below could also be made into a room sometime. Here the delights of just doing a conversion for ourselves, rather than as letting cottages, became clear. No Planning Board to consult, no building inspector to placate, we could make our own decisions and be responsible for the result. Raising the floor meant raising the cross-beam in the roof. No need for expensive structural engineer calculations, we just cut out the cross-beam and bolted it back eighteen inches higher, confident it would hold the roof and walls. Want a big window in the back? No need to worry the planners, who would be duty bound to say 'No', just knock a six foot hole in and build up the sides. What size of steel joist needed to span the floor? Oh, eight by four should be fine.

After the hassle of form filling, box ticking, being inspected and generally feeling the farm wasn't our own Geoff and I revelled in the freedom. Even in the twelve years we'd been at Fisherground the rigours of the Common Agricultural Policy and all the quangos who had an input into farming, the Lake District, and building seemed to have doubled and it was a delight to wave two fingers at the bureaucrats for once. By Christmas the dance floor had all its planks, and a party for Jen's 40th was on the cards. The girls took one look at the whitewashed lath and plaster end wall and decided it needed brightening up. '20's plenty; 30's flirty, 50's nifty, but 40 is… naughty' in foot high letters did the trick. Six year old Philip put his new-found climbing skills to good use, festooning the walls and beams with party lights, and by January 3rd everything was ready for her coming of age.

Jen and I had been running a 'sort of' youth club for a couple of years. Catherine, Sally, Elizabeth and Claire were just the right sort of age - early teens - not to be able to object, and their friends came along because they were the children of Jen and Anne-Marie's friends in the valley. This degree of obligation was needed because the youth club had a Christian bias, definitely not cool. To soften this bias I plagiarised a tranche of 'silly games' suitable for teenagers which formed the framework for each weekly club night. The kids wrecked our living room each Sunday night after 'The A Team' on telly.

The Annexe, decorated for Jen's birthday: 1989
Hilary joyfully steering her 'wheelbarrow'.

223

The strange thing was, adults, or at least the adults attracted to Fisherground, seemed to enjoy these games more than the kids, and Jen's party was perhaps the strangest orgy of silly games since Victorian times. The re-floored Annexe was partly to blame, with its acres of room and lack of anything breakable or even damageable, and no doubt the alcohol helped. By 11 o'clock 30 or more mixed adults and teenagers were well into plank racing, egg balancing, spoon threading, musical chairs and 'pass the parcel' with fiendish forfeits. Everyone agreed the high point was the 'blind jelly feeding' forfeit that pitted the 15-year-old Catherine against my friend Graham. Blindfold, they were each given a spoon and a bowl of jelly and required to feed each other. It was positively decorous at first, Catherine slightly in awe of this big man who visited from time to time, and Graham perhaps anxious not to offend his hostess. It grew less so as one of Graham's spoonfuls accidentally went down Catherine's neck, and decidedly war-like as she responded by tearing off her blindfold and tipping her bowlful over his head, scrunching it down for good measure. She ran off into the darkness cackling, Graham in hot pursuit.

We worked on the Top Loft/Annexe project off and on throughout 1989, and by the end of that year had completely transformed this ancient building. The maintenance bay took the entire Southern third, floor to roof, with an inspection pit to assist Geoff in his many projects on the tractors, cars and machinery, and a block and tackle hanging from the beam to lift out engines, gear boxes or whatever. Cars were simpler then - no computers or fancy tuning - and Geoff did all the servicing and maintenance on everything. He was a lot happier with a few garage comforts. Of course you couldn't drive a tractor through the same three foot wide doorway that had been fine for horses for 400 years, so I had replaced it with a nine foot wide version that went almost to the roof, cunningly camouflaged with an arched top that made it look like an original barn door.

We went to town on the Annexe itself, giving it a cathedral roof, a bedroom and its own shower room and loo. Jen was enjoying our new-found tourist-based wealth and replaced the kitchen units Geoff and I had made when we first moved in, so these found a new lease of life as the kitchen area in the new flat, and by the time we'd finished it was indeed a place Mamy and Papy could look on as a 'pied à terre' when they visited. It soon became the natural place for any visiting friends, and even developed its own booking calendar.

It also became the natural home for the youth group, having more space and fewer breakable ornaments than the living room. The kids seemed happier in a neutral room that was also somehow 'their' meeting place. Sunday evenings developed their own pace: parents brought the eight or nine kids for 7.30 and we started with a round-up of everyone's week, generally pretty anodyne. Half an hour in I introduced that night's particular silly game, this time a wall-building exercise with a point. Firstly there was a pile of bricks, ordinary house bricks, and I invited the kids to build a wall, with the cassette recorder playing Pink Floyd's *'Just another brick in the wall'*, followed by the Floyd's own lesson that so many people feel they are indeed just another brick in the wall of humanity.

Then we moved seamlessly on to Eskdale granite stones, and I invited them to build another wall with these. The book had advised leaving at least half an hour for the kids to produce even the semblance of a wall, but then, the book wasn't dealing with farmers' sons. Ten minutes later Mark had finished, and there stood a very passable stone wall, limited only by the fact that he'd built it properly, with two sides and a filled middle, and I hadn't provided enough stone for it to be more than a foot high. Still, it was an impressive wall, and a splendid demonstration of the moral of the evening: that each of us is an individual, filling a 'me-shaped' hole, touching those around us, and each important in our own right. The book claimed that if any stone was removed, the wall would fall down, demonstrating that each of us is vitally important. I removed one from Mark's wall, but it was too well-built to fall - which slightly scuppered the moral.

The Annexe had a real purpose, and filled it well. The same wasn't really true of the room below it - previously the farrowing pens - but as an act of pure hubris we decided to carry on, tart it up as well, and produce another large room, more or less just because we could. Again we knocked another six foot hole in the back wall, put in French windows, plastered everything and ended up with a very fine games room for the teenage girls and their friends, the youth group on occasion, and ourselves when we fancied a game of table tennis or pool.

It's just at moments like this, when you feel you have the world tamed, that everything is going smoothly, and that you've really achieved something, that life has a nasty habit of kicking you in the teeth.

Anne-Marie discovered a lump in her right breast. Just a tiny lump, the sort that is nearly always benign, just fatty tissue; but the doctor thought she'd better do a biopsy just to be sure. When she came back from getting her results Geoff was at work and I was bound up in whatever job I had on, and had forgotten that she'd gone for the result. It was Jen, her old friend from so long ago, who held her and dried her tears and assured her everything would be all right, that these days cancer was a word, not a sentence. Even if, after her own mother's experience, she didn't really believe it.

It was ten years since Jen's mother, Marjorie, had died from her cancer. Years which had blunted the painful memory, but certainly not erased it. Now the full horror of those long months of decline from rude health to skeletal agony washed over her again, even as she comforted her oldest friend and assured her that breast cancer was one of the easiest to treat. When we went over it alone together, that evening, Jen was a lot less confident, frightened beyond comforting that history would repeat itself and that sometime in the not too distant future she would find herself once again holding someone she loved beyond words as life slowly, painfully, ebbed away.

Chapter 31

The Centre for Complementary Care: 1990 – 2000

The doctors decided Anne-Marie's breast lump was not critical enough to merit a mastectomy, but they did send her to Newcastle Hospital for specialist radiation treatment. She also had to undergo a course of chemo-therapy, but eventually she was proclaimed cured, and could resume normal life, and so, slowly, could the rest of Fisherground. It had been an enormous shock, and she took all the advice on lifestyle very seriously. She had eaten very little meat before but now cut it out completely, living on a high vegetable, low carbohydrate diet. She ate so many carrots and took her doses of beta-carotene so assiduously that her face took on an orange hue till she toned down her intake.

Above all, though, she retreated into prayer and meditation, joining various groups. With impeccable timing a new centre opened in Eskdale Valley just as Anne-Marie needed support and help in meditation and healing. This was the Centre for Complementary Care, under its founder and lead practitioner Gretchen Stevens. The Centre became a major part of Anne-Marie's life, and she threw herself wholeheartedly into its work and organisation, filling envelopes, joining meditation sessions and chatting to clients. In its first years it had no paid administrative staff, and Anne-Marie joined a dedicated team of volunteers determined to make this experiment in healing and prayer work.

She discovered there was no easily accessible anthology of all the various strands of knowledge about living with cancer that she had found out for herself - nutrition, vitamin supplements, positive imagery, meditation - so she started to compile her own anthology, for use by the many cancer patients beginning to come to Gretchen for healing, in its broadest sense. It was a short step from there to Anne-Marie setting up the Centre's own Cancer Support group. This grew in stature over the years and was a source of comfort and knowledge to an ever-widening web of people recovering from the illness. Anne-Marie became known throughout West Cumbria and beyond, and found to her surprise how many homes the disease touched, and how many people needed comfort and support.

Anne-Marie and Jen, after the scare: 1991

Gretchen came by a roundabout route to Eskdale. She was American, and was taken on by Muncaster Castle as publicity manager, event organiser and in charge of bringing fellow Americans to spend a few nights and a large amount of money in a genuine English castle. She lived in with the owners, Patrick and Phyllida, and together they looked for ways to make the Castle earn its keep - or indeed, keep its Keep.

In her four years at Muncaster Castle Gretchen found her talent for healing and soothing more and more in demand. Patrick and Phyllida had a huge circle of friends, frequent visitors to the castle, and news of Gretchen's abilities became widespread, to the point where it was clear to her and her friends that she should dedicate her life to healing. She was adamant from the word go that what she offered was in no sense in competition with established medicine, but somehow a way of helping that medicine function more effectively. So her centre, when it came about, was very deliberately called *for Complementary Care.*

Ralph Waldo Emerson tells us that *'If a man write a better book, preach a better sermon, or make a better mousetrap than his neighbour, tho' he build his house in the woods, the world will make a beaten path to his door.'* The Centre for Complementary Care was in West Cumbria, possibly the most remote region of England. It was on a single track lane, with few passing places, off a minor road leading from nowhere to nowhere else. It ran on the principle that people paid what they could for an hour's treatment, which consisted of little else than Gretchen's soothing voice, soothing hands, and a lot of laughter. People came from far and wide, and people went away somehow better. Not necessarily cured, but better.

Anne-Marie was a part of this centre almost from day one of its existence, and the centre was a part of her. For the next decade the centre, her cancer support group and work, and her prayer and meditation groups formed the fulcrum on which her health and interests delicately balanced. She struggled with her understanding of what healing was, moving from her early terribly simplistic New Testament interpretation of Jesus' instruction to his disciples to 'heal the sick, raise the dead, cleanse lepers, cast out demons'(Matt 10:8) to a much more subtle understanding that body, mind, spirit, emotions and feelings are intimately inter-connected, and a sickness in any one part can cause symptoms in all.

Certainly her emotions and feelings had ridden a roller coaster over the previous few years, and perhaps because she never learnt to scream as her carriage hurtled down the rails she bottled up all the negativity inside, unable to confront, yet seething silently. She took her community to heart and the inevitable tensions in a household as complex as Fisherground, coupled with the wider strains as the new vicar, Peter, settled into the parishes after Michael left brought their own brand of stress for a church woman as dedicated as Anne-Marie. This was compounded by the heartache she and Geoff went through over young Philip's schooling, heartache that threw into sharp focus the strengths and weaknesses of small village life.

Eskdale School never numbered more than 40 on its roll, and consequently two and a half teachers had to split the entire school between them, meaning pupils spent several years with one teacher. This was great if they got on, hell if they didn't, and virtually impossible if one of the teachers was actually poor at the job. Anne-Marie and Geoff had already suffered considerable angst over their daughter Claire's early years with one teacher, and now that Philip was struggling with another it seemed time to make a stand. They weren't alone: Michael-next-door had also decided enough was enough, and in September they both removed their children to the local Prep School, where of course they had to pay for their education.

Here again life in a small village community brought stresses unimaginable to those used to the relative anonymity of town life. Anne-Marie had for a long time been a helper in the 'Mother and Toddler' group which met in St. Bega's Hall, and came back home in huge distress after what apparently started as a chance remark developed into this full scale row.

"Is it right, what I've heard, Anne-Marie? That you're thinking of taking Philip out of school?" asked one of the mothers.

"Well, yes, me, I find he's not learning anything."

"Well, he's only eight and..."

"Yeah, our Joe's the same, but it's a lovely school, and they're such good friends, and all."

" Me, I know what you say, but it was the same with Claire, and she never has caught up. And they're both dyslexic, and the head, he doesn't seem to make any, how do you say..."

"Concessions? Well, but he's got twenty to look after, he can't be spending too much time on the slower ones."

"Excuse me! Philip is not slow! He is a bright boy, but he finds words hard to read."

"Well, OK, but if you take Phil out, and Michael takes Tom, there's only our Joe and Helen left in that year group."

Another mother broke into the argument.

"If you take them out, and a lot of parents follow suit, and they might easily, the school could close. Do you want to be responsible for that - well, do you?"

"Well, is it not that if more of you had stood up for what you know is right, things might have been changed? Why are you all so, so ...."

"Now just a minute, Anne-Marie, don't you be coming in here with your foreign ideas. Eskdale School's been here a lot longer than you have, so stop rocking the boat."

Anne-Marie went home shaking with anger and shock that friends could turn on her - and to ask Geoff what it meant to 'rock the boat'.

At the same time Anne-Marie's siblings in France were going through their own inevitable traumas, divorce, trouble with children: all the problems that forty-somethings have. Other people might have merely ignored what was going on over the channel, but Anne-Marie wasn't made that way. She soaked up all the problems through the earpiece of the telephone and they churned around in her head, her heart and her insides, releasing all sorts of unhelpful hormones.

Wherever her cancer came from, she was determined to fight it with all the resources at her disposal, and to use all she had learnt from books, counselling and her medical contacts to help others who found themselves in the same predicament. So began her long relationship with Gretchen's Centre for Complementary Care. It started gently enough, with her just helping in all the admin jobs, folding newsletters, looking for sponsorship, making the tea, in return for sessions under Gretchen's gentle hands. She was always keen on the meditation afternoons and began to take a leading role, especially, of course in those designed to help cancer sufferers. It wasn't long before she was producing material for these sessions, material that grew into her anthology that began to be used as a valuable resource for sufferers across the West Coast.

True to the Centre's philosophy of being *complementary* to the medical services Anne-Marie's anthology and her approach were always keen to stress the critical role of surgery, radiotherapy and chemotherapy. Nevertheless, she saw her contribution as helping people to see how their cancer might not just have been a physical accident, but could be caused by stress, lifestyle, emotional problems, even depression and obsession. Her sessions tried to lead sufferers to a better self-understanding, a change of life choices, and a better balance. This chimed completely with Gretchen's own approach. Certainly there was healing in her touch, but equally she sought to help her clients recognise, and change, areas of their lives that were contributing to their sickness. As Peter, our new vicar put it, "You always come away from a session with Gretchen feeling more in tune with yourself and the world."

Chapter 32

The fête worse than death: 1994

"Oh God, it's the fête worse than death in three weeks." There was no way out of it, these days. Everyone at Fisherground was involved, and for most of us that took the best part of three weeks in August. Anne-Marie was in charge of all the stalls, which meant chivvying stall-holders, making sure they were up to speed, how many tables they needed, how much float, and so on. Jen was in charge of the bottle stall, with choir-master Kate, which meant begging, borrowing, stealing even, to get the 200 bottles they needed. Geoff was the treasurer and general dogsbody, and I was in charge of 'roadside publicity', setting up, taking down, and trouble-shooting on the day. The girls were all in a dance group that always performed, tap dancing on grass.

Roadside publicity was the reason for my latest rant. At the beginning of the week leading up to the fete I would spend two to three days touring the roads and shops in a 30 mile radius, asking shopkeepers to stick up a detailed programme of the fête's events, and nailing placards to telephone posts, trees, and any other suitable woodwork where drivers could read the bare bones: ESKDALE FETE, BANK HOL SUN pm. The placards were recyclable - except that this year I had to add an additional 'TREVOR & SIMON - Swing yer pants!!!'. I hadn't a clue who Trevor & Simon were, but the girls did. "Aw Dad, they're only the coolest act on the telly!"

"Yee-har, swing your pants, Daddy-doo!"

It was all Gretchen's fault. How could a healer working in darkest West Cumbria know such a dazzling array of celebrities and stars? Gretchen had a direct line to Harry

Enfield who had played in the back streets of London with her children. She provided the star attraction opener on several occasions, and this time it was to be Trevor and Simon. Just had to be publicised from every lamp-post for miles around.

The lawn was covered in the lurid pink placards, freshly printed and pasted. I was covered in wallpaper paste, and so was the kitchen table. The air was blue, Jen was seeing red: it was one of those rainbow days, and it wasn't going to get much better till the dreaded fête was over and done. Wistfully we harked back to the early days at Fisherground, when Geoff and I didn't even go to the fête, claiming the need to bale the hay, or some other excuse. Jen and Anne-Marie took the young girls, parted with a bit of cash on the Bring & Buy stalls, and slipped home gratefully, leaving others to tidy up. It had all changed under Michael's period as vicar. With a friend like that there was no escape from the fête committee and the burgeoning responsibilities, and once you started there was no way out but death or emigration.

Graham had discovered the same uncomfortable truth. With friends like Fisherground he too had to abandon everything else for the last weekend in August, and dedicate himself to the myriad embarrassments involved in parting visitors from their money. He arrived on Friday, and that evening he and I set out to 'do the pubs'; not a pub-crawl, but a pressurised raffle ticket selling spree. I dressed up in a dog collar to give us an official air, and we set off for the King George at 8 o'clock.

"You're not the vicar, you're the bloody campsite man. You woke me up at 8 o'clock this morning. You can't want more money, you nearly cleaned me out this morning..."

"Well, yes, sorry - and I'll probably be round at 11 o'clock tonight. But I am a sort of vicar, and it is a good cause, and there's lots of lovely prizes. Look, first prize, a weekend break at Fisherground! In the lodges, not just the campsite."

"Yeah, and look, second prize a full bloody week at Fisherground! Oh, go on then, how much are they? How much! You don't half know how to take the piss."

That night was a rough one on the campsite - Bank Holidays nearly always were. But at least I had Graham as henchman, and together we could jolly most groups into submission. All but one. A sullen looking man sat staring into the fire, a bit spaced out. His mates weren't playing ball with my usual patter. "No, why the fuck should we put the fire out. Listen, we've come for a weekend away from people like you, throwing your bloody weight about. Piss off, and stop creeping about in the dark." Suddenly the sullen man swayed to his feet, and lumbered over towards Graham threateningly. Graham tensed, but the punch, when it came, landed full in the face of the loud-mouthed mate, and a full-scale fist fight erupted. Graham and I looked on perplexed, and then melted into the darkness. Graham was rattled, "What the hell was that about?"

"Never happened before. D'you reckon he meant to hit you and missed."

"Don't think so. I reckon he was stoned and fed up with that aggressive bastard. What do we do now?"

"Well, I don't fancy going back. Sod it, perhaps they'll knock each other out and stay that way till morning. Let's give them half an hour…"

The main job next morning was getting all the gear to the Outward Bound Centre for the fête. We borrowed Michael-next-door's cattle trailer and towed it with the David Brown. Geoff was with us with a couple of his mates and we journeyed hither and thither, collecting all the chairs from the two village halls, the young children's playthings, and the traditional rustic fête games from the barn where they languished for 364 days a year. Bat the rat, ring the bell, hoop-la, throw the horseshoe… and a particularly contrary bike that someone had altered to make the steering go the wrong way. Total tat, but the very essence of a village fête. It took three of us two hours to set up, though. Last into the trailer were 40 trestle tables, so they could be first out on the big push on Sunday morning.

Saturday night, another trawl round the pubs. Together we sold over £400 worth of raffle tickets, generally had a laugh with the Bank Holiday drinkers, and got into the spirit of things. That night was wet: I didn't know whether to be glad or apprehensive. It made the 11 o'clock campsite round easy, with no fires and nearly everyone at least in their tents, but it boded ill for the fête car park which was on a greasy grassy sloping field. A wet day would also decimate the crowds and make everything hard work. We may have had just a drop too much whisky that night, but it had been a long day, and tomorrow was threatening to be worse.

Sunday morning, thank God, was bright and clear, and the forecast good. Anne-Marie, Geoff, and I were on the campsite by quarter to eight: Geoff cleaning the toilet block, as he could hardly speak that early in the morning; Anne-Marie and I taking a field each with a hearty "Goooood Morning. Tent rent if you please." No-one ever told us to piss off, though there were a few complaints about the hour, but on a sunny morning the campsite really was a cheerful place, with everyone stirring and determined to enjoy the day. With three fields full of tents just taking the money took the two of us well over an hour, so it was as well Geoff had finished so we could get off for a quick breakfast then out to the Centre to start setting up. Graham came in for some barbed banter from Geoff, but after all that whisky he did well just to be up. And it was his weekend off, as he loudly reminded anyone who'd listen.

At the Outward Bound Centre there were already several stall-holders waiting for their tables, and as soon as the trailer door was down a swarm of ants stripped it out, Anne-Marie valiantly insisting how many and what size table each could have. The marquees were up, with the WI ladies competing as ever for the best scones, the tastiest sandwiches.

237

They commandeered Graham as soon as he arrived - he claimed it was for his looks - and he was quickly busy setting up water pipes to the tea urns, electric cables to power them, emergency table levellers and so on. And of course he had to check the quality of the scones, cakes, sandwiches, and compliment without offending. It was a dirty job, but...

Jen and Kate started on the bottles, all to unpack and stack on their tables, all to ticket up with cloakroom tickets, for this was a tombola. Pay £1, probably win nothing, or perhaps a 50p bottle of ketchup, but just possibly the bottle of malt whisky. All in a good cause, madam, all in a good cause. Geoff hid himself away in the Mountain Rescue Centre, where he could dispense carefully counted floats, and take in large wads of cash as stallholders and the gate keepers sent it in. Anne-Marie bustled with Gallic efficiency, insisting that this stall went here, the bands were restricted to this area, the ice-cream man couldn't have that ideal pitch, etc. And I responded to every call made on the tannoy for me to come and sort out the fuses, help to set up the clock golf, explain to the volunteer cadet group how the sideshows were supposed to work... and a little later to run on down to the car park to use the tractor to pull out a car that had run off the track and got well and truly stuck.

Peter, the vicar then, was of course taking the services in two of the parishes, this being Sunday morning, but he arrived in time to hold a quick but heartfelt service of prayer and thanksgiving for the day to come. At midday the gates were opened and a steady stream of visitors swelled to a veritable flood by one o'clock. The star attractions, Trevor and Simon, had exerted their pull, and by 2 o'clock, the official opening time, the grounds were thronged with an unusually high number of kids who had dragged their perplexed parents along.

The grass bank rising up from the magnificent main entrance of this fairy tale castle was festooned with hundreds of excited kids sitting on the mercifully dry sward. Douglas,

Jen's brother-in-law, ratcheted up the tension on the tannoy. He'd had word that Trevor and Simon had broken down.... anguished groans... oh no, sorry, they'd broken down the gates and were even now driving in. A clown car, borrowed from a later act, bowled into the ring and two apparently terrified celebs fell out.

"Tttttrevor, what are those huge green things?"

"Don't be daft, Simon, they're trees!" "Tttrees, what are trees?"

And so on, and on. The adults looked on, bemused. The kids went wild with glee. There's nothing quite like humour your parents don't understand. Eventually the clowning pair proclaimed the fête 'well and truly open' and the crowds dispersed, only to find lots of the stalls had already sold out. Never mind, the WI ladies never let you down, buttering teacakes like mad. Graham was hard put to keep the urns topped up and the electricity working. Both gates kept on taking money from late-comers and Trevor & Simon spent the afternoon being escorted round the site by Peter, chatting to overawed kids and spreading their own specialized brand of magic over the afternoon. The dancing girls turned up and tapped the grass in perfect time - and astonished worms popped their heads out to see what was going on. The bands took it in turn to serenade the perfect afternoon, and T & S allowed themselves to be talked into doing a second set for those who'd come late.

By 4.30 there wasn't a scrap left on a single stall. Even the Bring and Buy, which generally reckoned just to recycle previous Jumble Sale stuff, had sold out. The plant stall had had a magnificent afternoon, raising hundreds of pounds and passing on arcane plant lore in broad Cumbrian to slightly punch-drunk visitors. The WI marquee raided the village shop and stripped it of every bun, loaf and scone. By five it was the turn of the car park attendants to man the field, pushing and cajoling the occasionally inept driver who had strayed from the track. Many hands made light work of dismantling all the stalls and tables, storing everything in the marquee for removal tomorrow. And with a very satisfied communal release of breath that had been held all afternoon everyone departed for home.

Rachel, Sally and Claire tap-dancing on grass

All except Geoff that is, and Anne-Marie who stayed with him to count the copious takings, to balance all the books, and finally to take it all to the nearest bank night safe. The helpers had arranged to eat together in the pub at the head of the valley, and were happily seated with a well-earned drink when Geoff and Anne-Marie returned, smiling through tired eyes, to announce takings of £11,580. All for a good cause! The church, the village school, the Centre for Complementary Care and the Mothers and Toddlers had good reason to bless the weather and thank Trevor and Simon - even if they had no idea who they were or what they were about.

Chapter 33

Flights of fancy:1992-4

August 24th, 1990, was a pivotal day for me. Mostly because of my own mathematical obsessions, partly for what turned out to be an accident of history, and partly because of one of my birthday presents. That day I was 42: significant to me in a way it probably isn't to anyone else. 42: six of my seven-year periods gone, and in my mind the half-way point of my life. I expected to live for twelve periods of seven years. Why? Well, it's a biblical sort of number, seven and twelve both being significant biblical numbers; and it just seemed appropriate. Somehow twelve distinct periods seem right, and I've found I have 'stages of life' that are each seven years long. There's a certain appropriate symbolism in thinking of each stage as a month, which fits well with the seasons, and I'd just finished with June. So I expected (and still expect) to die in 2032, the end of my December.

It turned out, though I didn't know it at the time, also to be accurately half-way through the time Jen and I lived at Fisherground, almost to the day. We were to have four seven-year periods there, my May, June, July and August. The birthday present that was such a central feature was from Jen. It was a series of lessons in paragliding. Anyone might find that significant!

My friend Tony Shepherd, principal by then of Outward Bound, Eskdale, took up paragliding earlier in the year and was an enthusiastic evangelist for the sport. He brought his paraglider to the farm and demonstrated how to handle it, and Jen could see I was intrigued. In the event it was another two months before I could use the four-day course, and it was early November when Debbie and I drove over to

Keswick to meet the tutor, Jocky Sanderson. Debbie was Tony's wife, and had decided not to be an aerial 'golf widow'. Unusually, for this extremely weather-dependant sport, the next four days were all flyable, as I quickly learnt to say, and Debbie and I drove back and forth the 100 mile round trip all week.

Unusually, too, for Cumbria, the wind each day was a gentle Northerly, so each day was spent on Wolf Crag, behind Clough Head, well away from any pub or even café for a mid-day break. Paragliding was in its infancy then, much derided by the hang-gliding fraternity who had been going since the mid '70s, initially based at Devil's Dyke on the South Downs where I had seen them in 1979 on a visit to Brighton. The canopies Jocky had for training were little more than souped-up free-fall 'chutes, but they felt like gossamer wings to Debbie and me. As in all sports there is a jargon you have to learn rapidly in order not to appear too much a rookie. Here's a quick glossary. The apparatus itself can be called a paraglider, a canopy or a wing. The activity can be called paragliding, flying or gliding (but not 'jumping' as Anne-Marie insisted on demeaning it). The person doing it is a paraglider or a pilot. That's all you need to know.

My canopy was an overgrown mattress, virtually rectangular, with only nine cells to fill with air. Its chances of actually flying were nil, but it could skim over the ground, as long as the ground was steep enough. Time after time on that first day I climbed to the top of the slope, 300 feet up, ran like a mad thing till the canopy blossomed above me, lifted me off my feet, and shot off down the hillside, reaching the bottom in about ten seconds. Ten seconds of sheer bliss, flying, or very nearly; followed by ten minutes of struggling back up the hill for another go.

By the third day I had graduated to what was almost a wing, beautifully curved, ten yards wide, with lots of lines attaching me to it. This could almost fly, and the trip down the hill could stretch to 20, 30 seconds even,. But the struggle back up didn't get any better. Jocky was a great teacher, phlegmatic, laid-back, unfazed by anything. While we students had our sandwiches and water for lunch, Jocky got out his hot ship, the cutely named Ninja, virginal white with a claimed glide angle of 8 to 1 (it could go eight yards forward and only drop one yard). My mattress was rated at 4 to 1, and that was optimistic. Jocky laid it out, 12 metres wide, slender, beautiful, but reputedly with a wicked sense of humour. He strapped himself into a mobile armchair, he turned and tweaked the lines, the Ninja sprang to attention, filled with air, and came up above him with just a gentle pull on its lines. He gazed up at it, still facing backwards, nodded thoughtfully to himself, turned and just walked off the hillside. No undignified running for Jocky. Then the strangest thing happened. He didn't shoot off down the hillside, he didn't struggle back up, he went upwards, and he carried on going upwards, circling in a thermal just as the buzzards did back at Fisherground. He flew.

He soared away from our safe hillside towards the nearby crags, where a crash would be fatal, not just the skidding along the heather we'd all done by now. Now he was four?, five? six hundred feet above the crag with all eyes on him. Suddenly we gasped in unison, as the Ninja fell behind him, curved into a perfect horseshoe shape, and started to fall rapidly... till Jocky released the brake he had intentionally over-used and the glider came out of his deliberate stall, surged over him and was brought back to perfect flying in the time it took us all to draw that next essential breath. Jocky was also a test pilot, employed to put gliders through their paces, see how they behaved in a stall, a spin, and all the other horrible things that might happen.

Would we ever be that good, that cool? Sure as hell we'd try, after that superb demonstration. On our fourth and last day I did manage to soar, just, for a few marvellous minutes, along the ridge in the updraught on the fell. It was enough, a promise of flight, of soaring free as a bird, of a weightless rising through the air; enough to hook me for ever, to ensure I went on with this dangerous but addictive sport.

November is far from an ideal time to take up a sport that depends on a fine, dry and preferably sunny day; a wind speed between 8 to 15 mph, if you're a novice; and enough daylight hours in the day to get your work done and be able to spend a couple of hours on a hillside. I did manage to borrow an old canopy from Jocky and to get enough time to walk up a few hills to try to fly, but hadn't really the experience to know which hill to choose. All I managed was to lose a lot of sweat climbing up and even more running down with the canopy flapping behind me.

Nevertheless, next spring found me full of enthusiasm and I bought a second-hand glider and got ready to fly. My first outing was on Muncaster Fell, near to home, and a long walk up with a heavy pack on my back. Yet again the wind was from the north, and rather stronger than anything I'd encountered on the four-day course. Tony agreed to help me launch. Facing backwards into the canopy as instructed I pulled on the lines and the wing shot upwards sharply, catching the wind, and pulling me forward with Tony hanging onto my belt. We stayed upright, more or less, and I reversed ready to fly. Tony pushed me to the edge of the hill and off into the rising air. This was where our lack of experience started to show: I went up in a satisfying fashion, but not out over the hillside; instead, inexorably backwards. The wing couldn't fly forwards as fast as the wind was flying backwards. I drifted up and back, unable to do anything except face the wind and await developments. They weren't long in coming. I started to come down, like a Chinese lantern running out of hot air, and landed right in the middle of a bog, over my boot tops, with my precious new glider settling soggily behind me.

We learnt from experience, Tony and I, though he was always the senior partner with an extra year's flying under his belt, and whenever we could we joined others, generally in the central Lake District, or slipped out for an evening's fly on nearby Hard Knott Pass, where we could drive nearly to the top. It was good to have a friend to fly with, to pit your skills against, and to share the rigours of a flight afterwards. We soon progressed to flying on Wasdale Screes, an awe-inspiring place to fly where we took off and were immediately hundreds of feet above the steepest crags and scree, falling a thousand feet to Wastwater. My heart was always in my mouth as we took off, but even if you lost the lift and started to descend, it would be easy to fly across the lake.

Eskdale Fête time was looming again and, always on the lookout for a spectacle for the crowd, Tony and I hatched a plan to fly a paraglider in from the hill behind, hand a parcel to a canoeist on the tarn who would appear to be shot at, roll his canoe, and fight his way to the edge, passing the parcel to a horsewoman who would gallop up to the opening ceremony and present it to that year's opener, the broadcaster Eric Robson, 'all because he loved Cadbury's Milk Tray'. Tony would have to fly in, as I would be busy organising last minute details, but I decided one evening to try a test run.

Take off was tricky, with no clear area to lay the canopy out, but to my delight I managed it with fewer than my usual flurries, and I started to fly out over the Outward Bound Centre. We had worked out on the map that we would need a glide angle of four to one to reach the lawn; but that was in a straight line, and I found I had to fly out over the trees that surround the centre, turn over the tarn, and then try to land on the lawn. I was running out of height and alternatives very quickly, and it soon became clear I couldn't make the lawn. From day one of the training course you are told that the worst possible place to land is in water, as your boots and kit drag you under, and you get entangled in your lines and quickly drown.

There was a jetty 20 yards to the right of the lawn, coming out from the trees, and with a cliff face beyond. It was my only, and very poor, alternative; but any alternative was preferable to drowning in the tarn. I aimed for it, and to my amazed delight hit it plumb centre, and even managed to let the glider fly over my head onto the shore. My delight was counter-balanced by the fright and embarrassment of a couple who thought they had chosen the ideal spot for a canoodle, but at least we all had a tale to tell. With his superior glider and my experiences to draw on Tony still reckoned he could fly in safely, and after a couple of successful trial flights indeed he did, and we had a brilliant opening to yet another Eskdale Fete.

My most memorable trip was quite early in my flying years. I was alone at Wrynose Pass, which can only be flown in an easterly wind, and today the wind obliged, with a gentle 10 mph breeze at the top. I took off without mishap, and spent a while beating back and forth looking for that elusive thermal to make me a buzzard for a day. I was about 200 over the top of the pass when suddenly a shriek from hell screamed past me, and a Tornado jet pulled away to the right, leaving me gibbering.

Eventually my heart settled, my palms stopped sweating, so I carried on flying and, in the way of these things, found a thermal that even I couldn't lose. Round and round, the biggest buzzard in the whole of the Lakes, round and round for ever, climbing a thousand, two thousand, three thousand feet, and drifting gently back over Wrynose top and out over the Duddon valley. Unknown aerial territory, but over ground that was leading homewards. I knew enough to expect another thermal over the top of Harter Fell, which was directly on my line of drift anyway, so when I eventually stopped going upwards, at 4,000 feet according to my altimeter, I steered straight for Harter, and on this magic day couldn't fail to find the expected thermal there. Round and round again, this time clockwise, just because I could. This time the climb peaked at 6,500 feet, an awe-inspiring height, well over a mile above my beloved Eskdale, all laid out below me. As I gazed down I glimpsed another Tornado screaming up the valley, but over 6,000 feet below me. I couldn't hear a sound.

Looking back up Eskdale from the paraglider. Fisherground in the foreground, the campsite beyond.

There is a profound alone-ness that far up, a solitary state hard to capture anywhere else. You are out in the open air, senses alert to every twitch of your canopy, every nerve highly tuned, and yet your two primary senses – sight and sound – are almost on the back-burner. The only sound is of the air streaming past you, and a faint hum of the Aeolian Harp of the lines, but you soon filter that out. You see the busy-ness of life on the ground - cars, tractors, towns even, but without their sounds they have a remoteness that removes them from your reality. You are truly alone: you cannot reach out to anyone else, nor they to you.

It was ethereal, to be floating gracefully a mile above my home, our farm, laid out like a child's toy. Why was I not going down? I wasn't in a thermal, it was just that all the air everywhere seemed to be rising, taking me with it. At the time I had no idea, and just delighted in the experience. Later I learnt that the east wind was meeting the westerly sea breeze, and with the two pushing against each other they and I could only go up.

If I went too far down the valley I would come to the sea, so I turned right and flew up the coastal plain. Then the huge no-go area of Sellafield nuclear site began to loom large, and I knew I wasn't allowed to fly anywhere near there. I should have turned inland, and would have if I had known I was in what is called convergence, but I was starting at last to sink, down to 4,000 feet, and opted to make my flight as long as possible to have something to boast about. Eventually I landed at Seascale, a village on the coast.

Not my longest flight, not my scariest, but far and away my favourite, for that unforgettable gentle wafting flight over the whole of the lovely Eskdale valley.

Incidentally, when I got home, much later, I redialled the number I had rung previously to notify the RAF of my intended bumblings on Wrynose, partly to complain, and partly to discover whether they knew I was there. I was assured the crew had seen me from two miles away and had had a whole 12 seconds to react.

Chapter 34

Lights, camera… action!: 1992

Fisherground's lovely cobbled farmyard was almost invisible under a battery of lorries: lorries with huge antennae dishes pointing to an invisible satellite somewhere to the south-west; a lorry serving tea, coffee, a mid-day meal; a lorry full of make-up magicians; a lorry powering a generator silenced to a whisper; and a lorry full of TV monitors with a small, intense man issuing crisp instructions into a microphone "Camera two, hold that shot three seconds more…and cut to camera one". Thick black cables snaked from one to another, and finally up to the Annexe, where a very nervous Jen and I were sipping water and gearing up for the moment the man lying on the floor said again "Five, four, …" and then did that three, two, one thing with his fingers, and the camera in front of us burned its red light again.

Half an hour's television, beamed from the farm to the entire nation. Worse, half an hour's LIVE television, transmitted out from little old Eskdale using the latest satellite technology. If we made a mess of it, a mess is what would go out to the nation. Jen looked cool and calm, with her hair specially done yesterday and the make-up lady's rouge, eye-shadow and lipstick on a face that rarely saw anything but sun cream. That was on the outside, inside she was less than calm. She had hardly slept the night before as her hormone system kicked into overdrive with adrenaline. I was getting by on my old trick, used every week in the pulpit, of acknowledging that nothing I said or did would matter much, and that really we were just holding a space for viewers to fill with their own thoughts and dreams.

This was the day; the day the BBC broadcast *'This is the day'*, a regular Sunday morning religious programme, coming today from Fisherground. The producers reckoned it gained enormously from being live, recreating the atmosphere of a shared act of worship of the type that went on week by week in churches throughout the land. The producer was Norman Ivison, who coincidentally had a double link to me. I had taught his sister Maths many years ago, but much more importantly Norman knew our friend Graham, because Graham had moved on from Methodist Youth Officer to being a presenter on the programme, amongst other things.

Graham it was who saw the potential for a varied programme based on Fisherground. Eskdale was a lovely valley, and the presenter could come in on the Ratty, a splendid intro. It would have been easier had Graham been the presenter and could have put us at our ease, but the management thought his connection too close, so we had a lovely lady, Linda Mary Evans, who did her best with a pair of nervous tyros. Jen and I could walk round the Outward Bound's picturesque tarn; and most spectacular of all I could be filmed paragliding for a cut-in sequence showing the peace and serenity of this graceful sport. Hmm, I thought, it may look graceful, but you have absolutely no idea of the contained terror involved in dangling 3,000 feet up from a few bits of nylon.

Norman arranged to spend the Monday before the programme with us, to film all the background sequences that would be cut in to give interest and depth to the output - and a much needed breathing space between the live bits for Jen and me. He wanted firstly to film the paragliding sequence, so I rang him the night before to say the weather forecast gave an easterly wind, perfect for flying at my old favourite site, Wrynose, where I had had my excellent flight the year before. We met there at 10 o'clock, Jen, me, Norman, his lone cameraman, Steve - and a reporter from the Whitehaven News, our local newspaper who had somehow got wind of the rendezvous. Again I had informed the RAF: a filmed crash between a fragile paraglider and a Tornado might be good television news, but hardly appropriate to a religious programme.

I was nervous. The potential for cock-up with a camera filming every fluffed attempt to launch was bad enough, but Norman also fitted me up with a two-way radio so he could tell me where Steve wanted me to fly, and I could tell him what I thought of the idea. Actually, we were lucky to be able to film at all. Conditions have to be right, and only are about one day in three. This was the day; well, it was bound to be. Growing in confidence I pootled about the sky while Norman confided to Jen that, as a matter of course, the BBC had me insured for £3 million just in case anything went wrong. He didn't transmit that titbit to me, but he did say the cameraman would like me to come in low over the small tarn so he could shoot an arty reflection take.

I was to come in as low as possible, keeping the tarn directly between me and the camera: that way there was bound to be a good reflection. I concentrated on the job in hand, Steve's voice in my earpiece, "Left a bit, left a bit, hold it there..."

Hold it there! What did he think I was, a helicopter? Obedient to the last I braked as hard as I could and held it, held it, held it... oh hell! The glider stalled and I dropped ten feet to land up to my waist in the tarn and its deep muddy bottom, acres of nylon, yards of line looping around my head and settling silently over me. The reporter took his own picture, and Norman threatened him with dire legal action if it appeared in the paper.

That was the end of filming for the morning, but Norman was confident they had quite enough footage, especially as we already had half an hour's sequence I had previously shot from a small video camera bolted to my helmet. On a different fell, admittedly, but Norman was confident the two would work well together.

Flying for the BBC: 1992. Wrynose Pass.

Back home I showered the mud off and changed into clerical gear for the afternoon's filming, while Jen made lunch for us all. This was to be a sequence in the glorious autumn colours of the Outward Bound grounds, and I was to give a short homily, which I had to write and learn, as I'd be looking straight into camera, and there was no auto-cue. Fortunately this part wasn't going out live.

It was a gorgeous afternoon when the four of us arrived at the Outward Bound, and Steve was soon hard at work taking background shots of the Virginia Creeper turning coppery gold in the slanting sun on Gatehouse Tower. All around the tarn Thomas Mawson's now fully grown trees showed off their autumnal glory. They were an exotic mixture, brought from every part of the globe to charm Lord Rea and his family, and perhaps to impress the villagers. Nowadays the villagers were welcome to wander at will and to enjoy Mawson's mastery.

Reluctantly, Steve was dragged away from the maples and the sweet chestnuts to the more mundane task of following Jen and me as we came up over the faux packhorse bridge and walked hand in hand to the precise place Norman had designated for me to share my thoughts on the story of Mary and Martha with the nation, or as many of the nation who might be up and watching. The first time I was so intent on placing my feet exactly where he wanted that all appearance of casual calm evaporated. Obediently Jen and I walked again, hand in hand, over the packhorse bridge. And again. We had Jen's favourite dog Mick, the bearded collie, with us, and even he was looking at us a bit quizzically as we returned again and again to the far side of the bridge.

Norman may well have been wondering how we would fare on the live transmission if I could make such a hash of simply walking and standing. But he kept his counsel and his cool, and eventually was satisfied that the lesson of Mary's laid-back acceptance of what came her way contrasted with her sister's continuous harassment and stress had been adequately drawn.

The presenter, Linda Mary, could only be in Eskdale for the day itself, so her outside sequence was shot on the first train up the valley, in a shower of rain that sharp-eyed viewers might well contrast wryly with the glories of our sojourn in the Outward Bound grounds. In the producer's lorry Norman was busy stitching all the sections to be cut in and carefully timing each. The programme had to start on the stroke of 10.30 and end on the dot of 11.00. There was no room for error, no chance of correcting whatever went out live.

The opening sequence of Linda Mary's trip up on the Ratty showed on our monitor, beaming out to the nation's televisions, her gentle Welsh lilt introducing the valley and the farm. The man lying on the floor counted us in, and she turned to us, sitting together on the sofa, and did the same, now live, for us. We smiled wanly into the unblinking eye of the camera and I launched into my much prepared and rehearsed opening remarks, before the camera turned to Jen for her to read the story of Mary and Martha. She was allowed to have the Bible open on her lap as any reader would, but she had rehearsed this so many times when she should have been sleeping that she told it word perfect, never needing to look down. The man on the floor put both thumbs up and grinned broadly, the red light went off and the monitor showed Monday's scene of us strolling effortlessly over the packhorse bridge, pausing casually as if to chat with a passer-by, and me delivering my take on the tale.

All three of us relaxed visibly, drawing a deep breath in unison, and settling in to enjoy the experience. The next live section was mainly Linda Mary's, all we had to do was look intent and focus on her as she invited viewers to treat the half-hour as a service in church. Again the thumbs-up from the man on the floor, and again the red light went out. This time the monitor showed the paragliding sequence, with music in the background, and a voiceover reading a poem about being at peace with oneself. Norman was right, the cut-ins from the head-cam were seamless, and even I didn't register the different fells. It would have been a brave producer who had kept the footage of me in the tarn!

Again the count in, again the red light, and this time we moved into the prayers. Linda Mary lit a candle and broke a small loaf of bread, her gentle voice reading out some prayers that viewers had sent in, and then it was Jen's turn again to speak out what was undoubtedly the most heartfelt prayer that morning. Anne-Marie was checked for her cancer every six months, and the recent check had confirmed a 'hot spot' again in her breast, and she was again on a course of chemotherapy. Jen prayed for her friend, simply but eloquently. I ended the programme with the blessing I used at every service, the red light faded for the last time, and the monitor showed the closing sequence.

Euphoria swept over us, we had done our best and nothing had gone wrong. We had even felt that it was a service of sorts, that the spirit of worship had survived the technology, the cameras, and the man lying on the floor. Graham rang to congratulate us, Norman seemed ecstatic, relaxing from the nervous tension of conducting a live broadcast under such difficult conditions, and Geoff and Anne-Marie were gushing in their praise.

We learnt later that day that the TV transmitter serving Eskdale had been out of commission as a result of a power cut, so none of our neighbours, indeed no-one in the four parishes, had seen the programme, or been able to make a video of it. I think on balance we were relieved.

Outside broadcast vehicles take over the yard

Chapter 35

Branching out: 1993

Jen and I were on holiday in York when we made the decision that ultimately changed the direction of our lives. It was a decision that Jen had had to fight hard for. I resisted all the way, and it took her three years to bring it to fruition. Her father Norman died at the end of 1989, having spent his widowed decade in Keswick, the town where he had been a well-loved English teacher for over 20 years, and she was determined her share of the inheritance wasn't going to be submerged in the Fisherground machine. This was the first time the simple formula of 'all earnings come into the general pot' had faced a serious challenge, and it needed a round table discussion to hammer the principles out.

Is an inheritance the same as earnings? Would there be a huge discrepancy in inheritances as the older generation slowly passed away? Indeed, might the remaining grandparents think twice about leaving their hard-earned bequests to a group, and favour their other children instead? The four of us had a bit of fun with the moral principles, but there was no real opposition to the understanding that inherited money belonged rightfully to the person it was left to. Mine was the only cautionary voice, and it wasn't against the principle of 'whose money is an inheritance', rather the question 'what can they legitimately do with it?'. This was a much more fundamental question. Jen's inheritance could easily be credited to her capital account, earning interest, able to be used for any Fisherground enterprise; but this wasn't what she had in mind.

Jen wanted her own property, in Keswick. She and I, with our growing girls, had enjoyed visiting Norman there, and it had reawoken her love of this pearl of the Lake District, and she wasn't prepared once again to sever all connection. She had spent the first 20 years of her life there and going back to visit Norman had reminded her of who she used to be. Not Ian's wife, the curate's missus, one of the Fisherground lot; not Catherine's mother, Sally's mother, Anne-Marie's friend, but Jennifer, a person in her own right. In Keswick she stopped on the street to chat to old school friends who knew and recognised her. In Keswick she was free, unlabelled, individual, and she wanted to hold on to that feeling.

So Jen wanted to buy a house in Keswick that we could let out to holiday makers in the same way we let out the lodges at Fisherground, but could also use ourselves for occasional weeks away. A pied-à-terre in her beloved Keswick, where she could relive her childhood and pass on to her kids the freedoms she had known. My problem was that pronoun 'we'.

"Who is 'we'?"

"Well, you and me, obviously."

"Not all four of us, the same as the lodges?"

"No, why should it be? It's our money buying it, - well, it's mine, in fact, if it comes to it…"

"And who'll have the profits from letting it out?"

"We will, we'll have bought it, I'll come over each week to clean it - it's nothing to do with Anne-Marie and Geoff. It will be ours. And let's face it, we can't live in Eskdale forever, we both want to retire to Keswick, always have."

"So you'll be working at least one day a week, I'll be coming over and doing jobs, mending, extending, all the usual stuff, and we'll be keeping the profits…"

"Well, what's wrong with that? It's my inheritance, I've lost both my parents. You've still got both yours, Anne-Marie still has both hers, I'm not going to lose my toehold in Keswick as well. I'll be the one travelling forty miles both ways, I'll be the one cleaning it. I'll have been the one buying it: yes, we'll be keeping the profits, or if you don't want them, I'll keep them."

What was wrong with that, as far as I was concerned, was that it went right against the principle that had served the four of us so well ever since we came to Fisherground. Jen would be working, and keeping her wages, whereas up to then everything earned by anybody was paid into the common pot, Fisherground. To me, it was a knotty problem, though the other three were pretty relaxed about it in truth. Fisherground was doing very nicely now, with its campsite, two cottages and three pine lodges. The early days of Family Benefit, free school dinners and dressing entirely from Jumble Sales were well behind us. Only I had a problem.

My mother provided the answer, an answer I could embrace, look squarely in the eye, an answer I could learn to love. Mum had been an accountant in her youth, and in retirement had taken on a part-time job again with a local accountancy firm. She got to hear of my dilemma, rather surprisingly, because I wasn't good at sharing that sort of stuff with my parents, and the answer was obvious to her.

"What happens to Geoff's pension payments from Sellafield?"

"I've never thought about it. What does happen?"

"Well, Sellafield pays some of his salary straight into a pension fund, and he has to pay some more in himself each year. None of that comes to Fisherground. Geoff will have a pension for life, and you and Jen will have nothing - unless you imagine Fisherground is going to go on forever, and he'll pay his pension into this wonderful 'pot' you keep going on about."

"So you mean…"

"So I mean, you silly boy, this property will just be your pension, and the work Jen and you do on it…"

"Is just the same as the money Sellafield are paying into Geoff's pension fund. Yes, I do see what you mean."

Dad couldn't resist taking the opportunity:

"You've always needed a bloody nursemaid. How old are you now?" It was true.

Jen started looking in earnest, and it wasn't long before she found just what she was looking for. 'Aysgarth' was a simple semi-detached three bedroomed house, built very much to the same design as the house she had been brought up in. It looked right in the estate agent's window - the same price as Norman's bungalow had raised: I liked that sort of coincidence. It looked right when we went to look round it; an unpretentious, hipped roof semi in a lovely position, right opposite the park, and with the bubbly river Greta just across the road. Nobody could build in front so we would always have that fabulous view of faraway Helvellyn, and look out from the main bedroom over the river in all its moods. It had a long garden stretching out the back, and a huge double garage to store all sorts of rubbish in. Jen loved it, and I put up only token resistance. On holiday in York we took the plunge, rang the estate agent in far-off Keswick, and offered the full asking price. He rang back an hour later to say it had been accepted.

What with Jen's inheritance and the money we had amassed in our Fisherground capital account we didn't need to take out a mortgage: how times had changed. It was February, 1993, before Aysgarth was finally ours; just a brief six weeks to get it up and running as a self-catering cottage.

There were of course several weeks when the house wasn't booked, weeks that Jen used to full effect. The little Mirror dinghy that never got much use at Fisherground found a new lease of life on Derwentwater as she took various kids over to St Herbert's Island to make dens, light a fire, and fry sausages and bacon. They always taste better when blackened and smoked on an open fire. True to her word she was off early each Saturday morning to clean up after the last guests and prepare for the next, mow the lawn, do the weekly supermarket shop, and usually fit in a walk round her old haunts. Roof down on the MG Midget she had also bought with her inheritance, she was in her element, reclaiming her youth and her independence.

Claire, Sally and Elizabeth on St Herbert's Island,
Derwentwater: 1993

The Lake District is justly famous for its rain, and on
31st January, 1995 it had another shot at the record books. I
saw on the local news that over four inches had fallen in the
last 12 hours, and that Keswick was in grave danger of
flooding from the River Greta - flowing just the other side of
the road from Aysgarth. Unsure of what I would do about it if
it did flood, I nevertheless decided to drive over. Apart from
anything else, the river in spate is an awe-inspiring sight, as I
had seen a few times in my teenage years in Borrowdale. I had
many a day off school when we were sent home before the
valley road flooded.

It was dark by the time I got to Keswick and let myself
into the house. All seemed well, but I could hear the rumble of
the river across the road, an ominous bass beat as huge rocks
were rolled along deep under water by the power of the
torrent. I climbed the bund, a grassy mound built by the
Environment Agency to turn Fitz Park into a lake and hold

billions of gallons captive, rather than flooding all the houses. The park was a maelstrom as far as the eye could see in the glow of the street-lights, an eerie swirling body of water where there should be cropped turf; a body of water lapping dangerously close to the top of the bund.

I turned and walked quickly down to the street called, with a certain irony, High Hill, which was always the first to flood. Here the Environment Agency had built a wall three feet high to contain the flow, to hold the river in its channel as it raced for the bridge. The wall was coping, just, and underneath the arches of the bridge there was only six inches of space above the raging waters. Leaning over the wall, I could easily hold my hand in the flow, a mere three inches below the top.

Out of the corner of my eye, in the gloom of the street-light, I caught a huge shape rushing down in the flow. It was an entire fallen tree, borne easily by the flood. It had probably been marooned somewhere upstream for years, but now it was making a bid for the sea. Running down to the bridge to see what would happen when it got there, I was just in time to see it stall for maybe half a minute, fighting for a toehold on the parapet, before it lost the fight and disappeared under water and grated along the underside of the old stone bridge, emerging battered and bruised on the other side like the world's biggest pooh-stick.

The sheer power of what was happening just the other side of the flood wall brought home the futility of my journey to Keswick. If I'd hoped to be able to stem the tides from Aysgarth, if the flood breached the bund and wall, the sight of that huge tree tossed around like kindling dispelled any such notion. Memories of the monumental floods of 1965 in Borrowdale came - well, yes - came flooding back. The lane at Thorneythwaite was gouged out into three feet deep ruts; the floods roared through the clipping sheds at a neighbour's farm, destroying the entire year's wool clip, and through his house, ruining everything to a depth of three feet. If the barriers didn't hold, there would be nothing I could do.

By the skin of the top layer of concrete on the wall, the barriers did hold. The rumour in the town the next day was that Keswick had had an almost miraculous reprieve. The force of water in a tributary way up Thirlmere valley had altered its course so that it diverted to Grasmere, the valley on the other side of the watershed, saving billions of gallons reaching the Greta, topping the defences. With the waters subsiding and Keswick breathing a communal sigh of relief, I drove back to Fisherground, in a hurry to check our insurance to see if we were covered for flood damage at Aysgarth.

Home, my tale told to a worried wife, I rang the NFU about the insurance. A somewhat bemused lady on the other end of the phone said she would check and ring back when things were clearer. She rang half an hour later, to say that not only was Aysgarth not covered for flood damage, it wasn't insured at all, at least not with the NFU. I looked at Jen, she looked at me, and the awful truth dawned on us. Not having had to take out a mortgage, there had been no-one to insist on proof of insurance, and it hadn't occurred to either of us to take any out. It was insured by that evening, with a special clause relating to flood damage.

Chapter 36

Plus ça change: 1995

"I wanted to tell you first, Ian, before it becomes general knowledge. Sue and I are moving on; I've got a parish in the Midlands that is a fair step up the ladder from Eskdale, and it lets Sue get closer to Worcester and her parents." Six years on, virtually a re-run of the bombshell Michael, the vicar, had dropped. But my reactions this time were very different. Peter and I had never really got on, and my feelings this time were of relief and exhilaration. I managed to stammer out some sort of good wishes, along the lines of "Well, I hope you'll be very happy there..." ...'cos you really haven't been here' hung unsaid. Partly, of course, the exhilaration was at the prospect of being in charge, in a sense, of the four parishes.

It's a heady thing for any curate to take on their first parish. They move into a prescribed role, with duties and responsibilities well-defined and understood by nearly everyone around - at least in a country parish. It's an even headier step for a non-stipendiary minister to become the vicar in all but name, for an undefined period which will, nevertheless, have an end point. For a while I was to be the first port of call for a funeral, a wedding or a baptism. For a while parishioners would ring and suggest that 'Mrs. Preston seems a bit low just now, do you think you could pop in...?'. or 'George is in hospital for a gall bladder op, he's always been good to the church.'

On the other hand, the churchwardens in all four parishes made it clear they were well used to keeping all their records up to date, chairing PCC meetings, dealing with the finances, and that usually, with vicars moving on fairly regularly, they managed pretty well. The message was clear:

an interregnum is when everybody connected with a church gets a chance to experiment a little, to exercise their own skills. And of course I still had to do all my own work on the sheep, the campsite and the lodges and cottages. Nevertheless, for six months or so I was, in a limited sense, vicar of the combined parishes of Eskdale, Irton, Muncaster and Waberthwaite.

Just into the New Year a large, rather florid man in a dog collar, squeezed into a clerical shirt that strained a bit at the waist, came up the garden path, with an equally large black and white Newfoundland on a lead. He had a mop of curly, greying hair, an infectious laugh, and he sat at our kitchen table insisting, wisely, that Jen should stay and be a part of the conversation. His name was Malcolm, and he wanted to be vicar of Eskdale. When he told us the dog's name was Bega (pretty well patron saint of Cumberland, and with the church in Eskdale Green dedicated to her) I thought he was maybe jumping the gun; but no, he and his wife Judith had a holiday home in Grange-in-Borrowdale, well within St. Bega's sphere of influence.

Malcolm reeled us in dextrously. He knew our relations with Peter hadn't been good, and was very careful to make it clear I would definitely be an equal partner in the Eskdale benefice ministry. Junior, but equal. Bega's junior, a collie pup Jen was hoping would be her new sheepdog, squatted on the kitchen floor and relieved herself, to Jen's embarrassment but Malcolm's uproarious laugh. He was a breath of fresh air in what had been a bit of an unventilated hothouse, and he cemented our vote in his appointment by chatting with the girls as well, then breaking off to leave with the words "Well, I'm off now. You girls don't want a boring old fart hanging around!"

He was to be inducted into the benefice in a major service in Irton Church, with the Bishop of Carlisle, the Archdeacon, the Rural Dean, and most of the civic dignitaries present to make him welcome. As local non-stipendiary minister I had my part to play, and sat beside him in the choir stalls as the service proceeded in all its pomp and circumstance. The Bishop sat in episcopal splendour in the high-backed, intricately carved throne that lowly Irton Church somehow possessed, and Malcolm knelt before him promising to serve us well, and was duly given the 'cure of souls' in the benefice. The archdeacon led him and the churchwardens round the various valuable artefacts, always an archdeacon's first concern, and elicited his promise to guard them carefully.

Actually, for a rural church in darkest West Cumbria, there were some surprisingly valuable artefacts. One, a stained glass window by no less a Victorian master than Edward Burne-Jones of a very seductive Sybil, was modelled on his mistress Maria Zambaco. Perhaps the archdeacon was unaware of its provenance. Another, a brass plaque dedicated to Admiral Skeffington, 'killed by a lunatic', mentions the Lutwidge family, one of whose scions, Charles Lutwidge Dodgson, is better known as Lewis Carroll. The Lutwidges owned nearby Holmrook Hall, now demolished, and their only memorials are this plaque and the hotel in the village named after them. Sic transit Gloria mundi.

Lastly, the archdeacon led Malcolm to the bell tower, containing a full peal of eight bells, and proffered a bell rope. Traditionally, an incoming vicar tolls the bell the number of years he hopes to serve in the parish, and to everyone's relief Malcolm tolled nine times, enough to see him to retirement; enough to see the parish into the next millennium; and enough to guarantee some stability. Throughout the service, sitting beside me, Malcolm had periodically leaned towards me and whispered "What the hell comes next, dear boy?" Winging it was always his way, and I was 'Dear Boy' from then on.

Like both his predecessors Malcolm was keen to introduce the Alternative Service Book as the main prayer book in all the parishes; and like them he met a great deal of opposition. Michael gave in, happy to let each parish choose its preference, which meant only Eskdale used the ASB. Peter fumed at their intransigence and often printed service sheets which were rip-offs from the ASB, but not in its covers. After being told in no uncertain terms by the various church-wardens of the opposition Malcolm simply carried on using the prayer book, but substituting his own language in a remarkably close parallel to that used in the ASB.

Malcolm, our new vicar, allowing me to preach al fresco.
Pentecost, 1995

True to his word, Malcolm involved me from the beginning in all aspects of parish life. In the early days he used me as a sounding board while he got up to speed, but it wasn't long before he knew far more parishioners, and far more details of their lives, than I did after living in the valley so many years. His greatest strength was his fundamental interest in people, and his memory for faces and family histories. He was a great networker, able to move among a group seeking out what he called the zeitgeist, the prevailing narrative of the individuals and of the group itself. I could only look on in wonder and admiration. Where the previous vicar, Peter, had been an introvert, Malcolm was in many ways one of the world's greatest extraverts. I felt like the middle bucket in the old three bucket test. You fill the right hand bucket with hot water, the left hand one with cold, and the middle bucket with tepid water. Put a hand in the cold for a minute, then in the middle and it feels hot. And vice versa with the hot. With Malcom in the driving seat I was very definitely the quiet one, the straight guy, the lukewarm.

Like Peter before him, Malcolm wanted us to share Morning Prayer at least once a week, at first on a Friday. Soon, however, this became as often as not a business meeting at breakfast following the service, as a procession of possible benefactors were invited to the vicarage for their views on a variety of schemes, and if possible their financial input. Parish work was much too small a canvas for this larger than life vicar, and he was forever dreaming up grandiose schemes to benefit the area, inspired by his successful conversion of an old mill into workshops in a previous parish.

"The Duke of Westminster has given us 30 grand!" Malcolm was excited, fired up over his latest project, grandly named 'The Muncaster Conference'. This was to be the umbrella for all sorts of plans and wheezes: for a University of West Cumbria; a conference centre in Muncaster Castle; an in-depth study into the needs and buying power of the local farmers. Such was his enthusiasm, his charisma, that he carried the great and the good before him, partly aware that the emperor had, at best, very scant clothing, yet caught up in the thrill of the possible, and the fun of the chase.

"Lighten up, dear boy, the time is ripe. West Cumbria needs a university, deserves a university, and it damned well shall have a university." He may well have been the first to christen the area 'the Energy Coast', trading on the nuclear industry at Sellafield and the long history of coal mining, iron ore and the latest development, wind turbines. He wasn't very impressed by my recollection of peat burning and the charcoal industry that had flourished till the end of the 19th Century - it didn't quite fit with the new vision.

In the event, only the farmers' buying group ever really got off the ground. The time was far from ripe for a new university; even the bits of tertiary education Cumbria did have - the Teacher training college, the agricultural college, the Art College - all struggled for continued existence. Muncaster Castle got its next generation of guardians with their own ideas for safeguarding its future, which didn't include a fancy conference centre. But we enjoyed spending the Duke's 30 grand, and the various other grants Malcolm conjured up - and it might have worked.

Chapter 37

The threshing machine: 1996

The ancient threshing machine must have weighed at least a ton. Now it hung suspended from the beam in the barn slowly rotating and swinging in the breeze that, long before such modern inventions, used to blow the chaff away from the grain as men winnowed the corn by hand on the 'threshold' of the big bank barn. The threshing machine had superseded winnowing in 1910 when Lord Rea moved with the times and installed the latest technology: now it was itself long obsolete, overtaken by combine harvesters. In any case, no oats or wheat had been grown in Eskdale since the end of the war, so it had already spent fifty years quietly rusting in the corner of the barn. Now even the barn was redundant: since the advent of big bale silage Fisherground, in common with most fell farms, had rarely made hay and so had no need for inside storage.

Along with my mate Graham we were loading it onto the trailer for removal the two miles up to Boot Village, where it would have a place as an exhibit in Eskdale Corn Mill, one of the last water powered mills in the Lake District still capable of working. Back in the 19th Century water wheels turned in virtually every beck and river throughout the county, powering mills producing flour, cloth, bobbins and sawn timber. You can still find their ruins in many valleys, but only a very few are kept and maintained as museum pieces, making their tenuous living from tourism. I was a founder member of the newly formed preservation society which took on the burden of Eskdale Mill, when the County Council decided it was an expense too far.

Graham, and the threshing machine.

Graham hung onto the rope on the block and tackle - fortunately he was a big man - while I backed the trailer underneath the gyrating thresher, then guided it down. It looked ungainly, top heavy, and sure enough as I pulled away it started to sway alarmingly. Another job for Graham, riding shotgun to make sure it didn't topple over on its slow last journey. Rather like a coffin on a hearse our procession braved the narrow road, backing occasionally to allow a visitor to pass, necks craning at the strange sight. Crossing the humped-back bridge over the Whillan Beck which powers the mill again started a mighty lurch, but Graham hung on manfully, and the cortege eventually pulled up beside the mill. If getting it on the trailer had been fraught, getting it off was worse and we were in danger of being crushed. But eventually it was safely stored and ready to be exhibited.

The thresher was the only machinery of any value still stored in the barn, and we emptied out the collected rubbish of the last 20 years, Jen again gleefully making a huge fire of the old hay. We ripped up all the 400-year-old floorboards, sadly worm-eaten and rotten beyond redemption, but the beams below were old oak, soft and flaky on the outside, but as hard as Eskdale granite at their heart. They should be worth something. Soft-hearted Jen sighed nostalgically as we tore out the old cattle stalls in the original byre, where she had milked Daisy and fed Buttercup not so long ago. There is a certain brutality about progress, and as I crow-barred out the old, patina worn, oddly shaped lengths of oak I couldn't help reflecting on the generations of farmers who had milked their few cows there. Lives spent moving to a gentler, quieter rhythm, surely, though no doubt physically harder, and unforgiving of serious illness.

Now the barn itself was old and sick, with bulging walls and sagging corners. It needed major surgery and a new function to justify the expense of that surgery. For many years now Fisherground had been signed up to the European Union's 'Environmentally Sensitive Areas' grant and subsidy scheme, designed to help farmers maintain walls, stone buildings and the infrastructure of attractive countryside. This scheme would pay up to 80% of the cost of the renovation, but we would still have to find over £15,000. The National Park Authority wouldn't allow conversion to houses, but were willing to allow either offices or workshops.

Anne-Marie was doubtful. "Do we really want strangers in the yard, renting a workshop, right on the top of us?" Geoff backed her up. "Yes, and think of the possible noise problems. Workshops and visitors don't mix." As usual, I was fighting a rearguard action. "Well, we have to do something, or it'll fall down and just be a heap of stones."

"Oui, mais why can we not just rebuild it as a barn?"

"'Cos it's pointless. We don't need a barn, and it'll just get full of junk again. And besides…" Jen cut in "Look, I agree we don't want workshops, but surely offices wouldn't do any harm. And why don't we make the upstairs into a

Badminton court? The visitors would love that, it'd be one of those, what d'you call them Ian..."

"USPs - unique selling points. Yes, that could work, guarantee more bookings in the lodges." Geoff again: "We'd have to make damned sure the campers didn't start using it though, or we'll be over-run."

Back and forth it went, for a couple of weeks, before we all four agreed to three offices, with a shared cloakroom/toilet, downstairs. And upstairs the complete 55 feet long, 24 feet wide area to be open for a Badminton court at least to start with, retaining the possibility to change it later. Part of that fortnight was also dedicated to the possibility of much more radical change. The Planning Authority occasionally had a change of philosophy; perhaps three more houses would be acceptable in later years, so let's make sure it could be easily modified. We drew up two sets of plans, one for three offices and a badminton court, and one, superimposed, for three houses and where they would need pipework, drains, walls and so on.

And now it was all happening. A winter of planning, applying for grants, trimming plans to satisfy grant specifications, trimming them again to satisfy the planning authority, finally eased into a summer of actual, real work. Work with stone and cement, with sweat and muscle - but for once, not our sweat. This was far too big a job for Geoff and me to take on, we needed builders. There's an approved way to get builders; you ask at least three separate firms for tenders, specifying the exact job, and you choose from their replies, taking account of references, local knowledge, and price quoted. However.....

Arthur Rothery and Fred Dent turned up in the yard saying they'd heard in the pub that there was a big barn job going, and they were the men for it. They said they loved working with stone, and had already done a couple of barns on the ESA scheme. More importantly, Fred said he'd been at school with me, way back in Waberthwaite Primary School, in

1954. Fred Dent: yes, I remembered. Not Fred, but his sister, Christine. First girlfriends are very important, especially when you're only six. Fred and Arthur got the job, without the hassle of tenders and such modern complications.

A month later I was beginning to panic as the radical nature of the surgery became apparent. Fred and Arthur propped up the immense beams that held the roof with 20 feet long metal pipes - then simply took away nearly half the walls. The cobblestones on the yard were buried under huge piles of walling stone which for 200 years had been neatly vertical and doing a fine job, till the tell-tale bulges had appeared and the barn developed its middle-aged spread. In the valley pubs bets started to be taken as to which particular night the wind would get up and the whole roof lift off and collapse, and the odd neighbour enjoyed winding Geoff up with tales of similar jobs that had ended in disaster. For all our lives Geoff and I had disdained Health and Safety laws, reviled insurance and risk analysis, and held that each person should be responsible for his own safety, taking responsibility for his actions. Suddenly that robust philosophy looked a bit threadbare: Fred and Arthur were jobbing builders, unlikely to have any insurances against collapse. Our own farm insurance was unlikely to cover an accident caused by cowboys who created a sort of steel and slate gazebo.

We needn't have worried. Fred and Arthur knew their business well, and when the wind did blow it simply blew right through and out the other side, and the immense weight of the roof held it firmly in place. Slowly, painfully slowly, the two men made new, proper, foundations and rebuilt those 20 feet high granite walls to the new specifications, with new windows and doorways in all the right places for offices and a badminton court in the short term, and perhaps three houses in the longer term.

The bank barn, stripped back to base: 1995

The whole job took the best part of a year, but by the end the transformation was complete, and Jen led her conscripts (any children still at home) in a mighty painting party, turning the rendered inside walls white. By now she was running a bit low on hands, with Catherine, Sally, Elizabeth and Claire all at university; but young Philip, at 14, was keen to help, and university holidays are long. Towards the end of 1996 all was complete, and the old barn had a new lease of life to celebrate its bi-centennial.

The end of 1996 saw another significant event; it would be our 25th wedding anniversary. Clearly the cue for a party, and where better than in the barn itself; that huge new badminton court crying out for a christening. Tricky time of year, between Christmas and New Year, but at least everyone was on holiday and could come. Party to start 8.00 pm prompt, and don't be late.

Catherine and I went into a huddle, secret plans were afoot: so secret even Catherine didn't know why she was to prepare enough dainty white bread salmon sandwiches for 16 people, and other finger buffet delicacies, to be packed into a hamper with plates and, most importantly, champagne flutes. What was the old man planning? Most unlike him, didn't think he had a romantic beat in his heart. All the girls were home for the Christmas break, most of them with boyfriends. Mid-afternoon I chivvied them all into cars, 16 including Betty, my mother, and told them we were off on a mystery tour. Through Eskdale Green village the procession turned left: hmm, heading for the coast then. What has the daft old beggar done? Bought a boat on the estuary? Surely not, he wouldn't dare without consulting Jen, would he?

Sure enough, though, the cavalcade turned into Ravenglass, on the estuary. Odds were shortening on a boat…. till it turned again, into the terminus of t'La'al Ratty. As the cars came to a halt we were greeted by Clifford, in his full pomp. Maroon dinner jacket, black bow tie, gleaming shoes reflecting the still perplexed faces surrounding him. "Ladies and Gentlemen, I am Clifford, your personal butler and guide on this special miniature version of the Orient Express. Please follow me to your carriage and take your seats when you are ready." Cliff scrubbed up well. He was more often to be seen on his back under a loco, grease and oil ingrained, but today he was most definitely Clifford.

Delightedly the family gathered round the impressive new carriage t'La'al Ratty had invested in, for just such occasions as this. Maroon itself, matching Clifford's regalia, it was fitted out with plush faux velvet seats, fancy table lights, delicate curtains, and with gold tracery inside and out. This was its first outing, and Clifford was determined to make it count.

After many photo calls, lots of banter at my expense, and rather nervous secretive glances between the assembled new boyfriends, wondering just how weird this household really was, I carried Jen into the carriage, to much applause. Being miniature, like the rest of the railway, the carriage was only five feet high, so it was more of a bundle than a carry, but the intention was good.

All aboard, the doughty steam engine gave a great blast on its whistle, and slowly pulled out of the station. Clifford moved with as much grace as one can in a carriage so low, dispensing champagne to the waiting flutes. Catherine unwrapped her canapés to huge applause, and the party got underway. Normally the journey from Ravenglass to Fisherground is only 25 minutes, so the driver was under special instruction to take it slowly, giving the boyfriends ample time to take in the magnificence of the route, with its views right up the valley to distant Scafell.

By the time we reached Fisherground and alighted the boyfriends had thawed, agreeing among themselves that while these two families might well be mad, they did seem good at enjoying themselves. Back home it was time to set up for the barn-storming to come, with tables groaning with food and drink. No need this time round, 20 years after the first disjointed barn party, for guests to pucker up at the first taste of home-brew; no need to slope off to the King George IV for reinforcements; and, thank God, no need for anti-histamines. The Annexe had been big for Jen's fortieth: the barn was huge, and allowed for ever more outrageous antics. First up was a 'come-all-ye' basketball challenge, where Sally's new man, Rob, showed his paces, and Jen's friend Hilary her refereeing skills. Then it was Jen's new friend Christine's turn to lead everyone firstly in aerobics, then line-dancing. As this was a good two hours into the party even the boyfriends had loosened up enough to join in, though the back row seemed always to be moving in a different direction from Christine.

Much later, very much later, the inner core sat around back in the snug kitchen. Anne-Marie had gone to bed, but Geoff, Jen, myself and a couple of the girls mulled over the day, and the twenty years we'd now been at Fisherground. For the girls, of course, it was their whole lives, until university had broadened their horizons. They had been lucky to be close enough in ages to be a gang, and had good memories of so many exploits together. Plays that Catherine had written: "Oh God, d'you remember Cinderella? Sally, you were such a tart!"

"Sally was always a tart, that's the way you wrote for her."

"Yeah, well, type casting."

"Is that why you always made Phil into a fairy?"

It had been a good day, a fitting celebration of 25 years of marriage, of 200 years of the big barn, and its house-warming into its new role... whatever that might prove to be.

Chapter 38

The best laid plans: 1999-2000

Pete, the National Park officer we'd got to know well over the years of planning applications, sat in the kitchen chatting about the continual changes in his job. For years it had had a simple planning brief and had been called the Lake District Planning Board. Somewhere along the line it became special, and incorporated the word, and now, 1998, it was morphing from the Special Planning Board into the Lake District National Park Authority. "Gosh" I said, and he grinned.

"But it is important, and it could affect you, Ian."

"How's that, then, Pete?"

"Well, there are going to be some elected members, for the first time, and I think you should stand."

"Me, why me? You know full well I've skated on thin ice for years with the planning board."

"Well, that's partly the point. If people in the west of the county see you are on the new Authority they'll realise it's not just there to say no to every proposal. I think you could be a good ambassador."

"Who's voting then, and why would they vote for me?"

"Well, parish councillors in this area. The idea is that there will be five parish council reps, one from each area, voted in by their peers…"

"You make it sound like the House of Lords, Pete."

"Delusions of grandeur, Ian, delusions - but give it some thought"

In many ways it was outrageous. We had sailed close to the wind for years; with planning permission for only 60 tents on three acres we had regularly had 200 + on eight acres. The

Board had had several complaints from the neighbour who objected to looking out over acres of tents. While I sympathised with his point of view, he did live half a mile away, well out of range from any noise. Same old argument: he could afford his holiday home, we were providing basic holiday homes – tents - for those who couldn't afford more. And all right, we did like the income too. Thinking nothing would come of it, I agreed to stand. It was another of those situations where one part of your life affects another in unforeseen ways. As a Non-Stipendiary Minister I had taken a lot of funerals - sometimes in neighbouring valleys - and while I knew very few of the people in the congregations they did know me, or at least my name. Narrowly, I was elected.

"Pete, you're not going to believe this..." The line crackled, but he came through loud and clear "I know! Hey, I'm really pleased. We need people like you on the Board, oops, sorry, the Authority. Look though, we need to meet, 'cos we have to get the campsite regularised. You can't be a member with such a glaring illegality; you'd be a sitting target." Did that mean we'd have to toe the line? No way could it be worth losing thousands of pounds just to be a member of an Authority I wasn't even sure I agreed with. The Planning Board. Code for a set of do-gooders who held back progress every time someone wanted to do something new. I couldn't imagine any neighbour having a good word to say about them... Oh God, it was US now.

He came to see us again, plan in mind. "Could you prove you've opened that other field for more than ten years without us acting against you?" Surprisingly, yes! Our accountants had always emphasised how vulnerable we were to inspections by the Tax Office, running a campsite dealing exclusively in cash, and insisted we count the number of tents each day and keep a record. This had served us well twice already, when we were able to prove the cash banked was appropriate for the number of tents. But the records also proved we had had well over 60 tents most weekends in summer, and all the holidays. Also, of course, Pete had a record of the complaints, and several aerial photographs showing tents on both fields.

"You need to apply for a CLEUD, that will regularise..."

"A clued, what's a clued? Haven't got a clued?" "

"No, not a clued, a CLEUD - short for a Certificate of Lawful Existing Use or Development."

"What's that when it's at home?"

"Well, if you can prove you've got away with something for long enough, the planning authority is obliged to say it's a legitimate use. For a house it's just four years, but for a campsite it's ten."

"That seems a bit immoral..."

"Not really. If a development hasn't caused a problem for that long, or enough of a problem for us to act, then I suppose you could say it's not doing any harm." Hmm. Anyway, if a CLEUD would do the job, we'd apply for one. "Oh, one more thing –"

"Yeees... what's that then?"

"Fifteen years ago when we gave permission for the campsite, one of the requirements was for a hedge to stop it being too visible."

"Ah."

"Ah?"

"Yes, Ah, as in I'll see to it, Sir. Honest."

If I had a pound for everyone who hooted with laughter and talked about poachers turned gamekeepers... I'd have a tenner. Well, a fiver at least. Nervously I took my place with 25 other members of the Authority, mostly old hands: county councillors, district councillors, appointed members - and five new, timorous parish councillors, adrift in this vast meeting room, with microphones, with the Press taking notes, with officers lined up on the top table. Haltingly I made my maiden speech, in favour of an application to convert a barn in an exposed position in wildest Wasdale. The officer patiently explained how contrary to policy this would be, and the vote turned it down 25 – 1. I had a lot to learn.

I had a lot to learn in every department. Planning policy was a 200 page book that needed to be at your fingertips. And planning was just one part of the new Authority: it had jurisdiction over Visitor Centres, over making new policy, over the Ranger Service, maintaining footpaths, bridges, even some byways. It owned Coniston Boating Centre, Brockhole Visitor Centre, lots of car parks, toilets, even a farm in Ullswater. It had to dovetail with the county council, the National Trust, the Friends of the Lake District. It had to enforce planning permissions and restrictions. It employed nearly 200 people, and I was on the Finance sub-committee.

What special voice could I bring to this august assembly? Yes, I was local, born and brought up a Cumbrian. Yes I was a fell farmer, fundamental to the maintenance of the infrastructure the Authority existed to protect. Yes, I was heavily involved in tourism, with a large campsite and self-catering. Even, at a stretch, as a Non-Stipendiary Minister I knew some of the anxieties and problems those living in the National Park experienced. I should have been uniquely qualified, and yet I struggled to find that voice. Perhaps knowing the strength of all sides of a discussion leads eventually to fence-sitting, or perhaps the sheer weight of policy and legislation makes any deviation impossible. For better or worse I decided to make those who live in the National Park my priority.

Uppermost among the problems facing those who live in the Park is how to find a home to live in. There are four pressures, each making it difficult. Firstly, demand far outstrips supply, and getting more houses without spoiling the unique appeal of the area is extremely difficult. Secondly, wages for locals are notoriously poor. Most of the available jobs are in the service sector, hotel work, bar work, cleaning, shop assistants - none of these pays much above the minimum wage. Thirdly, many of those who come on holiday learn to love the Lakes, and manage to buy a little cottage as a holiday home that they intend to retire to eventually. Often they finance this by letting it off as a self-catering cottage when they don't need it themselves. And fourthly there are the more professional self-catering cottages. Jen and I already came into this category, owning two houses near Keswick purely as a business, and a lucrative business at that. The reality was that any house that came on the open market was being bought not to live in, but either as a holiday/retirement home or a self-catering business proposition.

That phrase 'open market' hints of another market. For years the Planning Board had had a policy of allowing housing permissions with 'local occupancy' clauses, that specified owners must actually live in the houses, and could only buy if they had already lived in Cumbria for three years, or were coming to a job. The trouble was it was notoriously loosely worded and widely flouted. The Authority had a department labelled 'Enforcement', but generally seemed unwilling to enforce. It's a feature of poachers turned gamekeepers that they tend to be stricter than those born to the job, and I tried hard to stiffen both the wording of these permissions and the pursuit of those who flouted the rules.

I was well aware of the irony of my position, but it seemed the most honest contribution I could make, so I ignored the raised eyebrows, the disbelieving smirks, and the occasional outright protestation that a man who had 'got away with it for years' was ill-placed to sit in judgement on others' peccadilloes. It turned out that in many ways I was pushing at an open door, and over the eight years I spent on the Authority Affordable Local Housing rose to the top of the agenda, with new policies, new wording, and a greater recognition of the needs of those born locally. The only thing that didn't change much was Enforcement... the department even down-graded its name to 'Compliance'.

*****

While I was busying myself travelling an 80 mile round trip to Kendal for meetings, life was changing for everyone else at Fisherground too. Anne-Marie's health was always a concern, even though her cancer was in remission. Geoff, now 58, had the opportunity to take voluntary redundancy from Sellafield on exceptionally generous terms, and leapt at the chance. They began seriously to consider moving on and to look for their own retirement home. Jen and I had sold Aysgarth, the semi-detached house in Keswick, near the River Greta a couple of years previously, and bought, at her insistence, not one but two houses, in what was known locally as 'Millionaires' Row', the lovely hamlet of Applethwaite, just two miles out from Keswick.

Jen had been itchy for some time, with most of the children leaving home, and on her weekly trips to clean Aysgarth always took the opportunity to scan the Estate Agents' windows. She came home in great excitement. "Ian, guess what I've found?"

"A tenner on the pavement?"

"No, far more than that. Guess again." I hated these games, why couldn't she just tell me?

" A replacement for the Midget?"

"No, but you're getting warm - a replacement....for..."

"Oh God, another house?"

"Ooh, warmer still... keep going"

"What, a castle?"

"No! two houses! Sold together as one package. In Applethwaite! I've, er, I've made an appointment for us to look round it."

"Jen, are you mad? How could we afford even one house in Applethwaite, never mind two?"

"But that's the beauty of it! Because one of them is a converted barn, and they're both bound together by your beloved planning board's permission, who's going to want them except somebody like us who knows the self-catering business? And they really are cheap: well, cheap for Applethwaite."

Cheap for Applethwaite meant a crippling mortgage; and just into my fifties I really didn't want a mortgage. But that wasn't my only objection. I'd come to terms with Aysgarth and its being our 'pension', but it was a lot harder to justify what would be a major business, two self-catering houses, both big. Jen would be going over to Keswick two days a week, and I would no doubt have to spend some time converting, maintaining and so on. I knew it was another blow to Fisherground, that the fabric of the place was slowly unravelling, and I fought against the dying of the dream. Tooth and nail. Jen won, because in my heart I knew the endgame was coming, and that the Keswick of our youth was calling, ever more persuasively.

And now it was Geoff and Anne-Marie's turn. They had their own arguments about where to go, and when. Geoff had always disliked Keswick, with its glut of outdoor clothing shops, its cafés, its perpetually crowded streets. Somehow, its conservatism. Geoff had never quite lost that socialist streak and he rebelled at anything he called precious, smug, or, after a pint or two, up its own arse. Like Jen, Anne-Marie won, and they had their own offer accepted for a house in Keswick. The day contracts were to be exchanged, the seller suddenly raised an objection, delaying the sale. Geoff hit the roof: here was the excuse he needed, the demonstration of Keswick's perfidy.

With impeccable timing, Jen came back from cleaning her new Applethwaite investment to announce that the elderly lady next door was selling her house. Anne-Marie leapt on the news. Clearly, the failed purchase was 'meant', she and Geoff should buy this house beside ours, and when we all moved the cycle would remain unbroken. This little Lake District fell farm, such a failure in all things agricultural, had delivered in spades in its more appropriate industry: tourism. It had provided its temporary guardians with the means to move on, to maintain the dream of community that first moved us, quarter of a century before, to cast our lots together.

Anne-Marie and Geoff, celebrating his retirement: 1999

My work as a member of the National Park Authority, in particular on new policies for affordable local housing, meant I was closely involved in the developing policy allowing redundant barns to be converted specifically as local housing. We had two large redundant barns at Fisherground: the old original, presently serving as the Annexe, used as a bolthole by all visitors, and the huge renovated barn with its three largely unused offices and the little-used badminton court. There was a lot of spare space, just crying out to be made into houses. We wanted to leave a legacy in the valley, Fisherground Hamlet, and if we got planning permission and changed the two self-catering cottages into houses as well, there could be seven houses there, including the farmhouse. Houses for locals to buy and live in the valley. Houses to counter the pressure of ever rising prices. Plus of course the two businesses, the campsite and the self-catering lodges.

Of course, such a legacy would also add a lot of value. Even as local occupancy houses there should be a very good return on investment in the conversions. The others were convinced, and agreed to stay on to see the evolution of Fisherground completed. We dusted off the superimposed plans from the original conversion of the barn - the one showing how three houses could fit in, and brought them up to spec for a planning application. For a moment, in that millennium year, things were very good. Geoff and Anne-Marie bought the house next door in Applethwaite, and we ran all three as self-catering properties while we worked on the conversion of the barns into local occupancy houses. So it was that Fisherground celebrated the new millennium upbeat.

Wouldn't it be nice if the story could end there?

Chapter 39

The 'annus horribilis': 2001-2

Probably everyone over 60 remembers where they were the day President Kennedy was assassinated. Likewise, probably everyone over 30 remembers the same about Princess Diana's death. Every farmer remembers exactly where they were on 21st February, 2001. I was in Applethwaite, converting the end of Orchard Barn, the self-catering house Jen and I had bought as one of the pair. Also there was my friend Graham, working for the week laying a concrete floor for what would be a new sitting room. On the BBC news that night was the breaking story of an outbreak of Foot and Mouth disease. Apparently some pigs at an abattoir in Brentwood had tested positive for the virus, and the European Union, always quick to ban imports from the UK, had immediately issued a ban on all meat produced in Britain. Our own Ministry of Agriculture, Fisheries and Food was a little more hesitant, and was considering a possible restriction on the movement of animals. Any such restrictions were unlikely to last beyond the beginning of March.

In her speech marking the 40th anniversary of her accession, just four days after the Windsor Castle fire, Queen Elizabeth referred to the preceding year (1992) as her 'Annus Horribilis'. The year following the outbreak of Foot and Mouth (FMD) must rank as the ultimate annus horribilis for all of us at Fisherground, and of course for many others caught up in the maelstrom that developed. For us it was doubly poisonous, as Anne-Marie's fragile state of health became worse, perhaps in response to the stress of the times, and as that dreadful year ground on it became clear her cancer had returned.

Jen and I were staying in Keswick, working on the houses, the first time we saw the funeral pyres. One after another on the road from nearby Penrith, stinking black smoke rising from the gigantic heaps of cattle carcases, twisting in the flames as though life still flowed in their veins, smoke that bore hair, flakes of skin, and the nauseous odour of burning flesh, bone and hair. On the television news appeared a singular image of a cow hanging by its back leg from the serrated bucket of a JCB digger; an image that came to be the icon of the disease. On the local radio, farmers begged for the pyres to stop, certain in their own minds the smoke carried the disease, downwind, from farm to farm. Nick Brown, Labour's Minister of Agriculture, clearly already out of his depth, struggled to find means of containing a disease that spread like wildfire.

We were relative newcomers to the World Wide Web, with a telephone connection that allowed me to listen practically to a full CD while it painfully downloaded the Ministry's figures for the day: 20, 30, even 40 new farms affected. Pink Floyd's 'Dark Side of the Moon', with its screeching, keening first track became synonymous in my mind with the disease itself. By early March Cumbria was the major affected area, with farms going down like nine-pins, every one a heart-breaking disaster for the family involved - for these were all family farms, with a dairy herd built up over generations.

In the valleys of the Lake District we waited, hoping against sense that it wouldn't happen, for the news that the disease had got onto the fells. What would the much-maligned Ministry do then? Unfenced fells with one flock leading on to another with no physical barrier: would they decree all must be slaughtered? If they did, virtually the entire world-wide stock of Herdwick sheep would be gone, never to be replaced. What would become then of these rolling hills, kept grassy and walkable by these four-legged lawn-mowers? Every valley road sprouted its road-wide carpet, kept liberally soaked with the strongest of disinfectants, to try to prevent the disease coming in on vehicles or feet. And every day more and more of Cumbria succumbed.

On Saturday, 24th March, the first fell farm was confirmed to have FMD. It wasn't on the outskirts, close to the pyres of the plains, it was five miles from Fisherground, at the head of the next valley, Dunnerdale.

Sunday 25th March, 2001. A day so fraught with symbolism that I broke down under the stress and pressure, the sheer horror of all that was happening. I was to take the service in St. Bega's Church. It was Mother's Day, and as always Anne-Marie had gathered posies of daffodils for all the children in church to give to every lady there. This year she looked thinner and more vulnerable than ever. It was also Lady Day, the day in the year when traditionally farms change hands, if a new tenant is replacing an out-going farmer. It was the start of the lambing season, the start of Spring. It should be a day of hope, a day of joyful looking forward, a day when everything is possible. Instead, it was the day after Foot and Mouth came to the valleys, and as close to Eskdale as it could be. It was impossible not to imagine that a week from now all the Eskdale sheep and cattle would also be lying dead, slaughtered by the vets we knew and respected. Lying in piles to rot and stink till somewhere down the line lorries came to take them away. There were tales of carcasses being left for a fortnight, in sight and smell of the families who had cared for them year in, year out. Families who were not even allowed to leave their farms in case they took the disease with them.

I got through the liturgy, the hymns and the prayers, till we came to the sermon. As I stood in the pulpit I had grown to know and love my voice broke and failed me, and I felt hot torrents of tears flowing down my face, as I stood before these mothers, these children, and the full horror of what felt, for a moment, like the end of all things, swept over me. Betty, my sturdy church-warden, made of sterner stuff, bundled me off and took over, but not before other mothers, other children, caught my distress and wept with me.

Policeman on duty to prevent through traffic

Two more farms nearby, on the fell road out of the valley, were culled in the following week, then, almost miraculously, no more. A policeman stood at the junction by the King George IV, turning back anyone intending to drive over either Hard Knott Pass, towards the first casualty, or this fell road. Only those living in the valley could pass. Jen had a cheery word with him each morning as she walked to the post box with today's letters. The post box... the post man in his van, driving into every farmyard, and onto the next. Was that how the disease spread, was that how it travelled so many miles into the head of Dunnerdale? Rumour and speculation were everywhere. Suspicion spread in every pub. Such and such a farmer had deliberately brought the disease into his farm because the Ministry compensation packages were liberal. He was ready to retire, and he would get far more for his beasts in compensation than in the auction mart.

As March gave way to April the toll on the tourist industry began to be felt. The basic message on the news each night was that the Lake District was closed for business. You couldn't walk on any of the footpaths, you would be driving over disinfectant pads every time you go out in your car. If you came you could be the one who spreads the disease into the central lakes... The tourist industry was in disarray: on the one hand many couldn't survive a lost season, and who knew how long this pestilence would last; but on the other hand they recognised that the fells, cleared down to short grass by the very sheep that were at risk, were their unique selling point. Without hills to walk, who would come to the Lake District?

By the end of May, I found myself caught on the horns of this dilemma. We had sheep, and a fell, but made very little money from them. We had self-catering cottages and a campsite that depended on visitors coming, that paid our bills each year, and the visitors weren't coming. We were already thousands of pounds down on bookings and takings. We could, theoretically, clear all sheep from the lower part of our fell, which was fenced off from the rest, and allow walkers at least to exercise on it. This would have to be ratified by the police, the Ministry of Agriculture and the National Park Authority, who all agreed that a small area of fell that could be made available for walkers - visitors and locals alike - could only aid the Ratty, the campsites and the hotels in the area. On balance they thought the additional risk of disease spread was so negligible as to be justifiable. Our farming neighbours disagreed.

Maths had taught me to assess and to quantify risk: reward versus penalty. Three months into the crisis there had been no documented case of a walker spreading the disease. Apart from the bewildering outbreak in the Duddon Valley it seemed all the spread was from contagion, farm to farm. On the other hand, if a walker on this part of the fell did infect sheep over the fence, we could be responsible for the very

291

outbreak that took the Herdwicks from the fells. The Maths said it was worth the risk, for the risk was vanishingly small and the rewards, both for our own and neighbouring businesses, quite large. By now, tourism and farming were at loggerheads. Farmers certainly suffered huge stress and horror when their farm was hit, but they did receive very generous compensation. Tourism businesses received nothing to compensate for the empty beds, the deserted shops, the closed cafés. Maths taught me about risk, but nothing about valley values. We went ahead and opened those hundred acres to walkers and their dogs.

Bridget, with a holiday home in the village, was holding a party to celebrate Midsummer's Eve. Starved of anything to celebrate for so long I wandered along latish in the evening, to find the party in full swing, and some of the guests very definitely in the party mood, Jonathon among them. Jonathon was the son of farmers at the head of the valley, 28 now and in his prime, a fit, honed six-foot-three coiled up bundle of aggression. Before I'd even got a drink in my hand, he trapped me in the living room, everyone else enjoying the sun even at nine at night. "What the fucking hell do you think you're playing at?"

"Sorry, Jonny, what d'you mean?" – as if I didn't know.

"You know bloody well what I mean, you stupid little off-comer".

"Well, hardly off-comer, Jonny, I was born just ten miles ..."

"Don't give me that crap, you bugger off to college, then you come back lording it over the rest of us, off-comer's too good for you."

By now I was backed right into the corner, Jonathon looming over me, seeming at least a foot taller. I could practically feel the crunch of another broken nose as he head butted me, and I tensed and watched for the sign it was coming, but suddenly he drooped and moved out of my space...

"Bollocks, you're not worth it, you selfish little shit."
I never did get that drink, or anything to celebrate. I crept home, shame and righteous indignation struggling for supremacy.

The next day, midsummer's day, the Government announced a scaling down of some of the restrictions, and promised to re-open access areas as soon as possible. In the event, that meant 2nd August, too late in the season for many tourism businesses, that had already folded for lack of custom. On the 3rd August the Youth Hostel Association announced it might have to close a substantial number of its hostels, because usage that year had been less than a third of normal.

In the middle of all this suspicion, heartache and stand-off between the two major employers in the valley - farming and tourism - came confirmation of our own personal fears. Anne-Marie's cancer had returned and was confirmed on the 1st of June. She started a course of chemo-therapy which seemed to perk her up, but which did nothing for the pain in her neck. Jen was sure that was also down to cancer, but it was July before that was confirmed, and treated, this time with radio-therapy. These treatments take their toll, and throughout July and August poor Anne-Marie slowly became weaker.

Eskdale Fête that year was a sombre affair, all the more so for Fisherground. It was clear that for the first time in 20 years Anne-Marie wouldn't be able to play her part, organising stall holders, taking money and keeping account with Geoff. Jen abandoned her bottle stall, unable to face the hassle or the public. Grudgingly, Geoff continued as treasurer, but the heart had gone out of the job for him too. Graham and I manfully struggled round the pubs, selling the inevitable raffle tickets, but without the spark that could make the task a pleasure, or the wit to engage in repartee. We were walking in the valley of the shadow of death, twice over it seemed. Some said six million sheep and cattle had been slaughtered in the bid to end Foot and Mouth, which even now claimed a few more victims each week. Some said it was nearer 20 million. And the nagging thought that Anne-Marie might not, this time, have the strength to shake off her cancer lurked at the back of everything.

Sixteen days later came another terrible event, one that everyone in the Western world knows where they were when they first heard of it. The stories of Foot and Mouth had been fading from the nation's consciousness; suddenly, in a moment, they were wiped from it as cleanly as a student's slate. The day when we learned that Americans say the month before the day, when we all learnt that the 11th of September is 9/11.

Anne-Marie had been watching daytime telly, lying on her sofa harbouring her strength to cope with the rigours of the therapies that threatened to tear her apart. Suddenly she called out for Jen, busy in her kitchen downstairs. Jen came running up to see what was the matter, just in time to see the second plane plough into the second tower, live, in front of their eyes. As for most of us, it took time for the reality to sink in. This wasn't a disaster movie, this was real life, real death, and the horror of it all affected Anne-Marie in her fragile state profoundly. She was unable to move away, to switch off, to do anything but watch the ever-repeating clip of that second atrocity and the voiceovers as the day wore on. Pictures of people leaping, hand in hand, from infinite storeys high to certain death, rather than prolong the agony in the dying towers seeped into her soul, furnishing her dreams for weeks to come. Hour after hour she lay there, tears in her eyes, while the rest of us came and sat with her, then left, sickened after a short time.

Philip, youngest of the Fisherground children, had just left to start his Physiotherapy course in Manchester. For the first time in the 25 years we had been there, there were no children, and the four of us were together again against the world as we had been so long ago.

Where last time it had been a world full of promise, full of potential, this time it looked a bleak and desolate wilderness. On the global scale it was already clear 9/11 would be avenged, and that America's capacity for revenge could only bring carnage and bloodshed on an industrial level. In terms of the Lake District and FMD, while most of the valleys had been spared the worst of the culling and killing nearly all the gimmer hoggs which had been away for wintering had fallen victim. A generation lost: but not the entire Herdwick stock. The rest of Cumbria stood empty. Fields that should be full of cattle and sheep grew weeds; farmyards that should be full of bustle and life smelled only of disinfectant, as old men obeyed Ministry directives and patiently scrubbed and scoured every building in sight. Inside and out.

And at home the four of us tried to come to terms with Anne-Marie's failing health and worsening tumours. She had secondaries in her liver, in her neck, and now in her bones as well. She was on a huge daily dose of aspirin to help allay the pain. It brought her to her knees. Geoff and I were in the pub, seizing one of those moments out of the front line when you re-fuel for the hard road ahead, when Malcolm, the vicar, came in to find us. Jen had rung him to say Anne-Marie was in desperate straits, and could he find us and send us home. The aspirin had caused stomach ulcers and she had the worst case of diarrhoea and vomiting imaginable. Jen was ministering as best she could, and the doctor was on his way, as was an ambulance. She had four blood transfusions before the hospital got her stabilised, and of course the whole episode robbed her of what little strength she had left to fight her tumours.

This was just before Christmas. She was allowed out for the 'festivities', but it's hard for anyone to be festive when one you love is brought so low. Three days later was our thirtieth wedding anniversary. It passed without celebration. By New Year's Eve Anne-Marie was back in hospital, for rest and assessment. Her oncologist decided to try one last throw of the die, a course of heavy chemotherapy. He warned her she would lose her hair and be very ill from the cure itself, and Anne-Marie opted to have her hair shaved, rather than face the daily trauma of it coming out in clumps on her comb. Early in 2002 she had the first of what were to be five doses, and it practically killed her. It was clear to the doctor, to Anne-Marie herself, and to the rest of us that she simply didn't have the reserves to survive such potent chemotherapy. There were no other ways forward but palliative care and the best love and attention we could give, for however long she had.

It is immensely hard to watch someone you love die by degrees before your eyes. I had been scandalously unaware of Jen's pain 20 or so years ago when she went through the same process with her mother. This time I understood. Both Elizabeth and Claire were working full-time and couldn't be at home all the time, but Philip, as soon as he knew the gravity of the matter, left his course to be with his mother and father at such a time. Philip, just 19, with a maturity I was still struggling to reach.

Of course, Anne-Marie's parents wanted to be with her, and came to stay in the Annexe from late February. Anne-Marie's many friends wanted to visit and pray with her, and soon it all became too much for Anne-Marie in her fragile state. She asked Jen, already her chief nurse, to be gate-keeper too, and she had to be firm with so many and explain Anne-Marie simply couldn't cope. When people did come, Anne-Marie sat up in her living room, discordant blonde wig camouflaging her pallor. As soon as they went she discarded the thing, and the true grimness of reality showed in her pinched face, and powder puff skull.

Mothers' Day that year was early, on March 10th and Anne-Marie made a supreme effort to be one last time in her beloved St. Bega's church. Geoff wheeled her in in her wheelchair - she had lost the strength to walk - to a congregation who gathered round, inevitably knowing they were saying their last goodbyes to someone they had loved so long. Fortunately Malcolm was taking that service: I would have been in even worse state than at last year's Mothers' Day. There was an unbearable poignancy in her receiving her last bouquet of daffodils that brought many of us to tears, and as Malcolm gave her her last communion there was a tremor in the air. On the east window a Red Admiral butterfly opened its wings to the first warmth of spring.

It was time for Anne-Marie's extended French family to come over for their own tearful, traumatic goodbyes, and they came en-masse. Jen and Geoff had been a part of this family for so long that they became embroiled in their grief as well as their own. One by one, over a couple of days, they filed into Anne-Marie and Geoff's bedroom and she bravely dredged up her last reserves of strength to hold their hands as they prayed with her and took their tearful leave, each knowing it was the last time they would share her warmth. By the time she had gone through this 20 times Anne-Marie was exhausted, physically and emotionally drained. Jen, her mother's last days etched into her memory, could see that the end was coming, but Anne-Marie's family had to leave, knowing full well they would soon return for the last act, her funeral. In the event, they were half-way across the channel at 3 am on Sunday 17th March, Passion Sunday, when Geoff, lying beside her, became aware that Anne-Marie had left us.

Chapter 40

It fell to Jen, as so many things did around then, to wake Papy and Mamy in the Annexe around seven o'clock, to tell them of Anne-Marie's passing. It fell to her, too, to sit with Mamy in the conservatory, sharing their grief, and later to console Papy as he struggled to come to terms with the loss of a daughter. So many people, so much grief, when all she wanted was to be left alone for a while to sift through her own complex emotions. For 40 years, almost, she and Anne-Marie had been closer even than sisters, since they had chosen their sisterhood. For almost all that time they had shared homes, children, good times and bad times. So many memories now to be put in a box, tied up with string, and put away. Later, she would be able to dust them off, untie the string, take them out fondly and relive all that shared love, but for now she needed space. Space that was in all too short supply in the week after Anne-Marie's death, as well-wishers crowded round, as Mamy and Papy, adrift in a foreign country, needed her care. And as we once again welcomed all the family, almost turning round in Cherbourg to return for the funeral.

Anne-Marie's funeral was a painful affair. Virtually the whole valley turned out, plus so many friends from West Cumbria and beyond, that many had to stand outside St. Catherine's church. They came expecting the restrained, stiff-upper-lip half-hour service that usually sufficed for Cumbrian farewells, followed by as long a wake in the nearby pub as individuals wanted. They reckoned without Anne-Marie's French relatives, well over 20 of them, who threw their heart and soul into their grief and goodbyes. Malcolm took the service and wisely let them have their head as one after another stood up to pour out their sorrow and their memories. Outside the mourners shifted uncomfortably from foot to foot: inside stolid locals studied their fingernails, the backs of their hands, the floor. Anything but acknowledge or join in this very un-British outpouring.

Anne-Marie's memorial in St. Catherine's churchyard

Eventually, excruciatingly slowly, the whole dreadful week, the climax to 13 horrendous months, came to an end. The French contingent left, Philip returned to Manchester to pick up the traces of his course, and the four girls went back to their lives, chastened, saddened, but with the resilience of youth to see them through. Geoff, Jen and I wandered, shell-shocked, through a house that seemed to echo in its loneliness. Where once it had reverberated to the laughter, shrieks and chatter of five children and our very own French ambassador, now it held its breath to catch our hushed tones, reflecting our melancholy.

We are told, probably wisely, to make no major decisions in the year following bereavement, and so the three of us struggled on, implementing the planned conversions of the big barn, rattling around in that huge house that had seemed so recently to strain at the seams. One decision we did make – or rather Jen and Geoff made, and I went along with – was to sell the campsite. We could no longer cope with the hassle of the nights or the huge cleaning needs. It was time to move on, though I was unwilling to recognise it. I soon began to find that not only should I not make any major decisions; I was actually incapable of making any decisions at all.

In truth, I had struggled with a mild depression for years, fending it off with a bright 'sunshine lamp' and hefty doses of St. John's Wort. Now it leapt from mild to bitter, nothing seemed to have any point at all, and decisions were an irrelevance I couldn't be bothered with. I had no time or space for anything beyond the black hole inside my head. A black hole like those in space where anything that comes within range is sucked in and destroyed in an instant.

My father used to have a saying, one among many. "It's being so miserable as keeps him happy". I discovered how true this wry remark can be. My blackness seemed the sanest state of all, and those who laughed, who enjoyed life, seemed merely mad. So, for a while, I resisted Jen's insistence that I needed help, medical help. Why would I want to take a pill to take me out of this exalted sanity, this complete understanding of the immense futility of life and endeavour, and place me once again in the ranks of the foolishly optimistic? Fortunately, she prevailed, and for the next two years the chemicals in Prozac gradually restored the balance of chemicals in my brain, and I edged slowly back from the lip of the black hole.

Two years in which the long evolution of Fisherground from small-holding to small hamlet came to fruition. Geoff very soon decided that he needed two things in his bereavement: still to live in Eskdale, where he had so many friends, and where his wife was so recently buried; and not to continue living in the sad house she had left. He would be the first owner of the first of the three houses we were making from the big barn, and he took on the project management of its work, tweaking the plans to suit his purpose. By November it was complete, and with due ceremony we moved his furniture and memories journey by journey the 50 yards between the two houses.

By November also the sale of the campsite was in its final stages, contracts exchanged. Along with the site went Fellside Cottage, changed from self-catering to a permanent house for local occupancy. By the end of 2002, then, the evolution was half complete. The 'Top Loft' building, the old stables dating from the 16th Century had been a house for two years now. Fellside was now a house with a family living in it, hoping to make their living from the campsite when it opened next season. And Geoff was the first local occupant of one of the houses in the big barn. All that was left to do was to convert the other two and sell them and find a buyer for Beckfoot Cottage, still a self-catering house, and for the three lodges. And of course, if Jen and I were moving, a buyer for the farmhouse and land.

These conversions, this evolution, wasn't simple or straightforward. Until now all electricity to the various buildings had come from the farmhouse. All water came in a small-bore pipe from a single meter at the end of the lane. Suddenly every new house had to have its own electricity supply and meter, its own water meter, and its own telephone cable. Cue Joe and his JCB for perhaps the biggest of all the jobs he did over the years at Fisherground. After two days the farmyard, the orchard and the field leading to the road looked as if a giant mole had gone berserk, and they stayed like that for weeks. It all added to the air of dereliction, the feeling of displacement, that I found so hard to shake off.

Laying in water, electricity and telephone services for the new houses: 2002

Geoff made another huge decision, one he was sure of. He wanted to be free of all hassle, free of any shackles. He didn't want Derwent Lea, the house near Keswick earmarked for retirement for Anne-Marie and him. He didn't want the campsite, he didn't want any part of the lodges, and he definitely didn't want any part of the farm. In short, he wanted out. Selling the Stables, the campsite and Fellside Cottage just about made all this possible, as Jen and I used our share of the proceeds to buy him out of all his unwanted encumbrances. By the end of 2002 Geoff owned his new house and an awful lot of money: Jen and I owned an awful lot of property, and quite a big mortgage. We bought Derwent Lea from him partly because it would make our smaller self-catering business at Keswick self-contained, and partly because any other owner might make the rest of it difficult to run. So much for not making any major decisions in the first year of bereavement.

Mothers' Day 2003 passed off quietly, with only memories of the preceding two to ripple the waters. On Mothers' Day 2004 we took my mother and her friend May out for lunch, along with our daughter Sally and her long-term partner, Rob Fielding. Rob had been a fixture now for many years, ever since they met at university. He had lived with us for quite a few of those years, making himself a life in the Lakes, earning a reputation as a rock-climber and a living as a stone-waller. Work and play were both alike to Rob, continually erasing his finger-prints on granite rock. Sally and Rob had lived together in a village near Keswick since the millennium. During the meal Sally seemed a little distracted, wiping her brow with her hand, fluttering the air in front of her face. Eventually she cracked: "Look, for Heaven's sake, look!"

We looked, a shocked silence held the air for a moment or two, "Oh my God, Sally! Rob! Oh wow, after all this time!" Her engagement ring was gorgeous, a beautiful clean diamond in a simple setting, sparkling in the light. How could we not have seen it?

The waiter hovered. He had realised a good ten minutes before the rest of us, and now he broke into a delighted, wide grin, as we ordered champagne, and lots of it. The questions came, thick and fast. Why now, after all this time? When did Rob propose - was it dead romantic? Did Rob propose at all, or did Sally make a unilateral declaration? Was she pregnant? (No!) Where would they get married, and when? A lot went unanswered, but not the last two. This was going to be a wedding to sign off Fisherground with a party to outclass all the parties we'd ever held there. And it was going to be in the slurry pit!

Another stunned silence. The slurry pit had held all the pig muck for seven years, although that was a long time ago. We had put a roof on just five years ago, so it was now rainproof, but it had an open end, open to the North wind, and 40 feet wide. Please don't say the wedding will be in Winter… No, this was also going to be a wedding to give back some joy to the 11th of September. Well, we'd had some warm Septembers: it could be worse.

The week before the great day was balmy, Eskdale at its best. The sun shone, the bracken on the intakes was turning golden, the chestnut tree was shot through with many colours – from darkest yellow to an almost scarlet red. This crazy idea really was going to work, and throughout the week the momentum picked up. The marquee men brought all the insides of a marquee: the slurry pit was to deputise for the outside. They laid a wooden floor over the cracked, pock-marked concrete and set up three rows of tables and chairs, enough for 180 guests. Sally's friends turned up on Wednesday to decorate what we were now calling the Wedding Barn, feeling it deserved its capitals. By the end of the day the only smooth white wall was covered in what my mother described as 'lewd graffiti': the titles of every suggestive song from the 80s and 90s. I busied myself extending the electricity wires to bring in 30 amps, and looping coloured lighting over every conceivable beam, joist and rafter.

On Friday Rob's mother, Joy, came with a Transit van full of flowers – she was a professional flower artist – and set to work on the church and the Wedding Barn – creating perfect centrepieces for the tables and huge bouquets to make even the slurry pit vivacious. As it was still such lovely weather we set up more tables outside and strung yet more coloured lights all around, and from somewhere appeared scarecrows in various guises. A bride, dressed in Jen's wedding dress from 33 years ago. A groom dressed in a dinner jacket – not mine, I never owned one – and a priest dressed in my late uncle's high church regalia. Outside a drunken Scotsman slumped over one of the tables, his totally unrealistic ginger hair the only giveaway, and a farming figure seemed to be forever tending the mighty bonfire due to be lit at 9 pm, to 'warm the place up a bit'. Rob's father came hotfoot from a booze cruise to Calais with enough champagne to float the ferry he'd crossed on. Things were looking good.

On Friday night the wind got up, and the drought (a whole week of it) was brought to an end by heavy rain. We woke to devastation. All Joy's bouquets had blown over; the rain had blown 20 feet into the Wedding Barn and soaked everything in reach; and the poor Scotsman looked bedraggled as well as drunk. But the rain passed over, and all hands on deck soon restored some semblance of order. Geoff was sent off to collect a giant calor gas space heater to cope with the ten degree drop in temperature. In the house Sally was closely guarded by her sister, cousins and friends and given a complete make-over, real life at last benefitting from so many years of make-believe.

In keeping with Sally's fundamental theme for the wedding, she wanted to go to St. Catherine's Church driven by Jen in her open-topped Astra, but return in quaint style on the back of the farm trailer, pulled by me on the tractor, still in my priestly garb. I was to conduct the ceremony, leaving Jen to fulfil a father's role, walking proudly up the aisle and 'giving away' her daughter. I left a home teetering between calm and panic at one o'clock, on the tractor and trailer, to prepare myself and the church for the wedding at two. I walked into that ancient temple by the river to a sight and scent from Heaven. On the end of every pew Joy had fixed extravagant arrangements of white lilies and carnations and the deepest of red roses. They filled the air with a such a delicate perfume it almost seemed a sacrilege to walk through, disturbing the tranquil air. At the altar two large urns on finely wrought iron stands spilled over such luxuriance as to take my breath away.

Sally and her bridesmaids: Catherine, Claire, Elizabeth and cousin Louise. Proud mother beside her!

I had a few minutes entirely to myself in this simple valley church, surrounded by the beauty of Nature assisted by human art and craft. Minutes to meditate on what that building held for me. Most recently, of course, the immense sadness of Anne-Marie's funeral, and of so many funerals past, some of friends and neighbours after a full life, two of valley children, cruelly robbed of life on the cusp of adulthood. My dreams of priesthood and service to the community I lived in: for 14 years I had proudly fulfilled my role, but now I faced its end. Claire and Philip's baptisms, the sacraments marking their start in life. And the other sacraments, blessing and giving communion bread and wine so many times, to friends, to neighbours, and to so many visitors to this beautiful valley. The weddings past, often for friends and the children of friends.

The thought of weddings jolted me back to the present, and the need to set up the table and chairs for the register signing, writing out those registers in duplicate, and the marriage certificate. A marriage certificate, for my little Sally, who in my mind's eye slid back from the woman she now was to the bright-eyed graduate proudly receiving her degree, back to the pretty teenager marching off down the lane, a foursome of Fisherground girls rushing for the school bus. Back further to the tomboy days when the four of them roamed the farm, climbed the tree behind the house, making a tree house/castle to pour water on the heads of all who dared to attack. Back to the beautiful fairy she had been in those blessed few years before school, playing houses and babies with their dolls on the lawn. Right back to the moment of her birth, 29 years ago, to the panic when she wouldn't breathe, her umbilical cord wrapped twice around her neck.

And now, here came her man, her husband-to-be, Rob, looking as I had never seen him. Smart in a dress suit, one button at the waist. Smart with a crimson cravat round his winged shirt collar, disappearing down into a brilliant white waistcoat. Smart with his generally unruly mop of blonde curls neatly barbered. Even his glasses, usually scuffed from stone dust, sparkled like new. My God – they were new! He and his best man, Justin, sat nervously on the front pew as the church filled up behind them. The organist covered the buzz of conversations as old friends and families caught up with people they hadn't seen since the last wedding, funeral or baptism.

Sally and her man, Rob. 11ᵗʰ September 2004.

It was time, time for me to process in all my finery to the back of the church to await the bride and her mother. Even I was smart. Malcolm, the vicar, had insisted I borrow his best cope, a magnificent circle of gold threaded tracery embroidered on the finest of lawn linen. If I was imposing the bride was gorgeous. I stared at my daughter and my wife as they walked in state down the gravel path, momentarily overcome by their transfiguration. Sally shone, brilliant in shimmering white against a darkening sky that promised more rain to come. In her hand a bouquet to match the glories inside the church, at her throat her grandmother's pearls, and on her head a modest veil held by a glittering tiara. She always wanted to be a fairy princess; today she was.

It is a momentous thing to marry your daughter; to lead her and her chosen husband through the serious vows, the promises of faith, trust and companionship for a lifetime together. It is almost too great a responsibility to bear, and for the first time in a wedding service I caught my own voice on the brink of breaking, my own eyes pricking with the tears Jen shed so freely as she gave away our daughter. But I proclaimed them husband and wife in the time-honoured tradition, and at the end they left me at the altar as they slowly processed from me towards their new life, my final blessing still echoing quietly away.

They processed out into rain, rain such as the Lake District does so well. Rain that scuppered any chance of photos outside, rain that certainly ruled out a regal ride down the valley on a farm trailer, sitting on thrones of hay bales. Jen took them back in the Astra, with the roof firmly up. The congregation scurried for their cars, pessimists and realists under their wise umbrellas, optimists with no coats making the best of it. Eventually I was left with the momentary peace of our little church, before I too made a dash for the tractor. Infected with an unaccustomed gaiety I kept on my stole and scarf, carefully stowing away Malcolm's cope, and drove the tractor and trailer with a whoop of sheer joy through the downpour. For a couple of hundred yards the road down the valley runs alongside the Ratty railway track, and it happened that a train raced me down, side by side, the passengers cheering on the mad vicar on his steely steed.

Back at the Wedding Barn the champagne was already flowing, and the time just half past three. Trapped inside by the downpour conversations sprang up everywhere as old friends greeted each other, and the two opposing families hesitantly began to make contact and connections. The canapés appeared and disappeared with a regularity that kept the caterers on their toes, and eventually the rain stopped and revellers – after all that champagne we were all revellers – ventured out for more photos: ever more daring poses as climbers made a human pyramid with Rob at the apex. The bonfire flared, a little early perhaps, but it was a chilly evening and there was a mountain of fuel to maintain it.

At six o'clock the gong sounded for supper and the jostling throng struggled to find their assigned places. The hard-pressed caterers ferried food from the kitchen to the barn as the noise level, with everyone inside again, rose higher and higher. I'm sure the food was good, but after so much champagne, so much emotion, food was the last thing on my mind. More pressing were the speeches, and I had to wait nervously while Justin defended his groom's honour and Catherine reminded him just what a jewel he had been granted in her sister. I had said all I had to say in the address at church, but unaccountably I had worked up a little song, accompanying myself on the guitar. This isn't a great idea even when sober. However, it had a catchy chorus which was gratefully taken up with enthusiasm, possibly to drown me out.

Tables cleared to the side, the band struck up, and the serious drinking and dancing got under way. Sally was right, it was the party to end all Fisherground parties, and there had been a lot of competition over the years. Towards midnight the climbers decided it would be a great idea to burn the scarecrows. So it was that Jen lost her wedding dress. She and Anne-Marie had occasionally donned their full regalia and pranced around the lawn, just to prove they could still get into them. With Anne-Marie gone, and getting into it just a little bit harder, it seemed a fitting moment for it to go too.

After the party, after Sally and Rob left for their honeymoon, after Catherine, Elizabeth, Claire and Philip had all left, each with their own partners, it seemed a fitting time for the two of us to go, too. Six weeks later we left to spend at least the winter in our Keswick home, unsure of whether we would return. We never did.

Acknowledgements

First and foremost of course, my thanks to Jen, Anne-Marie and Geoff for sticking with the venture for a quarter of a century, and to the children – even if they weren't given the choice. It was a splendid way to spend so long together. Writing about it just reinforces my gratitude.

Thanks to Jen in particular for so many things. Most of the memories were stirred by the photographs she took throughout our time at Fisherground – photos I often objected to her taking at the time but have now depended on shamelessly. Many of the memories themselves have been hers and it has been fun dredging them up together. Last, but not least, she has put up with me hogging our computer and spending ridiculous amounts of time poring over it.

A few good friends have kept me going, insisting the material really was worth reading, and giving their time to suggest improvements, edit and proof read. Thanks then to Chloë Campbell, Graham Young, Robin Taylor and Keith Richardson for their invaluable support and suggestions.

The four of us together, New Year's Eve 2000/01.

72617748R00176

Made in the USA
Columbia, SC
24 June 2017